The Rope, the Chair, and the Needle

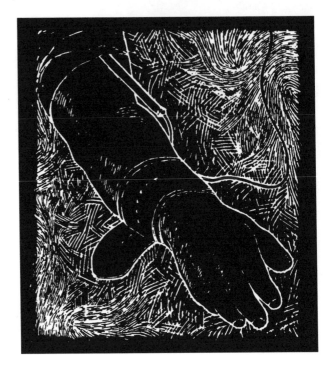

UNIVERSITY OF TEXAS
AUSTIN

THE ROPE, THE CHAIR, AND THE NEEDLE

CAPITAL PUNISHMENT IN TEXAS, 1923–1990

James W. Marquart

Sheldon Ekland-Olson

Jonathan R. Sorensen

Requests for permission to reproduce material from this work should be sent
to Permissions, University of Texas Press, Box 7819, Austin, TX 78713-7819.

⊗ The paper used in this publication meets the minimum requirements of
American National Standard for Information Sciences—Permanence of Paper
for Printed Library Materials, ANSI Z39.48-1984.

Library of Congress Cataloging-in-Publication Data

Marquart, James W. (James Walter), date
    The rope, the chair, and the needle : capital punishment in Texas,
1923–1990 / James W. Marquart, Sheldon Ekland-Olson, Jonathan R.
Sorensen. — 1st ed.
    Includes bibliographical references and index.
    ISBN 0-292-75213-X (alk. paper)
    1. Capital punishment—Texas—History—20th century.   1. Ekland-
Olson, Sheldon, date.   II. Sorensen, Jonathan R. (Jonathan Roger),
date.   III. Title.
HV8699.U5M35   1994
364.6'6'097640904—dc20   93-15717

This book is for George J. Beto.

CONTENTS

■ ■ ■

PREFACE

■ ■ ■

Texas has a long tradition of capital punishment. Mental images abound of frontier public executions and brutal illegal lynchings used as means to right some wrong. Executions and lynchings were deemed necessary to preserve the boundary between order and chaos, between "us and them," between good and evil. Violent ends for violent individuals appeared just and orderly. "You had to draw the line somewhere," it was said.

In the early 1900s, the frequency of local public hangings, as well as illegal lynchings, in Texas began to decline. By the 1920s the legal hangman's rope was replaced by the electric chair, and executions were moved from local communities to a state prison in East Texas. As the depression deepened state-sanctioned executions increased throughout the United States, but especially in the South, only to decline as the nation entered World War II. Postwar capital punishment levels declined, changing roughly in inverse proportion to a burgeoning civil rights movement, which was itself rooted in revulsion at the atrocities and injustices that had become so searingly evident in the European concentration camps. By the early 1960s anti-capital-punishment forces were carrying the day as a moratorium on executions was brought about.

This hiatus in executions reflected widely discussed concerns with injustice. Broadly drawn, the question was, had moral standards evolved to such a point that capital punishment was no longer tolerable, was no longer a punishment fit for any crime, was unconstitutional regardless of how it was carried out? Public opinion polls indicated a close call, with something like 50 percent of the population answering yes to the question "Are you in favor of the death penalty for persons convicted of murder?" More narrowly drawn, the concern with injustice was rooted in unequal application. A growing body of evidence suggested quite strongly that if you were poor and of minority status, your chances for being executed for any given capital offense were heightened. Such questions became grist for the U.S. Supreme Court deliberations in *Furman v. Georgia*—which concluded that capital punishment, as then administered, was arbitrary and capricious—and its two accompanying cases.

Like public opinion, the *Furman* Court was split. Even the majority in this 5–4 decision took different routes to their eventual agreement that capital punishment, as then practiced, was unconstitutional. Two in the majority concluded that capital punishment was cruel and unusual punishment, whatever the statutory form. The remaining three justices in the majority drew their rationale more narrowly. Capital punishment as then practiced was unconstitutional because it allowed for too much discretion and thereby opened the door to discriminatory practices. It was so infrequently applied and in such an unpredictable manner that it was likened to being struck by lightning. Furthermore, infrequent application meant that this punishment failed in respect to deterrence and thus, compared with available alternatives, did not serve a justifiable purpose.

What was needed, the Court felt, was more restrictive guidelines for jury deliberations. With the *Furman* decision in hand, state legislators across the nation went back to the drawing board and produced a number of guided-discretion statutes. Some were approved, others not. In Texas the legislature fashioned a statute that would be upheld and characterized as almost mandatory. The rather rigid guidelines would also eventually be tied to a new means of punishment—lethal injection. While the rigid guidelines were not replicated in other states, the new means of punishment was. By the early 1990s, twenty-two of the thirty-six states with capital punishment statutes had adopted this mode of execution.

Also by the early 1990s a clear-cut geographic distribution of executions was established. States in the former Confederacy led the way. And among these, as of mid-1992, twenty years after *Furman*, the leading state in terms of the number of executions was Texas, with fifty executions. Florida followed, with twenty-nine, and then Louisiana and Georgia, with twenty and fifteen, respectively. In sum, states in the former Confederacy accounted for approximately 90 percent of the total executions in the first two decades following *Furman*.

Any account of capital punishment must address this basic question: Why was there such a concentration of executions in a single region of the country? The common denominator, we will argue, is found in a cultural tradition of exclusion. Before it is possible to justify the termination of life, whether in the context of capital punishment, war, or abortion, it is morally necessary to define that life as lying outside the protective boundaries of the community.

Such exclusion was a basic element of the legacy of slavery. As the exclusionary legacy of slavery moved toward a more inclusive definition of the human community, several trends became apparent. Illegal lynchings gave way to state-sanctioned executions. Differences across racial and ethnic categories narrowed, with the possible exception of capital offenses involving the additional charge of rape. The procedural locus of discrimination became more concentrated in the practices of the prosecutors. Finally, in what is perhaps the most dramatic shift across the seven decades of our analysis, the time from conviction to execution lengthened.

The analysis that follows is the result of a data collection effort begun in September 1987. We first examined the individual records of 932 Texas capital offenders received on death row between August 1923 and December 1988. The Texas prison system maintains records on every inmate sentenced to death. From these records, we collected information that included the demographics of the individual offenders and victims, the circumstances surrounding the offenses, and various social variables. These data were recorded on individual code sheets. Not every inmate's file was complete, and to fill in gaps we surveyed newspapers for articles about the offense or execution of the offender, reviewed appellate information, and read trial transcripts located in the library of the University of Texas Law School. In several cases we contacted county clerks, who provided transcripts of trials. After these data were recorded, they were prepared for subsequent computer analysis. Data on lynchings in Texas were obtained from the Barker Archives at the Center for American History, at the University of Texas at Austin, as well as numerous publications cited throughout the chapters.

We compared the death-sentenced population convicted for murder with malice, robbery with a gun, or rape with offenders who were sentenced to prison for the same offense. Data for every inmate (nearly 12,000) who entered the Texas prison system between 1923 and 1972 for one of these three offenses were logged into a book and prepared for computer analysis. From this group of prisoners we selected samples of offenders for comparison with the capital offenders. We reviewed these sample inmate files to collect the same information we had on the capital offender group. We also utilized various Texas prison records (e.g., minutes of the Texas Prison Board meetings) to obtain information about the construction and costs of the original death row and an infamous escape from it. Former Texas prison employees who had personal experience with death row were also interviewed. All of this information was then compiled and organized and, where possible, was prepared for computer analysis.

While our account presents extensive statistical data on capital sentencing patterns over a period of seven decades, we have attempted to provide some detailed, individualized information on the men and women who occupied death row and the incidents that got them there. Each offense, victim, and offender offered a unique story worthy of individualized attention.

At the same time it is important to note that our account is neither an indictment of, nor a rallying point for, capital punishment. We have simply tried to do what social scientists are trained to do—provide dispassionate analysis. Sometimes this yields a rather bloodless story. So be it. The data are presented; let the reader decide. That is the overall plan; however, we depart from it somewhat in the final chapter, where policy questions and answers, as we see them, are presented.

In completing this project we solicited the help of many persons to whom we owe a special debt of gratitude. First and foremost is S. O. Woods. His penchant for keeping organized records along with his voluminous general knowledge of Texas prison history allowed the research to gain momentum during its very early stages. We owe a special word of thanks also to Melba Harris, who with great patience assisted us in gathering information on offenders sentenced to prison. We also acknowledge the entire staff of the Records Section at the Texas Department of Corrections for their help in answering our requests for assistance.

We acknowledge the extraordinary effort of a number of criminal justice graduate students at Sam Houston State University. Conrado G. Contreras worked extremely hard on assembling the data set on noncapital offenses. Robert J. Hunter, Paige Ralph, Edward Stadnik, and David Wagner sifted through dusty Texas prison records and microfiche to record data on inmates sentenced to prison. Madhu Bodapati made suggestions on early drafts and worked tirelessly on assembling Appendix B, and his efforts in this regard are especially appreciated. Dennis Longmire, associate dean of the College of Criminal Justice at Sam Houston State University, provided financial support at various times throughout the research. Rolando Del Carmen and Steven J. Cuvelier provided support and encouragement to complete the project. Edie Van Cleve was and is a valued friend and editorial critic. We owe special thanks to Lawrence R. Moran, who contributed significantly to the clarity of the manuscript. We are also deeply grateful to Carolyn Cates Wylie, managing editor of U.T. Press, who scrutinized the entire manuscript with extreme care and concern. Her suggestions and ideas contributed immeasurably to the work. Our thanks and appreciation goes to these friends and colleagues.

This book, like most, required a nearly compulsive effort and many nights and weekends away from home and family. We received deeply appreciated support from those we care for most—Cecelia, John, and Jessica; Carolyn, Brooke, and Scott; and Tracy and Amy.

The Rope, the Chair, and the Needle

"Single Cross."

Tombstones from Joe Byrd Cemetery, 1992.

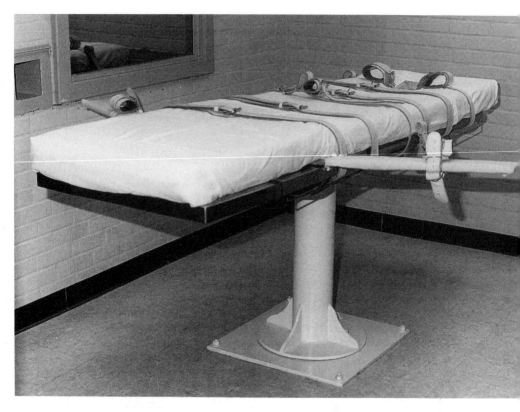

Above: Gurney.
Photograph © 1992 by Texas Department of Criminal Justice, Institutional Division.

Opposite: Electric chair ("Old Sparky").
Photograph © 1992 by Texas Department of Criminal Justice, Institutional Division.

Above: Old death row.
Photograph © 1992 by Texas Department of Criminal Justice, Institutional Division.

Opposite: Holding cell in death house.
Photograph © 1992 by Texas Department of Criminal Justice, Institutional Division.

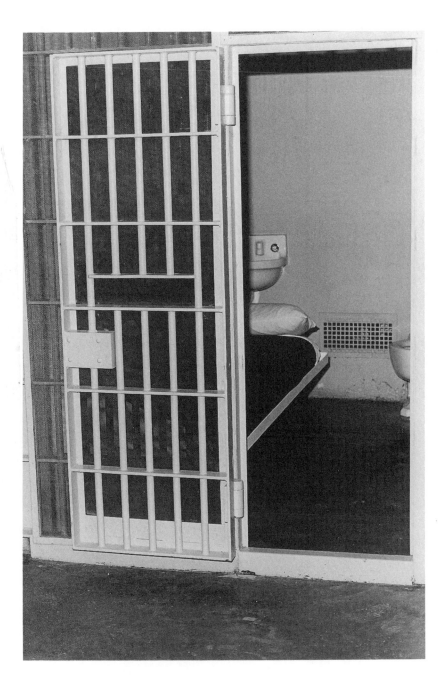

Ellis I Unit.
Photograph © 1992 by Texas Department of Criminal Justice, Institutional Division.

Death row garment factory.
Photograph © 1992 by Texas Department of Criminal Justice, Institutional Division.

CHAPTER I

FROM LYNCHINGS
TO ELECTROCUTIONS

■ ■ ■

The calculated killing of a human being by the State involves by its very nature, a denial of the executed person's humanity.[1]

If you [the jury] turn a deaf ear to the thousands of mothers who have daughters of her age [the victim was 15] haven't you formed a league with death and a covenant with hell? . . . This negro is a lustful animal, without anything to transform to any kind of valuable citizen, because he lacks the very fundamental elements of mankind.[2]

In late summer of 1923 legal hangings disappeared from local communities throughout Texas. They were replaced, beginning in February 1924, by electrocutions at the state penitentiary in Huntsville. Legislators were moved to pass laws mandating this change by the specter of mob lynchings in the immediately preceding years. In this sense, the link between illegal lynchings and the 1923 capital punishment reform statute is clear and direct. They are rooted in a long, common cultural history. We begin the story during Reconstruction.

Reconstruction, Lynchings, and the Spirit of Lawlessness

Reconstruction

The legal stage for the eventual reforms was set by passage of the Thirteenth and Fourteenth Amendments to the Constitution and the Civil Rights Act of

1871. Ratification of the Thirteenth Amendment was announced on Decen
ber 18, 1865. It provided closure on the central issue of the Civil War
outlawing slavery and involuntary servitude "except as punishment of crin
whereof the party shall have been duly convicted." Through this loophol
states throughout the recently disbanded Confederacy drove laws for leasin
prisoners to maintain plantations and to rebuild public accommodations, a
well as laws to impose capital punishment.

In Texas it took barely two months following ratification of the Thirteenth
Amendment to enact legislation that established the Board of Labor, whose
members were given the task of forming contracts for the use of prisoners. At
the same time, prisons themselves took on a plantation-like character. They
were located on large sections of land in East Texas. Inmates were used to
raise cotton and corn, to tend livestock, and to maintain such public accommodations as roads and waterworks. Order within prison was maintained
much as it had been under the old system of slavery. Physical domination was
paramount. Whippings were permitted and dog packs chased down escapees.
Prison units were segregated: Black inmates were more likely than their white
counterparts to be found in the fields picking cotton. These prison plantations
would remain very much in evidence a full century later.[3]

The same can be said for patterns of capital punishment, both legal and
illegal. It is important first to note, as others have done, that the line between
legal and illegal hangings was often razor-thin. In his now classic study of
lynching, published in 1933, Arthur Raper put it this way: "In the efforts to
prevent a lynching, or prevent further mob outbreaks after a lynching, peace
officers and leading citizens often make promises which virtually preclude
impartial court procedure."[4] More recently George Wright, in a study of Kentucky executions between 1870 and 1940, has reiterated the same point.[5]

It is clear that life in Texas in the years immediately following the Civil War,
as in other regions of the former Confederacy, was dominated by the political
and economic struggle to define the new relationship between the authority
of local, state, and federal government officials.[6] Central to this struggle were
the recently redefined relationships between persons in the white and black
communities. Much of this struggle was permeated by an underlying climate
of coercion, both threatened and real. From all available accounts, white aggression and black victimization was the dominant form of violence—violence
used by whites to keep blacks in their "place," excluded from political, legal,
economic, and social institutions.[7]

Records of violence during this period come from two sources. Concerned
with the rising level of lawlessness, the 1868 Texas Constitutional Convention
established a special committee to gather relevant statistics. Reflecting the general suspicion of the time, the Freedmen's Bureau organized its own data-
gathering effort for the same topic and time period (1865–1868). While both

sets of records contain flaws that stem from lack of systematic coverage, the Freedmen's Bureau records appear to be the more complete.[8] Complete or not, both reports are consistent in their conclusion that, as the Texas Constitutional Convention's special committee put it, "the great disparity between the numbers of the two races killed, the one by the other, shows conclusively that the 'war of races' is all on the part of the whites against the blacks." Anecdotal support for this conclusion is abundant.

For example, in mid-1868, in the small community of Millican, about ten miles north of where the Navasota and Brazos rivers join on their way to the Gulf of Mexico, black members of the community protested when the murderer of a politically active black minister and voter registrar went unpunished. In response, members of the newly formed Ku Klux Klan incited a riot that resulted in the killing of at least six prominent members of the black community. In Washington County, just south of Millican, a former slave who was protesting his continued enslavement by his former master was shot for his "boldness" and as a consequence had to have his arm amputated. Further north, in the East Texas County of Rusk, just south of Longview, a relatively large community, a black mother and her baby were killed when she tried to seek new employment opportunities. In McLennan County, near Waco, a freedwoman was shot by her former master because "she gave saucy words to her mistress."

Not all regions of Texas were equally infused with a tradition of plantation life and slavery. Circumstances seemed to be worse in locations where slave plantations had formerly dominated the rhythm and substance of life. In 1836 Texas had become a republic, and with independence from Mexico slavery had been legalized. A large influx of white planters from other slave-holding states began almost immediately. In the main, this influx first concentrated in counties along the Sabine River where it forms the state's eastern boundary, especially in San Augustine, Sabine, Shelby, and Nacogdoches counties. It was not long, however, until slave plantations expanded all along the Sabine, Neches, Trinity, Navasota, and Brazos rivers: Harrison, Rusk, and Smith counties in the northeastern region of the state and Walker, Montgomery, Grimes, and Washington among the more central counties led the way.[9]

By the time the Civil War broke out, Texans were paying taxes on over 200,000 slaves, who constituted almost one-third of the state's population (Map 1.1). Following the end of the war and emancipation, the growth of the recently freed, but still highly dependent, black population slowed dramatically. However, with the exception of some out-migration to urban areas and northern states, as late as 1930 the descendants of Texas slaves maintained residence largely in East Texas in much the same location as their ancestors. It was in these counties that the disproportionate amount of violence and lynchings in the post–Civil War period occurred.

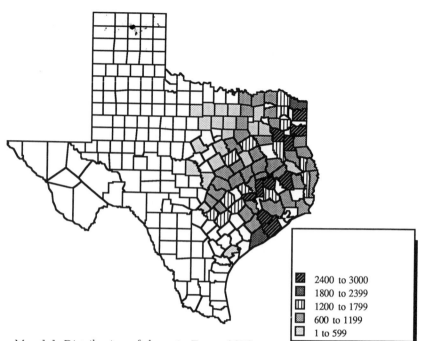

▨	2400 to 3000
▦	1800 to 2399
⊞	1200 to 1799
▨	600 to 1199
☐	1 to 599

Map 1.1. Distribution of slaves in Texas, 1858.

In 1868, General Reynolds, commander of the Fifth Military District, reported that "civil law east of the Trinity River is almost a dead letter" and that "murder of negroes is so common as to render it impossible to keep an accurate account of them."[10] In his attempt to analyze the veracity of this conclusion, Barry Crouch noted that in 1868 there were some 5,000 pending homicide indictments in Texas. Between the end of the war and 1868, there was only one recorded legal execution, that of a Houston freedman.[11]

In addition, the records from the Freedmen's Bureau's investigation of post–Civil War violence in Texas that were examined by Crouch reveal that white-against-black violence was far more dominant than any other combination. Rates of victimization constructed from these data reveal that white violence against blacks was recorded at a rate of 601.2 incidents per 100,000 blacks in the population. By contrast, the comparable rate for black violence against white victims was 7.4 incidents per 100,000 whites.[12] While these figures offer a clearly imperfect view of the *level* of violence that occurred during this time, in all likelihood they reflect the basic *pattern*.

It is further established in Cantrell's analysis[13] that the incidence of violence during this time rose dramatically when freedmen won the right to vote and began to register, join Union Leagues, and vote for Radical delegates to the constitutional convention. Thereafter, violence became a not so subtle tool to keep blacks in their traditional political, social, and economic position. This practice of exclusion became the cultural bridge between lynching and the South's near monopoly on the practice of capital punishment.

Lynchings in Texas: 1888–1918

The tragic consequences of exclusion continued with a vengeance following Reconstruction and soon became intertwined with the sectional struggle over federalism and states rights. In 1888 Senator Richard Coke found himself before his U.S. Senate colleagues explaining the particularly egregious lynching of Joseph Hoffman in Washington County, Texas. Denying a race problem, and asserting instead that the incident resulted from human nature "under excitement," Coke replied to his critics bluntly:

> It is reserved for the South to have to stand face to face with the black man and solve the problem of joint government and joint residence, and we are solving it. If you will let us alone, we will solve it.[14]

The solution, however, was slow in coming. This pace is documented in several related sources. The best figures, albeit incomplete, come from the Tuskeegee Institute and from the *Chicago Tribune's* efforts to document lynching incidents beginning around 1882. This information was later compiled, expanded, and analyzed in *Thirty Years of Lynchings in the United States, 1889–1918*, a document published in 1919 by the National Association for the Advancement of Colored People (NAACP) as part of their antilynching campaign.

By the time the *Chicago Tribune* began chronicling lynchings in the early 1880s, hangings and vigilante justice were a well-established tradition on the frontier, including the frontier in Texas.[15] Lynchings, as one form of vigilante justice, were thought by many on the western frontier to be a guardian of the otherwise precarious social order. In practice they were visited disproportionately upon groups marginalized by the dominant community—African-Americans, Mexican-Americans, Asians, Native Americans, and Southern European ethnic minorities.[16] Most particularly in the Reconstruction South lynchings increasingly became one tool (along with coercive labor contracts, various crop lien laws, and tenant-farming practices) in the continuing struggle between black members of the community who had obtained or were striving for a better position and whites who saw their status threatened.

According to *Thirty Years of Lynching*, during the period 1889–1918, Texas ranked third in terms of the number of lynchings (335), behind Georgia and Mississippi. Seventy-eight percent of the individuals lynched in Texas had their familial roots in Africa, a figure somewhat below the percentages in other former states of the Confederacy—for example, 97 percent, 94 percent,

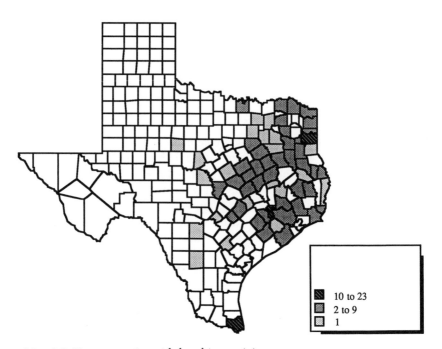

Map 1.2. Texas counties with lynching activity.

93 percent, and 90 percent in South Carolina, Mississippi, Georgia, and Florida, respectively. When these lynchings are separated according to the county of occurrence, the 335 reported lynchings in Texas during this time are concentrated in geographical locations such as Harrison, Upshur, Rusk, McLennan, Limestone, Freestone, Waller, Grimes, and Brazos counties, where the tradition of plantation slavery was the strongest and the proportion of African-American citizens was the greatest. (The Southern Commission on the Study of Lynching would later report[17] that between 1900 and 1929 lynchings in Texas counties with a black majority population occurred at a rate of 3.79 per 10,000 blacks, compared with a rate of 1.94 per 10,000 blacks in counties with less than one-quarter black population [see Map 1.2]).

Data from *Thirty Years of Lynchings* reveal that in the first decade of this period (1889–1898) well over 95 percent of the recorded lynchings (in some cases race was not recorded) were of blacks. The incidents were largely concentrated in the northeastern triangle of the state (bounded roughly by Paris and Longview in the north, through Nacogdoches, and continuing along the Neches River to Beaumont and Port Arthur), as well as within a fifteen-mile corridor along the "bottoms" of the Brazos River running south from Waco. There was not only a geographic but an episodic concentration in that a number of lynchings would occur in the space of a few months and then there would be a lull. For example, 1897 was particularly brutal, with four multiple lynchings between April 27 and May 18; the following twelve months were relatively free of lynchings.

In the second decade of this thirty-year period, between 1898 and 1909, the basic episodic and location patterns continued. There was a general "diffusion" of incidents along the Trinity River as well as in the corridor between Waco and Longview through Athens and Tyler. The link between this violence and political and economic social control was repeatedly demonstrated.

In 1900, in Grimes County, a political struggle between local factions resulted in the assassination of two black leaders, and the eventual exodus of many local citizens.[18] Five blacks were lynched on October 3, 1901, in Harrison County in a quarrel over "profit sharing." In 1907 there was an outbreak of four lynchings in two months in Montgomery County, near Conroe, just south of Huntsville. The year 1908 proved to be one of the most violent in Texas in the twentieth century in terms of lynchings, with a total of twenty-one.[19] Nine blacks were lynched on a single day in June of that year in Hemphill, close to the Sabine River on the East Texas border. In 1909, some sixty miles north of Hemphill, four more lynchings were carried out in the space of four days, again in Harrison County. Scattered in clusters between these multiple-victim incidents were single-victim lynchings.[20]

In many instances lynchings were motivated by an underlying agenda that had to do with imagined insults or lack of respect for existing conventions. Frequently the focus was relationships between black males and white females, or what would eventually come to be called a "peculiar form of chivalry." It mattered little that the assertions were removed from the facts in any particular case. What mattered was dominance and control. A 1905 editorial in the northeastern Texas newspaper, the *Times Clarion* (Longview), is illustrative.

> Almost every day some negro brute assaults a white woman in this state, and often one to a half-dozen murders are committed in an effort to hide the crime. . . . If rape and murder by brutish negroes are to become common, the negro must expect extermination.[21]

Such gross exaggerations were obviously designed to whip up emotion, rather than rational discourse. Such emotions were, of course, not restricted to Texas. Again evidence provided by the NAACP's 1919 report demonstrates that nationwide during these years some 140 African-Americans, compared with six whites, were victimized by lynching without being charged with a specific crime. Instead published accounts in these cases reported accusations of "testifying against whites," "suing whites," "wrong man lynched." In addition approximately 760 lynchings of African-Americans were precipitated for unspecified crimes against the person or property, not including murder or rape.

Responding in large measure to the social, political, educational, and economic injustices illustrated by this brutal pattern of selective repression—which were evident as well in the less brutal but more pervasive arenas of travel, employment, and education—twenty-nine African-American professionals and intellectuals met in Niagara Falls in the same year that the Longview *Times Clarion* editorial was published. Led by William Edward Burghardt Du Bois, they adopted at their second meeting (1906), a resolution that read in part:

> We shall not be satisfied with less than our full manhood rights. . . . We claim for ourselves every right that belongs to a free-born American—political, civil, and social—and until we get these rights, we shall never cease to protest and assail the ears of America with the story of its shameful deeds toward us.[22]

Some of the persons associated with what came to be called the Niagara Movement, further energized by publicity surrounding continued lynchings during this period and a race riot in Springfield, Illinois in 1908, joined forces with others to initiate what became the National Association for the Advancement of Colored People.

"The Call" for a Lincoln Emancipation Conference, in celebration of the centennial of the birth of the man who presided over the Civil War, brought these people together with this lament:

> If Mr. Lincoln could revisit this country he would be disheartened by the nation's failure. . . . He would see the black men and women, for whose freedom a hundred thousand of soldiers gave their lives, set apart in trains . . . in railway stations and in places of entertainment, while State after State declines to do its elementary duty in preparing the Negro through education for the best exercise of citizenship. . . . Added to this, the spread of lawless attacks upon the Negro . . . even in the Springfield made famous by Lincoln—often accompanied by revolting brutalities, sparing neither sex, nor age nor youth, could not but shock the author of the sentiment that "government of the people, by the people, for the people shall not perish from the earth."[23]

Back in Texas, in the final decade of the thirty years of lynchings, the basic distribution of race-linked vigilante justice continued. Two months after the NAACP's founding a race riot broke out in Palestine, Texas, claiming the lives of eighteen blacks.[24] Some five years later, in 1916, a particularly egregious lynching took place in Waco, dubbed the "Waco Horror" in light of the reported fact that a seventeen-year-old black boy, accused of killing a local white woman, was removed from the jail, dragged through town, mutilated, hanged, and eventually burned.

Elizabeth Freeman, an active member of the Women's Suffrage Movement, was engaged by the newly founded NAACP to conduct an investigation. Her report appeared in a special July supplement in the *Crisis*, a publication of the NAACP, edited by W. E. B. DuBois. As part of a campaign to publicize the incident, copies of Freeman's article on the Waco Horror were distributed to all members of the U.S. Congress, 750 newspapers across the country, and 42,000 *Crisis* subscribers. As Joel E. Spingarn, chairman of the NAACP Board of Directors, put it, "The publicity we gave Waco has roused a fighting spirit we must not let die."[25]

By the end of 1918, lynchings had been declining for a number of years and antilynching reform efforts, spearheaded by the NAACP, were beginning to see results.[26] While lynchings continued to be a serious problem, statistics on the number of *prevented* lynchings also began to appear, signaling the efforts of local citizens who largely through local church groups were attempting to turn the tide.

At this same time, soldiers began returning from the battles of World War I. Black veterans who had fought for freedom and had come to know the trenches, fields, towns, cities, and regions of France returned home to many of the same prejudices and threats they had left. It was a situation made for renewed conflict; an article titled "Returning Soldiers," written by W. E. B. DuBois from the point of view of the black veteran, in the May 1919 issue of the *Crisis*, said it loud and clear:

> This is the country to which we Soldiers of Democracy
> return. This is the fatherland for which we fought! . . .
> It was right for us to fight . . . Under similar circumstances,
> we would fight again. But by the God of Heaven, we are
> cowards and jackasses if now that the war is over, we do
> not marshal every ounce of our brain and brawn to fight
> a sterner, longer, more unbending battle against the
> forces in our land.
> We return.
> We return from fighting.
> We return fighting.
> Make way for Democracy! We saved it in
> France, and by the Great Jehovah, we will
> save it in the United States of America, or
> know the reason why.

Racial Violence in Texas: 1919–1922

The general downward trend in racial violence was reversed just seven months after the Treaty of Versailles was signed and one month after the above *Crisis* article appeared. The most violent episode in Texas occurred in the northeastern community of Longview. It began on June 16, 1919, in the small town of Kilgore, just outside Longview, with the killing of a black dentist from Illinois for associating with a prominent white woman. While both the dentist and the woman had reportedly graduated from the same college, local citizens were incensed by the dentist's lack of respect for his "rightful place." More general socioeconomic tensions mounted when white members of the community began opposing the founding of the Negro Business Men's League in Longview at this same time.

Violence was precipitated on July 5, when local citizens saw copies of a Chicago *Defender* article that suggested that the dentist and the woman were lovers. Thus aroused, these citizens, including the woman's brothers, threatened to lynch the article's author, a prominent black Longview schoolteacher and community leader. Five days after the Chicago article appeared, its author was severely beaten and threatened with lynching unless he left town.

A crowd of white men formed to carry out the threat. A group of black citizens responded in defense. Shooting ensued, with several injuries to members of the white crowd. A larger white crowd, estimated to be about one thousand strong, gathered in the town square, and began burning houses and businesses. Governor William P. Hobby declared martial law and sent some three hundred National Guardsmen and several Texas Rangers to Longview to enforce the peace. By July 12 quiet was restored. One week later rioting broke out in Washington, D.C., and in Chicago. What would eventually be referred to as the "Red Summer of 1919" was under way. Racial violence would occur in Chicago, Washington, D.C., Knoxville, Philadelphia, and Indianapolis and would finally climax in October in Phillips County, Arkansas.[27]

In the same summer in Austin officers of the NAACP, after issuing a particularly strong plea for racial equality at their June 1919 conference in Cleveland, were summoned to court to show why thirty-one branch offices of the NAACP in Texas should not be closed. The NAACP responded in late August, by sending John R. Shillady from New York, who among other things was a prominent member of the organization's effort to get an antilynching bill through the U.S. Congress.

The previous year, shortly after assuming the duties of executive secretary of the NAACP, Shillady had written a particularly strong letter of protest to Governor Hobby, condemning the killing of six members of a single family in Walker County, reminding the governor that some 157,000 Negroes were fighting in France for freedom, and appealing to the governor's patriotism to stop such violence. Governor Hobby, reflecting the delicate balance, in public sentiment in 1919 Texas, between "states' rights" politics and revulsion at this and other recent incidents of violence aimed against blacks, reportedly told the NAACP and Shillady "to go to hell," while simultaneously asking the Texas legislature for stricter measures designed to reduce the occurrence of lynchings.[28]

Whatever the governor's response to lynchings and the protest correspondence from the NAACP, Shillady did not receive a warm welcome when he arrived in Austin to address the charges being leveled at NAACP organizing activities in Texas. While walking back to his hotel in downtown Austin after making his case for the NAACP before the court, Shillady was accosted and beaten by a group of men, including a local judge and sheriff. In an interview many years later, the assaulting judge recalled, "[On] my forty-first birthday, Ben Pierce, Charlie Hamby and I, met John R. Shillady . . . on the corner of Brazos and 6th Street. He was apparently advocating social equality of the Negroes and Whites. We gave him a pretty good thrashing."[29] This thrashing left Shillady a "shell-shocked soldier." Returning to New York, he resigned his leadership role in the NAACP within a year. It was later charged that these injuries led to complications that eventually caused Shillady's death.[30]

While the Red Summer of 1919 was clearly a racially violent period in the history of Texas and the United States, there were also countersigns that the boundaries of "place" were becoming more inclusive. On June 28, 1919, Texas ratified the Nineteenth Amendment to the U.S. Constitution guaranteeing women's suffrage. A concerted campaign against lynching brought together such organizations as the Texas League of Women's Voters, the Texas Interracial Commission, branches of the missionary societies of the Methodist Episcopal Church, the Young Women's Christian Association, and eventually the Association of Southern Women for the Prevention of Lynching, headed by a Jessie Daniel Ames, who was born just twenty miles from Longview.[31]

Reaching a more inclusive definition of the human community became the centerpiece for this loose-knit coalition of reform-minded organizations. While lynching remained the most dramatic manifestation of injustice, leaders were tenacious in their insistence that lynchings would cease only when the descendants of slaves were given an equitable place in the educational, economic, and political institutions of society.[32] This insistence notwithstanding, success was slow in coming, signaled most vividly by the halting progress of L. C. Dyer's antilynching bill through the U.S. Congress.[33]

As information on the pattern of lynchings accumulated, however, it became evident that most incidents occurred when local citizens worked themselves into a kind of frenzy after a black male was accused of either murder or rape of a white person. Unwilling to wait for the law to run its course, citizens opted for the more expeditious procedure of lynching. This tendency was tragically illustrated on May 6, 1922, when three blacks were "burned at the stake" in communities about seventy miles east of Waco in Freestone County for their alleged participation in the slaying of a young orphan girl the day before. Black members of the community threatened revenge for the brutal burnings. Governor Neff sent Texas Rangers to ensure the peace. Two days later another black man was lynched. Natural calamity intensified tensions when heavy rains caused record flooding and heavy losses along the East Texas rivers. Within two more weeks a total of nine blacks had lost their lives to lynch mobs.[34]

Legal Hangings in Texas

We do not mean to suggest that illegal lynchings were the sole factor that led Texas lawmakers to enact the reformed electrocution statute in 1923. Illegal lynchings and the social movement aimed at their elimination were important, but *legal* local hangings by the 1920s were a long-established part of the state's landscape. Indeed, one of the most enduring stereotypes of Texas surrounds the public hanging of cattle rustlers on the range or in dusty frontier hamlets.

Prior to 1923, convicted capital offenders in Texas were executed in the county of conviction, under the supervision of the local sheriff. These hangings were by design a public show, "carefully arranged beforehand and attended not only by the rabble, but by persons of rank and fashion, of intelligence and sensibility."[35] Capital crimes in the pre-1923 era at one time or another included treason, piracy, murder, kidnapping slaves, selling free persons as slaves, rape, robbery, burglary, counterfeiting, and arson.[36]

The best set of data for legal hangings in the United States during this time has been compiled by Watt Espy.[37] He has collected (and continues to collect) information on 14,634 executions in this country since 1608, of which 394 took place in Texas between 1819 and 1923. With the "Espy files" we examined these early Texas executions.

Murder and felony murders constitute the large majority of cases. Of the 394 offenders, 390 were hung and 4 were reportedly shot, all in the county of conviction. Nearly all were men (391). The three women were hung for murder. The ages of the condemned ranged from fifteen to eighty. The primary types of occupation of those executed were farm labor of one sort or another, though in some instances the occupation was listed more specifically as bandit, bandit leader, buffalo hunter, slave, cowboy, or rug peddler.

The race and ethnic breakdown of those executed was 60.5 percent African-American, 26.5 percent Anglo, .5 percent Native American, and 12.5 percent Latino. The records reveal that eight slaves were legally executed. Most of the executions of African-Americans (some 60 percent) were carried out during 1867–1899, the most lethal decade being the 1890s, when sixty-five African-

Americans were hung according to then operable laws. As noted earlier, however, the line between legal hangings and illegal lynchings was often very thin.[38] Both often appeared to be administered as much to maintain the caste-like system of domination as to even the scales of justice. Nevertheless, it was the outbreak of brutal lynchings in central Texas in May of 1922 that eventually precipitated reform of the then operating statute.

The Road to the Electric Chair

Appalled by the level and sheer brutality of illegal lynchings in the 1920s, J. W. Thomas, from the small community of Rogers (not far from where the brutal burnings had taken place and a short distance from Waco), ran for the state senate on the platform that hangings should be removed from the emotional atmosphere of local communities to the more remote prison in Huntsville, where citizens, both black and white, could be brought more securely under the equal protection of the law. At the same time, Thomas advocated a shift from the rope to the electric chair as a more progressive and humane means of execution. Neither the shift to centralized state-imposed executions nor that to the use of electrocution was unique to Texas at the time; both reflected national trends of the day.

The initiation of centralized state-imposed executions in the United States is generally linked to an 1864 execution in Vermont, but the momentum for removing these events from the emotional fever of local communities began to build during the height of lynchings in the 1890s. Most of the initial reform statutes appeared first in the northeastern, followed by the midwestern and western regions of the nation, and then finally in the South, where Virginia, Kentucky, North and South Carolina, and Arkansas enacted statutes between 1908 and 1913. Florida, Georgia, and Texas followed in 1924. Mississippi, in 1955, and Louisiana, in 1957, were the last.[39]

In New York, on August 6, 1890, William Kemmler became the first person to be executed by electrocution. His death followed a decade-long controversy involving such famous personages as Thomas A. Edison and George Westinghouse. Throughout the 1880s, a controversy swirled around the types of current (alternating or direct current) to be employed in homes, businesses, and public areas. Edison favored DC, while his opponent and rival Westinghouse advocated AC. Edison's DC current was winning the "marketing war" because it was cheaper to install. Westinghouse countered by charging that DC current was dangerous to humans. Putting this danger to work for the state, Harold Brown, in the mid-1880s, invented the electric chair, a device to execute criminals more humanely in a "quick and painless" manner.

Joining the debate over the expanding uses for electricity, on January 1, 1889, the New York legislature approved electrocution as the new means to carry out capital punishment. The "chair" replaced the gallows, and Harold Brown was authorized to oversee the execution of Kemmler. Three used generators were purchased to carry out the new statutory provisions.[40] While the new execution technology was being refined, Kemmler was fighting to avoid it. His attorney petitioned the United States Supreme Court to review his case. The Court, however, decided against Kemmler, noting that electrocution did not offend the Eighth Amendment's prohibition of cruel and unusual punishment.[41]

Kemmler's electrocution, much like the later lethal injection innovations, started a trend. Following New York's lead in the North were Ohio in 1897, Massachusetts in 1901, New Jersey in 1907, and Pennsylvania in 1915. Southern lawmakers also became advocates: Kentucky adopted electrocution in 1907, Virginia in 1908, Tennessee in 1909, North Carolina in 1910, South Carolina in 1912, Arkansas in 1913, Texas in 1923, Florida and Georgia in 1924, and Alabama in 1927.[42]

Thus, by the time the freshman senator from Rogers proposed his 1923 reform execution statute (in Senate Bill 160), electrocutions had become an "acceptable" form of capital punishment in the United States.[43] However, not everyone agreed. Two of Thomas's colleagues in the state senate are quoted in the senate journal:

> Whereas, The Electrocution Bill passed by the Second Called session of the Thirty-Eighth Legislature is in contravention of all rules of civilized treatment of prisoners by hauling them hundreds of miles over the State subject to the gaze of the public; and
>
> Whereas, those bereaved and near in kin to the unfortunate one will be denied the last few days of association with the unfortunate one—and only the wealthy can accompany the condemned person and thus the poor whose heartstrings are just as tender will be discriminated against, which is contrary to all laws of Democratic institutions; and
>
> Whereas, it will be unfair to the inmates of the State penitentiary to use their confined place as headquarters for executions; and
>
> Whereas, there is a State education institution located where this place of execution is designated.
>
> Now therefore, we recommend that the provisions of this bill be not carried out, and that all humane organizations are requested to use their best efforts to defeat the carrying out of this uncivilized act.[44]

Such opponents, however, were in the minority and Thomas' bill passed in slightly modified form during the Second Called Session of the Thirty-eighth Legislature. The law is reprinted in Appendix A.

Persons would now be electrocuted when convicted of capital offenses involving robbery, rape, and murder. The new law enumerated a variety of provisions, including specification of the timing (after midnight and before sunrise), and a $5,000 appropriation for the construction of the electric chair. A "Death Row" of nine cells and one shower was to be constructed to house and serve capital offenders awaiting executions. The newly fashioned electric chair (soon given the name "Old Sparky") was embedded in the concrete floor of the death chamber and became operable in the Huntsville prison unit on December 1, 1923.

When the electric chair came on line, it marked the end of an era for legal hangings in Texas.

Bexar County's [San Antonio] rope which has hanged two men and which was retired with the installing of the electric chair in the State penitentiary at Huntsville will hereafter be used by the sheriff's department to tow automobiles. The well oiled and pliable piece of Manila hemp was taken from the locker in the sheriff's office Friday, the hangman's noose untied by Deputy Sam James and was tossed into another locker and re-named "tow rope."

The rope was purchased by former Sheriff John W. Tobin for the execution of Clemente Apolinar. After the execution of Apolinar the rope was lent to the sheriff of Brewster County for the hanging of a man. It was returned to Sheriff James Stevens after being used in Brewster County. The rope has been treated with oil, stretched and whipped until it was pliable as fine silk fishing line. The deputies predicted it will last for years as a tow rope.[45]

On January 1, 1924, Captain R. F. Coleman, warden of the Huntsville prison and therefore the legislatively designated executioner, submitted his letter of resignation to be effective January 15, 1924. The first scheduled electrocutions were to take place on January 16, 1924. In an interview with reporters, Coleman gave as his reasons, "It just couldn't be done, boys. A Warden can't be a warden and a killer too. The penitentiary is a place to reform a man, not to kill him."[46]

Walter Monroe Miller, a former sheriff of Johnson County, just south of Fort Worth, assumed duties as the new warden in Huntsville on February 4, 1924. His views on performing executions varied from those of his predecessor. "It's a case of duty to me," Miller told reporters. "I have hanged several men while I was Sheriff and to touch the button or pull the switch on an electric chair means no more to me than pulling the lever of the gallows. . . . At any rate it's more humane—the chair."[47] Four days later, Miller oversaw the electrocution of five men, all black, shortly after midnight on February 8, 1924. After the brief increase in illegal lynchings between 1919 and 1923, there was a consistent decline in these incidents until they basically disappeared, with sporadic exceptions, in the 1940s.[48]

The rejection of vigilante justice was facilitated by a broader shift in the definition of "place," in this instance as defined by standing before the law. By expanding the protections of rational-legal due process, encouraged by a more centralized system of capital punishment, the exclusionary beliefs and practices aimed at citizens whose roots were African-American became less stark. This shift in the spectrum of beliefs was, to be sure, a matter of shading rather than sharp contrast. The legacy of an overrepresentation of blacks among the executed population would continue for several decades.

Conclusion

As the implications of Thirteenth Amendment's loophole for maintaining what so many had died to eliminate became apparent, the Thirty-ninth U.S. Congress drafted and passed legislation that at the time was referred to as the Reconstruction Amendment, and that when ratified on July 23, 1868, became the Fourteenth Amendment to the U.S. Constitution, ensuring that within the states citizens were more fully protected by the clause ". . . nor shall any State deprive any person of life, liberty, or property without due process of law, nor deny to any person within its jurisdiction the equal protection of the laws."

Still, the slaves-of-the-state imagery for the convicted felon remained. By 1871 a Virginia court held in *Ruffin v. Commonwealth* that

a convicted felon . . . as a consequence of his crime, not only forfeited his liberty, but all his personal rights except those which the law in its humanity accords to him. He is for the time being a slave of the state. He is *civiliter mortuus*; and his estate, if he has any is administered like that of a dead man. (p. 796)

This same year, as the newly established legal battlefield against the remnants of slavery took shape, the U.S. Congress passed further protections for former slaves, this time in Section 1983 of the Civil Rights Act of 1871—a measure designed to curb the lynching and terrorizing activities of the Ku Klux Klan. On this legislative and judicial battlefield politicians and citizens alike shaped the character of criminal justice in the post–Civil War years.

The most obvious historical fact that sets criminal justice in the former Confederate South apart from the rest of the country is the legacy of slavery. We have noted that in *Lynchings and What They Mean*, the 1931 report published by the Southern Commission on the Study of Lynching, the geographic concentration of illegal lynchings was dramatically documented. However, figures compiled by the NAACP Legal Defense and Educational Fund reveal a similar picture for state-sanctioned executions. As this is being written, no southern state is without a death penalty statute. Of the top fifteen states, ranked in terms of the number of executions carried out between 1930 and 1992, twelve were members of the Confederacy. If we look only at executions in the post-*Furman* years (1977 onward), as of mid-1992 90 percent of the 167 executions took place under death-sentencing statutes in southern states.[49] Texas led the way with 50, followed by Florida with 29, Louisiana with 20, Georgia with 15, Virginia with 14, and Alabama with 9.

But how might slavery be linked to capital punishment, both legal and illegal? How do we account for the fact that within the United States, illegal lynchings and legal executions have been disproportionately concentrated in the southern tier of states? The source of this southern concentration of both illegal lynchings and state-sanctioned executions is rooted in a cultural readiness to engage in what we would call a logic of exclusion. Across time and location slavery, as a social system, depends on beliefs and practices that place some persons in a category apart, separate from rights and duties otherwise applied.[50] As numerous writers have suggested, and as mountains of empirical data have confirmed, there is a deep moral significance in the idea of one's "place" in the human community. When we go to war, when we advocate abortion, when we legitimize capital punishment, and when we tolerate lynchings, we engage in a kind of logic of exclusion whereby the life being terminated is placed outside the security of the "bounded" community. As Justice Brennan wrote in *Furman v. Georgia*, "the calculated killing of a human being by the State involves by its very nature, a denial of the executed person's humanity."

Normally immutable, the sanctity of life becomes less secure once the boundaries of community membership are crossed. "Place" in this sense is central to the power of our cultural myths.[51] A culture of exclusion, once established, is not easily extinguished. Although the Civil War and the ratification of the Thirteenth Amendment ended slavery, the logic of exclusion as a cultural system of beliefs continued. In this sense, the foundation for state-sanctioned capital punishment in the United States can be found in the period of Reconstruction, as can the process of reform.

First and foremost, the progression from illegal lynchings to state-sanctioned, centralized electrocutions was driven by what Gamson, Fireman, and Rytina have called encounters with unjust authority.[52] Much of the scourge of lynchings in the Reconstruction South originated in the struggle for legitimate authority between local and federal officials. Legitimacy remained an unsettled issue, an issue often resolved in local fact by the situational dispute-settling mechanism of lynching. The central proposition of local beliefs that allowed this to occur was embedded in the tradition of slavery and the inherent logic of exclusion.

Thus, the central issue for those who would reform existing practices became the definition of "place" in the social, economic, and political life of the community. The core problem for reformers was to convince others that "the unimpeded operation of the authority system would result in an injustice."[53] Lynchings were the most dramatic example of the implied injustice and thus provided a solid ideological basis for early efforts toward more broadly based reform. Thus the obvious and tragic inequities of lynchings became, with deep irony, instrumental in getting the NAACP off the ground.

The NAACP spent a great deal of energy in its formative years concentrating on redefining beliefs and practices in regard to lynchings. The report *Thirty Years of Lynchings* is the most obvious example; the efforts in support of federal antilynching legislation are another. By publicizing potentially dramatic incidents such as the "Waco Horror" in 1916 and the Longview and Chicago riots in the summer of 1919, NAACP leaders hoped to generate a "sudden, discontinuous change in [their] capacity for collective action."[54] It is just such an incident (the burning of three persons accused of a crime) in 1922 that spurred a local Texas politician to push for and pass capital punishment legislation.

In the summer of 1923, the Texas legislature, following a national trend and touting electricity as a "clean, efficient and humane" means of execution, enacted a law to centralize capital punishment in the state prison in Huntsville. The legislative change was precipitated most directly by a rash of racially motivated hangings in the immediately preceding years. The hope was that this new statute would reduce the emotional tension surrounding local hangings and these public spectacles would soon recede into a dimly remembered past. While remnants of this past would continue to show up in ugly detail,[55] by adopting state-controlled electrocution for more secluded executions, Texas legislators hoped to demonstrate that their state was in greater concord with evolving standards of decency.

While lynchings continued to occur in the immediately ensuing years, they eventually ceased. Leaders of a coalition of social movement organizations generated enough awareness of the injustice to concentrate more fully on the core issues of educational, employment, and voting rights. These efforts, in turn, were eventually buttressed by awakened sensitivities to civil and human rights that were occasioned by World War II and the Nuremberg Trials.[56] Once awakened, the broad-based civil rights movement in the last half of the twentieth century would succeed in fashioning a more inclusive understanding of the human community, an understanding still very much in the process of evolving. But this is a subject for later chapters. First, it is important to survey the patterns of legal executions that emerged from the 1923 capital punishment statute in Texas.

CHAPTER 2

THE INITIAL "HARVEST OF DEATH": 1924–1972

■ ■ ■

Therefore, it is the further order and judgment of this Court that the warden of the State Penitentiary, at Huntsville, Texas, be, and he is hereby, directed and commanded to, at some hour before sunrise, on the fourth day of June, 1937, take the said Dwight Beard, the defendant herein, into a place provided by the State of Texas, and there to pass through and cause to be passed through the body of the said Dwight Beard, said current of electricity until the said Dwight Beard is dead, dead, dead.[1]

The new capital punishment statute took effect the morning of February 8, 1924. Shortly after midnight, 12:09 A.M., Charles Reynolds walked through the entrance to the room housing "Old Sparky," was strapped by guards into the electric chair, and after three surges of electricity was pronounced dead at 12:16 A.M. In quick succession, Reynolds's death was followed by the execution of Ewell Morris, George Washington, and Mack Matthews. While these four men were being electrocuted, Melvin Johnson obtained a last-minute, one-hour stay of execution from Acting Governor T. W. Davidson. No additional reprieves were forthcoming, however, and Johnson was electrocuted and pronounced dead shortly after 2:00 A.M.[2]

Thus, within two hours of its initiation, the new capital punishment statute resulted in the execution of five offenders. All five were of African-American descent; all were from rural East Texas counties. A contemporary observer labeled these executions a "harvest of death."[3] Between February 1924 and July 1972, a second, more prolonged "harvest" occurred. It reflected broader national trends, was organized by legal procedures and prison informal rituals, and became enveloped by an evolving body of folklore.

Overall Trends: 1923–1972

The five decades between 1923 and 1972 saw 510 capital offense convicts sentenced to die in Texas's electric chair. Tables 2.1 and 2.2 illustrate the outcomes by offense and racial-ethnic breakdown of all 510 pre-*Furman* pris-

Table 2.1. *Outcome of Pre-*Furman *Death Row Population by Offense*

	Murder		Rape		Robbery		Total	
	(n)	(%)	(n)	(%)	(n)	(%)	(n)	(%)
Executed	257	50.4	99	19.4	5	1.0	361	70.8
Commuted	75	14.7	10	2.0	7	1.4	92	18.0
Reversed or dismissed	7	1.4	1	.2			8	1.6
Deceased[a]	1	.2	1	.2			2	.4
Furman[b]	38	7.5	7	1.4	2	.4	47	9.2
Total	378	74.1	118	23.1	14	2.7	510	100.0

[a] Two prisoners died on death row while awaiting execution.
[b] Death sentences of 47 inmates were vacated by the Supreme Court's *Furman* decision in 1972.

Table 2.2. *Outcome of Pre-*Furman *Death Row Population by Race/Ethnicity*

	Anglo		African-American		Hispanic		Other		Total	
	(n)	(%)	(n)	(%)	(n)	(%)	(n)	(%)	(n)	(%)
Executed	107	21.0	229	44.9	24	4.7	1	.2	361	70.8
Commuted	38	7.5	37	7.3	17	3.3			92	18.0
Reversed or dismissed	6	1.2			2	.4			8	1.6
Deceased[a]	1	.2	1	.2					2	.4
Furman[b]	22	4.3	20	3.9	5	1.0	_	_	47	9.2
Total	174	34.1	287	56.3	48	9.4	1	.2	510	100.0

[a] Two prisoners died on death row while awaiting execution.
[b] Death sentences of 47 inmates were vacated by the Supreme Court's *Furman* decision in 1972.

Table 2.3. *Distribution of Pre-*Furman *Death Row Population by Offense and Race/Ethnicity*

	Murder		Rape		Robbery		Total	
	(n)	(%)	(n)	(%)	(n)	(%)	(n)	(%)
Anglo	145	28.4	21	4.1	8	1.6	174	34.1
African-American	191	37.5	90	17.6	6	1.2	287	56.3
Hispanic	41	8.0	7	1.4			48	9.4
Other	1	.2					1	.2
Total	378	74.1	118	23.1	14	2.7	510	100.0

oners convicted of capital offenses. Of that total, 378 (74 percent) received the death sentence for murder, 118 (23 percent) for rape, and 14 (3 percent) for armed robbery. Table 2.3 presents the distribution of offenses by race/ethnicity. Figure 2.1 depicts the trend in death sentences, and Figure 2.2 charts actual executions. As was the case nationally, the highwater mark in Texas was reached in the mid-1930s.

Of the 510 persons sentenced to die, 361 were eventually electrocuted; 71 percent were executed for murder, 27 percent for rape, and 1 percent for armed robbery. In all, 56 executions occurred in the 1920s, 122 in the 1930s, 78 in the 1940s, 76 in the 1950s, and 29 in the 1960s, prior to the moratorium in 1964. Again, like death sentence patterns, executions in Texas paralleled, and contributed substantially to, national patterns over these decades.

A reporter who witnessed some 190 of these executions and spent a good deal of time talking with the men on death row, described the characteristics of those he had met:

> It took no study for me to accept that simple, ignorant men committed more crimes of violence than did sophisticated men of means. And, it took but little to realize that when sophisticated men of means did commit crimes of violence, they seldom were executed for them. Those who were electrocuted were the blacks, Mexican-Americans, the poor whites and whites out of favor in their communities for one reason of another, having nothing to do with the criminal allegations for which they died.[4]

While this reporter felt little study was required to establish the class, race, and ethnic characteristics of the death row population, the implied inequities would occupy the attention of researchers, legal scholars, and appellate court judges for decades. The resulting body of writing suggests that the reporter was not far off the mark. Gender was the largest difference within the death-

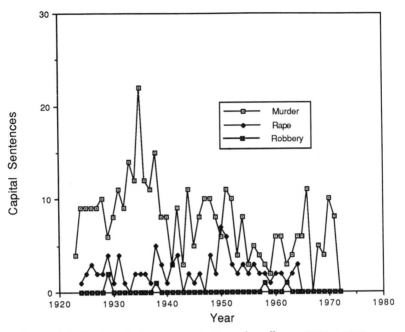

Figure 2.1. Total capital sentences in Texas by offense, 1923–1972.

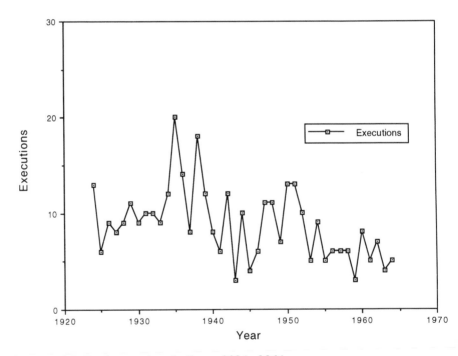

Figure 2.2. Total executions in Texas, 1924–1964.

sentenced population, which consisted of 507 males (99 percent) and 3 females. Between 1924, when the first execution took place, and 1972, when the Texas death penalty statute was overturned, no females were executed. Sixty-three percent of those executed were African-American, 30 percent were Anglo, and 7 percent were Hispanic. The average age was thirty years.

The work histories of the condemned population were episodic and unstable. The predominant occupation was that of common laborer (66 percent), mostly in agriculture. The men arriving on death row had been dairy workers, log cutters, sawmill and ranch hands, fruit and cotton pickers, or tractor drivers. A minority were in non-agricultural lines of work. For example, G. C. "Clem" Gray (#22) was a former deputy sheriff, butcher, and reputed town bully from Mount Pleasant, who was executed on August 7, 1925, for the murder of a local doctor's son.[5] Approximately 1 percent (6 individuals) were categorized as being employed as professional or managerial personnel. The education of the 510 death-sentenced prisoners was limited. Slightly over half (52 percent) had less than a sixth-grade education; ten percent reported that they had never attended school; 90 percent had not graduated from high school.

Over the full five decades, 54 percent of the condemned population came from small non-urban counties.[6] As Texas became increasingly urban, this characteristic shifted. Between 1923 and 1972, rural counties sent 276 offenders to the death house in Huntsville. Seventy-one percent of these began their stay on death row between 1923 and 1950. After 1950 the majority of offenders came from urban counties.

While the large majority of death-sentenced offenders were members of minority groups, it is important to note that this disproportionate representation changed over the years. In the 1920s less than 30 percent of those arriving on death row were Anglos. By the 1960s this had risen to almost 50 percent. There was no comparable shift in the demographic makeup of the state. Taken in conjunction with information discussed in subsequent chapters, this trend suggests quite strongly that changes in the administration of justice in Texas were well under way by the time they were given accent by the landmark Supreme Court decision *Furman v. Georgia* in 1972.

While arrest records are no doubt incomplete, the majority of the death-sentenced offenders do not appear to have been "three-time losers." Available records indicate that 28 percent of the death-sentenced inmates had never been arrested for a prior offense, 36 percent had been arrested once or twice, and 36 percent three or more times. Six percent of the offenders had nine or more prior arrests. In regard to prior violent activity, twenty-one death-sentenced inmates (4 percent) had been convicted of killing before, 4 percent had been convicted of a prior rape, and 8 percent had had a previous robbery conviction. Twenty-four percent had a record of at least one prior conviction for a burglary. Finally, 65 percent had no record of previous incarceration in an adult penitentiary. Those with prison records, the most dependable set of data, had been convicted primarily of petty theft (e.g., chicken, horse, turkey, cattle) or burglaries.

Once sentenced to die, blacks were more likely to be executed, 61 percent of the condemned whites having been eventually executed, compared with 82 percent of the blacks. Among Hispanics, the comparable figure was 50 percent. Conversely, 34 percent of the sentences for white offenders were commuted, whereas only 20 percent of the black offenders received clemency. Interestingly, 46 percent of the Hispanic inmates received a commutation.

As to the characteristics of the victims of the death row inmates in the five decades before *Furman*, 80 percent of the offenders had been convicted of offenses against Anglo victims. Approximately 15 percent of the offenders' victims were African-American and 5 percent Hispanic. Among cases in which white victims were killed, 73 percent resulted in executions. By contrast, 62 percent of the cases involving African-American victims and 46 percent of those involving Hispanic victims eventually resulted in the execution of the offenders.

Statistics such as these would eventually become the fulcrum for reversing capital punishment statutes in the 1970s. These patterns will be examined more precisely in the following chapters. For now it is enough to note that many of the patterns reported in the post-*Furman* years[7] were present in stark detail during the early years of execution by electrocution in Texas.

The Path to the Chair: Forms and Rituals

The Death Warrant

When a defendant was found guilty of a capital crime and given a death sentence, a death warrant was issued. The following warrant, issued when executions were at their peak in the 1930s, is a typical example.

On the 12th day of March, A.D. 1936, this cause was called for trial, and the State appeared by her District Attorney and the defendant Elmo Banks, appeared in person, and in open Court, his counsel also being present, and the said defendant Elmo Banks, having been duly arraigned in open Court, and having pleaded not guilty to the indictment herein, both parties announced ready for trial, and thereupon a jury of good and lawful men, to-wit:— LFC, and eleven others, was duly selected, impaneled and sworn, who, having heard the indictment read and the defendant's plea of not guilty thereto, and having heard the evidence submitted, and having been duly charged by the Court, retired in charge of the proper officer to consider of their verdict, and afterwards on to-wit:— March 13th, A.D. 1936, were brought into open Court by the proper officer, the defendant and his counsel being present and in due form of law returned into open Court, the following verdict, which was received by the Court, and read by the Clerk in open Court, and is here now entered upon the minutes of the Court, to-wit:—

"We the jury, find the defendant Elmo Banks, guilty of murder with malice aforethought, as charged in the indictment, and assess his punishment at death."

It is therefore, considered and adjudged by the Court that the defendant Elmo Banks is guilty of murder with malice aforethought as charged in the indictment herein and as found by the jury herein, and that he be punished as has been determined by the Jury, that is, with "Death," in accordance with the law and that he be remanded and is committed to jail to await the further order of this Court herein.

And the defendant, Elmo Banks, is hereby remanded and committed to the custody of the Sheriff of Lynn County, Texas, who will transport him to the State Penitentiary in Huntsville, Texas, and shall deliver him and the said death warrant into the hands of the Warden of the Penitentiary, and shall take and receive from said Warden, his receipt for the said Elmo Banks, and for said death warrant, and said Sheriff shall return said receipt to the Clerk of this Court.

These are therefore to command you to execute the aforesaid judgment and sentence at any time before the hour of sunrise on Friday, the 23rd day of October, A.D. 1936, at the State Penitentiary at Huntsville in the room arranged for that purpose by causing to pass through the body of the said Elmo Banks a current of electricity of sufficient intensity to cause the death of the said Elmo Banks, and by the application and continuance of such current through the body of the said Elmo Banks until he is dead.

[*Elmo Banks was executed, as scheduled, on October 23, 1936, 7 1/2 months after his conviction.*]

Death sentences were routinely appealed to the Texas Court of Criminal Appeals. Until this initial appeal was decided, inmates remained in the county jail. If the conviction was affirmed, the offender was brought a second time before the trial judge, who pronounced a sentence of death and then set an execution date, which could not be less than thirty days later. However, once a death date was set, it was "an unbroken custom" from 1936 [to 1972] for Texas governors to grant a thirty-day stay of execution, beyond the initial date.[8] With sentence and execution date set, the offender was transported to Huntsville to await execution.

Initial Death Row Processing

At admission to the prison in Huntsville, the convicted offender was photo-graphed, given an execution number in sequential order, and interviewed by a prison classification officer. Information gleaned from these interviews became the basis for the inmate's "social summary," which included date of sentence, criminal history, personal history, subject's version of the event that gave rise to conviction, family data, work and military history, mental status, recreational interests, and a general summary of the prisoner's current situation.

In addition, prison officials sent letters to previous employers, schoolteachers and principals, county welfare or relief personnel, and personal friends or contacts who might be able to provide information related to later appeals for clemency. These letters contained questions about the inmate's character (e.g., dependability, use of alcohol, ambition, honesty, intelligence). Some inmates wrote on their own behalf to the governor for assistance. Upon completion, the inmate's file was sent to Austin, where officials reviewed the material and made a recommendation to the governor for or against commutation.[9] The clemency process is discussed at length in Chapter 5.

Descriptions of the condemned offenders contained in these records provide a glimpse into the beliefs and practices of the day:

Subject is a short, heavy-set negro with copper complexion, extremely black hair, and dark maroon eyes. During the interview, he told his story in a disconnected, emotional fashion. He appeared to be very nervous and unable to concentrate on anything but the offense. His language and vocabulary are poor, and consists of many colloquialisms which seem to have had their origin in pre–Civil War days. His manner is that of the semi-illiterate plantation negro.
[From the file of Johnnie Banks, #191, who was executed April 29, 1938.]

The subject is a husky youth of average stature, red-haired, frank in attitude, serious of mien, whose general behavior is that of the town-dwelling youth of the better than average laborer's level. His history would seem to indicate that he is an amoral youth capable of vicious behavior.
[From the file of Burton Franks, #229, who was executed June 7, 1940.]

Subject is an average-sized, ebony skin, well-built Negro, with a rather bullet-shaped head and prominently Negroid features. His vocabulary is consistent with his reported grammar school education and his mannerisms are those of the average urban Negro laborer.
[From the file of James Miles, #214, who was executed April 23, 1939.]

The subject is an average-sized, well-built, rather good-looking Mexican youth, with a skin which is lighter than the average run of Mexicans. His vocabulary and language are poor, and his stock of knowledge is limited, as is consistent with his reported Mexican labor background.
[*From the file of Frank Salazar, #223, who was executed December 16, 1939.*]

The subject is a tall, well built, muscular, ebony-skinned negro. He says that he is about six feet, three inches in height and weighs probably 195 pounds. His language and vocabulary are poor, and his intelligence seems to be about the level of the average East Texas back-woods negro. . . . He admits a history of rather wide heterosexual activities, but these do not seem to be widely different from those of other negroes of his general background.
[*From the file of Florence Murphy, #231, who was executed August 30, 1940.*]

The subject is of about average height and is rather thin. During the interview he assumed an attitude of cooperation, straightforwardness and sincerity. He made no effort to hide his own guilt and made it a point to assume all of the guilt in his version of his offense. He is very clean cut and his mannerisms and vocabulary indicate his reported rural back-ground and sixth grade education. The subject seems to have turned his every thought toward religion and he says that if his life is spared, he intends to preach.
[*From the file of James Alford, #241, who was executed May 8, 1942.*]

The subject is a rather small, but strongly built, heavy-set negro with dark skin. He assumes the attitude of the urban, sophisticated, negro play-boy, but his thought process, language and vocabulary are those of a person of limited education and background. During his ten years of living in Corpus Christi, he apparently picked up a good many surface tricks of speech and manner of the urban sophisticate, but the adjustment never went very deep and his manner is quite unconvincing. During the interview, he assumed a suave, sailing, devil-may-care attitude and his story was replete with quips, wise-cracks and indefinite answers. However, he was quite nervous and this seemed to be a device to keep up his courage.
[*From the file of George Griffin, #234, who was executed April 20, 1941.*]

The subject is a short, pudgy, negro with a slight external strabismus [squint-eyed]. When interviewed he was emotionally aroused against his co-defendant, whose story he had heard while the co-defendant was talking to the interviewer. For several minutes he threw himself about his cell and shook the bars like an angry ape. The subject may be described

■ ■ ■ 27

briefly as an amoral, drifting, self-indulgent, unstable negro of average intelligence who, although superficially polite and periodically well-behaved, is the rest of the time a selfish criminal with little social feeling.
[*From the file of Robert Manning, #228, who was executed April 28, 1940.*]

The subject is of very average stature and is of slender build. His general manner is consistent with his reported background as a laborer and is consistent with that of the Mexican laborer in the Texas urban center.
[*From the file of Jesse Palanco, #207, who was executed August 19, 1938.*]

Reprieved from the Chair

Although every offender arrived on death row with an execution date, it was customary for the governor to grant one thirty-day reprieve to allow pardon officials time to review the case. During this time many of the letters, both for and against additional consideration, would accumulate in the inmate's file. The following is a typical example of a reprieve document.

WHEREAS, Albert Carr was convicted in the District Court of Harris County, Texas, in September, 1934, in Cause No. 40236, for the Crime of Rape, and was convicted and given the penalty of death; and the date for this negro convict's execution has been set for May 8, 1935; and

NOW, I, AS GOVERNOR, am requested to grant a thirty-day reprieve to this condemned convict in order that the Board of Pardons and Paroles may further investigate his application for a commutation of this death sentence to life imprisonment. In a report dated May 7, 1935, the Board of Pardons and Paroles recites that they have not had sufficient time to investigate the facts in this case, and, "The Board feels that where human life is at stake that sufficient time should be taken to thoroughly investigate apparently essential facts and circumstances not satisfactorily explained in the Statement of Facts in the record of the case; and in view of the fact that this man is now lodged in the death cell at Huntsville and can be surely and safely restrained there, nothing will be lost by granting him a thirty-day reprieve from the execution of his sentence."

In matters concerning the taking of human life, I am of the opinion that a full and complete investigation of facts and circumstances surrounding each case be made. In order that the Board of Pardons and Paroles may have additional time to complete their investigation,

NOW, THEREFORE, I JAMES V. ALLRED, Governor of the State of Texas, by virtue of the authority vested in me under the Constitution and laws of this State, for reasons herein set out, do hereby grant Albert Carr, a THIRTY-DAY REPRIEVE FROM HIS SENTENCE OF DEATH.

Albert Carr, the 145th person to arrive on death row, was executed on June 7, 1935, after being convicted of rape. Between 1924 and 1971, 137 (27 percent) of the condemned prisoners received no additional reprieve and 113 were executed on their first execution date. Eight of the 510 capital offenders received nine or more reprieves; four of them were eventually executed. .

Generally a couple of weeks before the reprieve expired, the prison warden would write a form letter to the condemned man's family about arrangements to pick up the body. Three options were available. First, the family could make their own arrangements. Second, if the family could not afford a burial or failed to notify the warden about funeral arrangements, the condemned was buried in the prison cemetery, the Captain Joe Byrd Cemetery, named, following his death, after an assistant warden and executioner at the Huntsville Prison who had begun working for the prison system in 1936 and died on the job in 1964. As a third option, the condemned man or his family could donate his body to the State Anatomical Board for dissection and study.

An example of a letter sent to a family member of a man convicted in Limestone County just northwest of Waco and eventually executed August 24, 1941:

It becomes my sad duty to inform you that unless the Board of Pardons and Paroles in Austin, Texas, intervenes in behalf of _____, the death penalty assessed him in the District Court of Limestone County will be imposed during the early morning hours of August 24th—shortly after midnight next Saturday.

As you are the one your brother listed to be notified, I would appreciate being informed as soon as possible whether or not you or other relatives intend to claim his body in the event that the above mentioned is carried out.

The State of Texas does not furnish transportation in these cases, and it will therefore be necessary for you or other relatives to engage an undertaker to call Huntsville Prison the night of August 23rd. We wish to have our arrangements agree with the wishes of you or other relatives as much as is possible under the circumstances, and as our preparations must be made in advance, we will appreciate being advised by return mail regarding any arrangements you may wish to make. If you intend to claim the body, please have the undertaker advise this office by letter immediately. If you do not wish to claim the body, burial will take place in the Prison Cemetery here in Huntsville with full Christian rites.

For your information, please rest assured that everything possible is being done to make your brother's last hours as happy as is possible under such conditions, and the Prison Chaplain is in constant attendance.

Some of the inmates' files contained responses from the family, many of which reflected their social and economic circumstances:

Many thanks to you for the information. It is my desire to claim the body of my hopeless son, but I am unable financially, to bear the expense. [*From the file of Elmer Pruitt, #178, executed May 30, 1937.*]

To the Warden at Huntsville, sir in reply to your notice though it pains me to my heart to tell you, I cannot claim the body of my son, I am not able to bring the body here so you will be doing a great favor by giving him a Christian burial there. Also in your statement you have tried to make his last moments as happy as possible. I thank you in God's name, tell him I hope he has made his peace with his God. [*From the file of Bennie Randall, #215, executed May 7, 1939.*]

Execution Rituals

After family and relatives were notified, local newspapers and national wire services were contacted with the press release of the impending execution. If the governor did not intervene, the prisoner was executed. An eyewitness provides a glimpse of the basic ritual.

And then there is a loud *crunch*, a noise from outside death row—and all the chaplains raise their voices. But the noise swells into a whine, the whine to a snarl that overcomes their voices. It mounts higher, subsides, mounts, subsides, then fades away.

They all know what that sound means. Joe Byrd is testing his equipment, swirling the needle in the gauge above the switch to 1,800 volts, back to 500, up to 1,300, back to 500, hold, then a purring away to silence. . . . A knock. The green door is pushed open slightly. The warden peeks in. "We're ready," he says. . . . The big clock says 12:02 A.M.

Assembled in the Death Chamber are those who joined the cast for the final act of the ritual.

The warden nods to the condemned man and steps back a few inches to make room. He glances briefly at the one-way window at his shoulder to alert the executioner standing so quietly beside his switchboard.

The prison physician, to the left of the chair, is nervously fiddling with his stethoscope.

The three guards place themselves at the back and on both sides of the chair. They wait.

To the condemned man three of the four men standing behind the black railing directly in front of the chair are strangers. They are the official witnesses, and the one he knows is the newsman who had talked with him, joked with him, offered him cigars—and had heard him out without comment as he tried to explain the events of the brutal and bloody day that had brought him here to this little room.

Now the warden's eyes recheck the scene, finding every person in the right place. He turns to the man, addresses him by his first name, asking in an almost kindly voice: "Do you have anything to say?"

The man sweeps the witnesses with his gaze. "I hold no malice against anyone," he says softly. "I'm not mad at anyone. I want to thank all of you people for being so kind to me." It is as if by rote.

The warden nods. He speaks, and the words seem strangely derisive, but they are words wardens before him have spoken, and his voice is firm and polite. "Have a seat, please," he says.

The man moves to the chair and sits down. The guards move quickly, efficiently, to strap him in, to position electrodes on his head and left leg, first dampening the shaved spots with a saline solution to facilitate the smooth flow of the electric current.

The man is pale. His arms are lashed to arm rests, his legs to the chair legs, his body to the chair with a broad strap so taut that it straightens his spine to the chair back.

He smiles—but he tries to cringe away as a guard stuffs cotton in his nostrils to trap blood that might gush from ruptured veins in his brain.

A mask is placed across his face. The guard steps back quickly. The warden glances around once more; every man is in his place. He turns and nods in the direction of the one-way mirror behind which Joe Byrd is waiting.

The *crunch*. The mounting whine and snarl of the generator. The man's lips peel back, the throat strains for a last desperate cry, the body arches against the restraining straps as the generator whines and snarls again, the features purple, steam and smoke rise from the bald spots on head and leg while the sick-sweet smell of burned flesh permeates the little room.

The generator purrs to a halt.

The warden does not move. Neither do the guards. But the physician steps forward. He places his stethoscope against the steaming chest, listens intently. He turns to the warden.

"I pronounce this man dead," he says.

It is 12:08 A.M.

The ritual has ended . . .

On death row the men are silent. The guard sips his coffee and reads the newspaper.[10]

Following the physician's pronouncement, a death certificate was issued along with the "Warden's Return after Execution." Clay Whittle's execution on July 30, 1944 provides an example.

WARDEN'S RETURN AFTER EXECUTION

RECEIVED: The Death Warrant, together with the body of the named, CLAY WHITTLE, [#262] from the Sheriff of Houston County, Texas, May 18, 1944. Said Death Warrant ordering the execution of the above named, CLAY WHITTLE, on June 30, 1944. A.D.

FURTHER: In accordance with the judgment of the District Court of Houston County, the said, CLAY WHITTLE, was duly executed on the 30th day of July, 1944 A.D., at the hour of 12:08 A.M. by Warden H. E. Moore, causing to pass through his body a current of electricity with sufficient intensity to cause his death. The said, CLAY WHITTLE, was pronounced dead by Dr. M. D. Hanson, Medical Supervisor of the Texas Prison System, ten minutes after application of the electric current.

FURTHER: The body of the said, CLAY WHITTLE, was buried in the Cemetery of the Texas Prison System, Huntsville, Texas, July 31, 1944 A.D.

Electrocution was not free. The statute stipulated that the county of conviction was to pay the state prison system twenty-five dollars for services. This "service charge" included the cost of feeding, housing, and executing the offender. In addition, the county of conviction was required to provide $8.47 for the burial clothes. The latter fee was increased in 1943 to $19.92 ($10 for the casket, $8.92 for clothing, and $1.00 if needed for a tombstone).

While waiting for the process to run its course, many of the condemned jotted letters, poems, and diaries that provide some clues about how they approached their execution. Some inmates wrote confessions, others revealed impressions of prison personnel. Some desperately fought for survival, others were fatalistic, quietly resigned. Still others "got religion," read the Bible, and wrote last statements witnessing their conversion and faith:

To "Keep Up With The Joneses" many blindly form pardnerships with the Devil. Carefully hoarded material gain gives a false happiness, shared with none and desires never satisfied.

Finally they are divested of earthly gains and never know peace, then the Devil seeks another pardner.

Others take God in pardnership, the treasures so gained are never hoarded but joyfully shared with all men. Tho freely shared this treasure increases and gives peace everlasting as God dissolves no pardnership.

To shake hands with God and accept him as a full time pardner is surely the only way to "Beat The Devil."
[*From the file of Charles Clark, #371, executed March 25, 1954.*]

I have wanted to write this letter to you right from the beginning. But due to circumstances beyond my control, I have not been allowed to until now.

My purpose in writing is to let you know, in my own words, exactly how sorrowful I am for what I have done. I hope that my degree of grief will someday help you to begin to understand me when I say that I never could have willingly and knowingly done what I did. If sorrow could ever be so great that it could restore life, then J. would be alive today through my sorrows. I am truly repentant.

Those are the most sincere words I have ever spoken and they are spoken from my heart in hopes that they, in some small way, will tell you that I am not so bad as newspapers and rumors have depicted me.

I have asked the Lord to forgive my sins and to instill some forgiveness into the hearts of those who feel badly toward me now for what has happened.

Again I say that I am sincerely sorry for what I have done not only to J. but to you and the rest of your family as well.
[*From the file of Walter Witaker, Jr., # 379, executed September 1, 1954.*]

Facts and Folklore

As the decades passed and executions accumulated, stories of sadness, courage, humor, folly, and just bare facts became part of the folklore surrounding the death house, Old Sparky, and those who came and left death row.

- *The first person electrocuted:* Mack Matthews, February 8, 1924.

- *The last person electrocuted:* Joseph Johnson, July 30, 1964.

- *The youngest offender:* Henderson Young (#196), a convicted rapist of African-American heritage from Harrison County. Born on May 15th, 1921, Young was executed on May 6, 1938, less than nine days short of his seventeenth birthday.

- *The oldest person electrocuted:* Clemens Matura, who was sixty-seven when executed for murder on July 2, 1937.

- *Five executions in one night:* February 8, 1924.

- *Three executions in one night:* This occurred three times—on December 29, 1933, February 9, 1934, and July 10, 1936.

- *Two executions in one night:* This occurred twenty-two times.

- *First execution in which a female reporter was allowed to witness:* E. M. Snow, executed on August 12, 1927.

- *First inmate executed for killing a Texas prison guard:* Luke Trammell, August 20, 1937.

- *First inmate executed for killing another Texas convict:* Sam Phillips, May 14, 1926.

- *Brothers executed:* Frank and Lorenzo Noel (executed July 3, 1925), S. A. and Forest Robins (executed April 6, 1926), Oscar and Mack Brown (executed July 10, 1936), Roscoe and Henderson Young (executed May 6, 1938).

In addition to these facts, a number of incidents were recounted in response to inquiries of what life was like for the condemned on death row. One such event was the electrocution of Arthur Adams, sentenced to die for a murder committed in the Fort Worth area. After the customary thirty-day stay the execution was set and the execution rituals begun, only to be interrupted by faulty equipment. In his written statement, a prison officer reported:

> A few minutes after 12:00 midnight, we strapped Arthur Adams in the chair. And when we were strapping him in, we broke the left leg electrode and it had to be repaired. We released the man from the chair and he was taken back into his cell where he remained with the chaplain until he was brought back to be placed back in the chair. It took about an hour to repair the broken electrode. The man was calm and wasn't upset when he was placed in the chair the second time, which was at 1:00 A.M., and he was legally pronounced dead at 1:05 A.M.
> When asked if he had anything to say, he said, "I am alright and have no grudge against anyone."
> The man had ice-cream for supper.
> [*From the file of Arthur Adams, #293, executed September 5, 1947.*]

A second series of stories that found their way into the folklore of life on death row illustrated the economic straits of many families. One involved a request by an executed inmate's mother, who attempted to obtain "gate money," money inmates received at the time of discharge from the prison system. Writing to the warden, this mother noted:

Mr. kind sir, am I not supposed to have 50 dollars discharge money for my son J. B. Stephens? When a boy leaves they give him 50 dollars and my dear boy is gone never to come back?
[From the file of J. B. Stephens, #266, executed December 19, 1944.]

The $50 discharge money was not given to the inmate's mother following the execution of her son.

In addition to stories about "hitches" in the execution process and the economic straits of families of those awaiting execution, death row stories included accounts of how scheduled executions, with the accompanying gloom among inmates, could be affected by extraneous circumstances. During the 1940s numerous temporary stays of execution came about as a result of the radio broadcast "Thirty Minutes behind the Walls." The following letter from prison personnel to the Board of Pardons and Paroles shows how.

The execution of L. C. Newman of Polk County, is set for Thursday, July 18th [1946] and is to take place a few minutes past midnight, Wednesday, July 17th. Our 430th broadcast of "Thirty Minutes Behind the Walls," is scheduled for Wednesday evening, July 17th, at 10:30 [P.M.]. That means just a little more than 1 hour's time will elapse between the ending of the broadcast and the execution of Newman if it is carried out that date.

Last Wednesday evening we had 373 outside visitors in the auditorium for the program, and approximately 40 inmates. We will probably have more than that for the broadcast tomorrow night. We do not have sufficient means to notify the public of any change or cancellation of the program. And too, the "gloom" among the inmates is always "heavy" on execution nights.

In view of the above, we respectfully request your honorable Board to make recommendations to Governor Stevenson that L. C. Newman be granted a 24-hour extension of time so that the program and execution will not conflict.

A precedent will be broken if this request is not granted. In the more than 8 years "Thirty Minutes Behind The Walls" has been on the air several execution dates have been postponed so there would be no conflict in the two.

In making this request we urge you to take immediate actions, so in the

event the execution date is not advanced we will have sufficient time to cancel the broadcast from the prison here.
[*From the file of L. C. Newman, #277, executed July 19, 1946.*]

The postponement was granted.

Perhaps the most sensational event in death row folklore involved the attempted escape of six prisoners on July 24, 1934; three from the general inmate population and three from death row. Any attempt to escape from death row would be newsworthy. This escape became particularly infamous because of the involvement of two members of the notorious Bonnie and Clyde gang. Joe Palmer and Raymond Hamilton had been sentenced to death after killing a prison guard (a second guard was shot but survived) in an escape on January 16, 1934, at the Eastham Unit in the Texas Prison System. They were assisted in their escape by Bonnie Parker and Clyde Barrow (a prisoner at the Eastham Unit in the early 1930s), who hid guns in the field where the prisoners worked, picked up the escapees in a waiting car, and drove them to freedom. Following this prison break and murder, both Palmer and Hamilton were apprehended, convicted of capital murder, and sentenced to death.

Some seven months after this initial escape-murder and subsequent apprehension and conviction, Palmer and Hamilton, along with a third death row inmate, Blackie Thompson, again attempted to escape, on July 24, 1934. They were accompanied by three general population inmates, Charlie Frazier, Whitey Walker, and Roy Johnson. The incident began on a Sunday around four o'clock in the afternoon, during feeding time. As a guard and his two inmate waiter-helpers entered the cellblock to distribute meals, they were confronted by a general population inmate who had a .45-caliber pistol.

All three were ordered to keep quiet on threat of death. Charlie Frazier then took the guard's keys and forced one of the inmate helpers to open the cells of Joe Palmer and Blackie Thompson. Other prisoners in the cellblock were told that if they wanted to attempt an escape, they should just call out. Raymond Hamilton was then released. Before the escaping inmates left death row, they locked the guard in one of the vacated cells.

The convicts left death row for the prison yard, where they obtained a ladder from the prison paintshop and placed it against the wall near the gun tower (picket 7). On their way to the picket they encountered another guard and two inmates, who were subdued and locked in a nearby captain's office. Upon reaching their intended escape route, the inmates set the ladder against the perimeter wall, where Raymond Hamilton, Joe Palmer, and Blackie Thompson climbed over and descended to the outside. A fourth inmate was shot and killed while on the ladder. The two remaining would-be escapees were shot and wounded. The prison officer who shot these men would later report:

The first thing I saw was a man in stripes reaching over a ladder leaning against the wall, in an effort to reach the platform of picket #7. I immediately called the front. I told them there was trouble at #7. Next I got my gun and shot at him, and the convict fell off. One dressed in white then came up the ladder. I shot him and he fell. Then the man in stripes came up the ladder again and I shot at him and he fell. A man in stripes came up the ladder the third time and when I shot he swung around under the ladder and I shot again and he fell. Then came another in white and I shot once or twice at him and he fell. I do not know how many times I shot at each man.

When I emptied my gun, I called the front again. Then I called Mr. Rains on #9 and asked him to come across, as there was trouble at #7.

I saw one man cross the street running parallel with the walls.

I shot nine times, one shot gun shell snapped, and I picked up a rifle and attempted to reload it, and could not get but one cartridge in it. I used the rifle first until I emptied it and then I picked up the shot gun and fired until it snapped.

In the escape, Whitey Walker was killed and Roy Johnson and Charlie Frazier, who masterminded the escape, were wounded. Joe Palmer, Raymond Hamilton, and Blackie Thompson managed to escape. On December 16, 1934, Blackie Thompson was killed by police officers near Amarillo, Texas. Hamilton and Palmer were eventually recaptured and executed on May 10, 1935, just under one year after their second escape.

Conclusion

Shortly after midnight on February 8, 1924, 5 condemned murderers, all black and all from rural East Texas counties, were electrocuted. Thus began the era of the electric chair in Texas. Between February 1924 and July 1964, 361 condemned men were executed. Executions reached a peak in the mid-1930s and declined thereafter. Ignoring this variation, on average one man was executed every five weeks. After July 1964, a moratorium suspended all executions in Texas until June 1972, when the Supreme Court in *Furman v. Georgia* decided that capital punishment was being administered in an arbitrary and capricious fashion, particularly in respect to the race and social class of the defendant. In concrete terms this meant that for the same offense blacks were more likely to be executed than were whites. In the chapters that follow, we will examine this basic pattern as it relates to those condemned to death for rape and murder in Texas and how this pattern shifted over time.

CHAPTER 3

RAPE, RACE, AND A "PECULIAR CHIVALRY"

■ ■ ■

The subject is a negro of average height, sparely built. His skin is dark brown and lustreless. The eyes and nostrils are wide apart, the nose short, the upper lip long, protruding and infantile; the chin recedes. His vocabulary and pronunciation are those of the average ignorant East Texas farm negro. It would appear from the interview and correspondence that the subject is of low average intelligence, emotionally immature, oversexed, preoccupied with his own penis, sadistic in his sexual relations, self-indulgent, silly, disrespectful, trouble-making, and maladjusted to the negro life-situation.[1]

Rape has been morally condemned and formally sanctioned by death for as long as laws have been written. The death penalty for rape is found in the Code of Hammurabi and in the laws of ancient Israelites, as well as in the statutes fashioned by colonists in Massachusetts. However, in the eighteenth century, guided by the Quaker-designed statutes in Pennsylvania, many legislators began softening their stance until most northern, western, and eastern states eventually enacted statutes wherein rape became punishable, not by death, but by a prison term. By contrast, in southern states rape remained a capital offense throughout the nineteenth and well into the second half of the twentieth century.[2]

The tenacity of the link between rape and capital punishment in the southern tier of the United States was intimately bound to race relations and what would eventually be referred to as a "peculiar form of chivalry." From the Biblical stories surrounding the curse of Ham to the earliest accounts of the little-known and less-understood peoples of "Barbary," "Lybia," "Numedia," and "Land of the Negroes," charges of sexual tension and lustful, bestial behavior permeated characterizations of these "sooty-skinned" people, and indeed eventually rooted much of the dishonoring exclusion used to justify the slave trade in the eighteenth century.[3]

Once thus excluded, slave women, deemed especially passionate by nature, became freely available objects for sexual favors.[4] Slave men, presumed emboldened with freedom, became objects of fear, their purported beastlike passions leaving white women vulnerable and calling for absolute repression. Whereas the evidence of sexual attacks by slaves, even in the most intense slave revolts, was rare or nonexistent,[5] these early constructed images were long-enduring. Violent repression of the black male became widely accepted, as did the sexual exploitation of slave women by white owners. Both patterns would be reflected in capital punishment statutes of the twentieth century.

Between 1930 and 1972, 455 men were executed for rape in the United States. Four hundred forty-three, all but a dozen, of these executions occurred in former Confederate states.[6] In Texas, between 1924 and 1972, 99 rapists (82 blacks, 14 whites, 3 Hispanics) were executed, more than in any other state. This chapter examines the general sentencing patterns over this five-decade period, the background of the individuals charged and convicted, the characteristics of their victims, whether any significant differences existed between rapists sentenced to death and those sentenced to a prison, and finally whether the patterns generated at trial were ameliorated by the appeals process.

General Sentencing Patterns

Ed Henderson was the first man in Texas to be electrocuted for rape. He had been the twelfth man admitted to the Huntsville prison death row, on May 9, 1924. He was electrocuted one month later in the early morning hours of June 9, 1924. Over the ensuing decades an additional 117 men were transported to Huntsville to await electrocution on rape convictions. Over these same years, prison records indicate, 2,190 persons began their sentences of five to ninety-nine years for rape convictions.

The trend in the number of death sentences per hundred prison sentences for rape is summarized in Figure 3.1. A death sentence for rape became much more likely in the years following World War II. Thereafter there was an

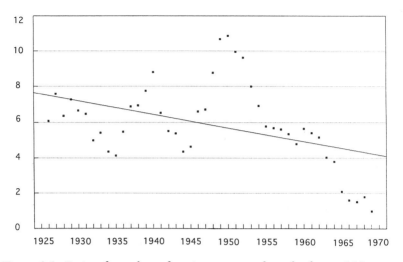

Figure 3.1. Ratio of number of rapists sentenced to death per 100 rapists sentenced to prison (five-year moving average).

equally dramatic decline. The highest number of rape death sentences occurred in 1951 (seven), followed by 1950 (six) and 1938, 1939, 1952 and 1956 (five each).

Of the 118 individuals convicted of rape and awaiting execution at Huntsville, 99 (84 percent) were eventually electrocuted; again the peak period was the 1950s, a decade in which Texas saw 31 executions for rape. As Table 3.1 suggests, this peak came later in Texas than in other southern states and the District of Columbia, where capital rape statutes were in effect. The peak execution decade for almost every other state was the 1940s, with a precipitous decline thereafter. For example, Maryland executed 19 rapists in the 1940s and none in the two subsequent decades. In North Carolina executions for rape peaked at 27 in the 1940s and then fell to 5 and 1 in the next two decades. Similar patterns are found in Arkansas, Georgia, Tennessee, and South Carolina.[7]

Background of the Texas Rapists

The background and characteristics of the 118 men sentenced to death for rape between 1924 and 1972 are summarized in Table 3.2. Over this five-decade period approximately 54 percent of the capital convictions came from urban areas of the state. Reflecting shifting population concentrations in the state, this pattern was not consistent across these years. In the 1930s, 26 percent of the death-sentenced rapists came from the six major Texas coun-

Table 3.1. *Total Executions for Rape in Southern States by Decade*

	1920s	1930s	1940s	1950s	1960s
Alabama	0	10	7	5	0
Arkansas	0	8	7	3	1
District of Columbia	0	3	0	0	0
Florida	6	7	17	10	2
Georgia	6	19	26	15	1
Kentucky	6	6	4	1	0
Louisiana	0	0	0	2	1
Maryland	3	5	19	0	0
Mississippi	0	0	0	5	4
Missouri	1	2	1	1	2
North Carolina	12	16	27	5	1
South Carolina	5	6	23	5	4
Texas	**13**	**23**	**20**	**31**	**12**
Tennessee	5	10	12	2	1
West Virginia	7	0	1	0	0
Virginia	10	3	9	9	1
Total	**74**	**118**	**173**	**94**	**30**

ties: Bexar (San Antonio), Dallas, El Paso, Harris (Houston), Tarrant (Fort Worth), and Travis (Austin), as did 54 percent in the 1940s and 63 percent in both the 1950s and the 1960s.

The majority of these death-sentenced rapists were in their twenties at the time of their crime. The two youngest were sixteen. One of these two, Henderson Young (#196), was convicted along with his brother Roscoe (#195) of robbing a young Anglo couple and raping the girl. Henderson was two months shy of his seventeenth birthday when put to death for rape in May 1938. Roscoe was also executed on the same date for the part he played in the robbery. Bennie Randall (#215) was 16 when he raped an elderly woman; he was electrocuted in May 1939 at the age of seventeen.

John Coleman, fifty-seven years old at the time of the offense, was the oldest rape offender on death row during these years. He was sentenced to death on April 23, 1948, in Longview. Coleman's experience in his own words:

Before the trial, several Negroes were lined up against a wall and I was among this group of Negroes. The victim of the rape was brought in, would not say that I was the one who raped her at first, but finally said that I was the one who raped her after the man who was with her insisted that I was the one who raped her. I did not know this man. At my

Table 3.2. *Percentage Distribution of Death-sentenced Rapists by Personal Characteristics, 1924–1972*

Variables	%
County of conviction	
Bexar	4.20
Dallas	20.30
El Paso	0.80
Harris	21.20
Tarrant	5.10
Travis	2.50
Others	45.90
Age at arrest	
14–19	10.40
20–29	54.50
30–39	22.10
40–49	5.20
Over 50	7.80
Race	
African-American	76.30
Anglo	17.80
Hispanic	5.90
Marital status	
Married/common law	50.00
Divorced/separated/widowed	13.60
Single	36.40
Occupation	
Skilled laborer	12.80
Unskilled laborer	87.20
Years of education	
0	12.40
1–6	42.00
7–8	18.60
9–12	25.60
Attended college	1.40
Prior convictions	
Property crime convictions	
0	61.50
1–2	28.20
3 or more	10.30
Violent crime convictions	
0	80.30
1–2	18.80
3 or more	0.90
Rape conviction	
Yes	0.80
No	99.20
Prior adult prison terms	
0	68.40
2	25.60
3 or more	6.00

trial I testified that I had signed a statement because I had been beaten. Nevertheless, I was sentenced to death. After 4 or 5 days later a deputy came to my cell at the Gregg County jail and told me that I had gotten the chair because I testified that I had been beaten. The deputy sheriff told me that I would have gotten 4 or 5 years if I had not told about getting beaten. [*From the file of John Coleman, #304.*]

With only two weeks of formal education, this offender was judged to be illiterate. He had two prior misdemeanor arrests and no record of serving time in state prison. He was executed on July 8, 1948, three months after his conviction.

This elderly black man with little formal education was not alone. Three-quarters of the death-sentenced rapists were African-American. Almost 90 percent had been employed in some kind of unskilled work. Their work histories were spotty. Most were yard workers, dishwashers, warehousemen, bakers, cooks, service station attendants, hotel porters, odd jobbers, and handymen. Some 70 percent had no record of a prior prison sentence in Texas. The majority had less than a sixth-grade education. Many signed their death row classification papers with a simple "X."

Illustrative of the limited educational background found among death row inmates is the following summary from the file of a man executed February 1, 1949, following his conviction for rape in Harris County (Houston):

Subject first started to school in 1926 when he was 7 years of age and completed the 1st grade at Wharton, Texas in 1929. He then went to a colored school at Bolton, Texas, but did not complete any grade. From 1930 to 1933 he attended the A. W. Jackson Colored School at Rosenberg, Texas and completed the 2nd grade. He last attended the Jones Creek Rural School at Foster, Texas in 1933 and 1934, and was in the third grade when he quit school. Subject states he could not go to school regularly since he had to help work on the farm.
[*From the file of Wilson Moore, #310.*]

The data in Table 3.2 reveal criminal activity of rather minor and sporadic nature. Excepting the offense for which they were sentenced to death, the petty offender image becomes more clearly focused in death row interviews:

Richard Robinson was born December 11, 1903 in Harris County, near Houston, Texas in the Loving Canada Community. He lived in this community and the City of Houston all of his life. The subject was married October 2, 1927 at Houston, Texas and was divorced in September, 1939 after he had come home and found his wife with another man. After the

divorce, the subject had continued to contribute about half of his salary, six dollars a week, to his family for support of the children. The subject says he does not know how his wife is being supported at this time. The subject states that his father is a green tender for the River Oaks Country Club at Houston. He states that he attended the Hart School, in Harris County, near the Loving Canada Community, completing the seventh grade. He reports that he liked school, although he didn't get to attend as regularly as he would have liked to do, because of occasional odd jobs. He says that he dropped out of school to go to work, to help the family pay for an appendectomy for his mother. His work has been that of yard man or house man for various residents of the River Oaks Country Club Estates. The subject admits two previous arrests. The first was in June 1924 in Houston, Texas, on a gambling charge, for which he paid a seventeen dollar fine in Harris County Court. The second charge was in June, 1932, in Houston, Texas, on a second gambling charge, for which he paid a fine of thirteen dollars.
[*From the file of Richard Robinson, #239, who was executed on February 15, 1942.*]

Allen Williams was born in Alto, Texas in Cherokee County on November 2, 1910. At the age of 7, the family moved to Houston, where he finished school to the 6th grade. At the age of 12, the subject states that he went to sea as an Able Bodied Seaman and was there until approximately 12 years ago, when he got full employment in the port of Galveston and Houston, where he has been doing Yacht and Tug work and some other work in the harbor. He states he went to school in Houston, Texas and completed the 6th grade, The subject was first arrested on 5-28-1931 by the police department, Houston, Texas for burglary and was given a two year suspended sentence. He was next arrested on 1-10-1932 by the police department, Lufkin, Texas for petty theft, and was fined $14.00, after he had stolen an overcoat, which was returned. His third arrest was on 12-21-1933 when he bought a watch for his wife and he found out that the watch had been stolen and he was convicted as a receiver of stolen goods and released.
[*From the file of Allen Williams, #337, who was executed on March 21, 1951.*]

Allen Matthews was born on March 4, 1927, and was reared in Houston, Texas. He states that he attended the Lucky Colored School in Houston, Texas, from 1935 until 1943, completing the seventh grade. He states that he failed one year because he was ill with double pneumonia and a rare form of typhoid fever. He states that he enjoyed school and made fair grades. He quit when in the seventh grade, to go to work to

support his mother. He worked as a yard boy, securing short jobs only. He then secured work as a delivery boy for the "Banana House" and a grocery store. He worked there for about four or five months. He then secured work from the Pepsi-Cola Company, Houston, Texas, as a truck driver. He worked there for about a year, and was laid off because of slack business. He was arrested on 7-2-1950 by the police department, Houston, Texas on a charge and released. This was his only prior arrest.
[*From the file of Allen Matthews, #347, who was executed on September 5, 1951.*]

While the majority of death-sentenced rapists did not have a prior prison record in Texas, about one-third did. For example, the second and third persons to arrive on death row following a conviction for rape were, like the Henderson and Roscoe Young, brothers. One had been convicted of rape as a juvenile in 1918 for which he served twenty-two months at Gatesville State School for Boys (in Texas) before being paroled in 1921. On April 12, 1925, he and his brother robbed a young couple in Dallas and raped the woman. Prior to their trial a mob stormed the jail. Police and firemen were called in and during the resulting melee one citizen was shot and killed by the police. The two brothers were convicted of rape shortly thereafter in separate trials that lasted a total of eighty-one minutes. They were both executed in the morning hours of July 3, 1925.

Another death-sentenced rapist had been previously convicted of rape in 1933 and given a twenty-year sentence in the Texas prison system. He spent most of his time in the Ramsey prison unit, where he worked on the plow squad. After maintaining a clear conduct record he was released on conditional pardon on December 23, 1936. The following account, taken from his file, describes his version of his arrest, alibi, and second conviction for capital rape, two and a half years after his release.

The subject states that on 8-9-39 he was working for Mr. WB about six miles south of Terrell, Texas [a small town just east of Dallas]. He claims that Mr. WB brought him in from work that night, and as he was passing a negro cafe, one of the employees told the subject that a mob had been looking for him since he was supposed to have raped a [47-year-old white] woman that day. He says that the fact of his own previous conviction for chicken theft and sentence to prison for rape, his father's conviction and sentence to prison, and the fact that his brother is now serving time in prison, were all brought out as evidence against him. The subject says that on 6-19-39, he had visited a relative in Overton, Texas and at that time had visited a "sporting lady" and had contracted a case of "blue ball and chancre." After he returned home to his wife, this developed into a more serious case and about 15 days before he was arrested on the pres-

ent charge, he was separated from his wife and went to Terrell, until such time as he could be cured. He also claims that at the time of the trial he was suffering so much from the disease and was hurting so much that he paid little attention to what was going on.
[*Florence Murphy, #231, was executed on August 30, 1940.*]

Some fifteen years later, John McHenry was admitted to death row. He had been previously arrested as a juvenile for burglary and rape by force in March 1953 in Visalia, California. He was given an indeterminate sentence and committed to Preston School of Industry. He was released sometime in 1954. He came to Texas, where he was convicted of rape and sentenced to death in October 1956. McHenry described his arrest and conviction.

I was fingered and arrested by two officers. They said I was spending too much money. They said they had been looking for me and watching me for a long time and they took me and showed me some jewelry which they said I had given to some girls to sell. I sat and talked to them about some burglaries I had pulled and about giving some jewelry to two girls. One of the girls was Catherine and I do not remember the name of the other. I talked to the officers about an hour. They then took me to the line-up. In the line-up the other fellows were dressed in jail clothes, and I had on a sport jacket and slacks. I stood out like a red apple in a barrel of green ones. In the line-up I heard an officer say "That's him," and then "yes, that's him, isn't that him." I thought I was being identified on burglary cases. They had me say, "Where is your husband," and had me put my finger on my mouth and say, "Shhhh, or I'll kill your kid." The woman testified in court that she did not see the face of the person who assaulted her and the only way she knew he was colored was by the way he said, "your."
[*From the file of John McHenry, #398, who was executed on January 3, 1957.*]

Background characteristics other than criminal record are also summarized in Table 3.2. Behind these figures lie stories of life circumstances rich in detail and only imperfectly revealed in short transcripts of interviews conducted early in the inmates' stays on death row. Two common themes that emerge from these transcripts are social, educational, and economic marginality along with a disrupted family life:

Tommie Wells was born in June 1915 in Gayles, Louisiana. He claimed that his father died in 1919 of alcoholism. He stated that his mother died in 1923 of tuberculosis. He did not know the occupational or general situation of either his mother or father. The subject's brother's whereabouts is unknown. The subject claims to have attended the Ravenwood School near Shreveport until 1932 and he claims to have completed the third grade there. His aunt reported that the subject was always "hard to learn." The subject worked on farms until about 1932 or 1933. Subject moved to Little Rock, Arkansas in 1936. He reported that he worked as a dishwasher at the Belvedere Cafe at Little Rock. He also received relief from the Transient Bureau at Hot Springs. The Federal Fingerprint report shows several arrests for vagrancy and night walking and disturbing the peace. With reference to the night walking and vagrancy charges, the subject stated that he was innocent of any intentional wrongdoing in these connections and that the charges had simply resulted from his having been caught out late at night and having been unable to explain his business.

[*From the file of Tommy Wells, #200, who was executed on June 17, 1938.*]

The personal background of offenders is only one part of the montage of information that guided the outcome of cases involving the charge of rape. Equally important, if not more so, were the circumstances of the offenses and the characteristics of the victim.

Victim and Offense Characteristics

In 90 percent of the cases a single victim was involved. Ninety-six percent of the victims were white females. The fact that four out of ten of these rapes occurred in the home suggests that there may have been some additional crime involved, perhaps burglary or robbery. Lack of detailed information in many of the inmate files made it difficult to determine how frequently this was indeed the case. What we can surmise from the data in Table 3.3 is that in some 70 percent of the cases either a gun or knife was used as a weapon for coercion; slightly over 50 percent of these victims were teenagers or younger; and in three-quarters of these death-sentence rape cases the victim and offender were strangers.

Clearly, this bare-bones tabulation of offense and offender characteristics does not fully portray the mixture of offense circumstances, courtroom demeanor of the defendant, competence and quality of the defendant's attorney, and personal prejudices influencing jurors and judges charged with dispensing justice. Nevertheless, taken together with the vignettes culled from inmate files, these facts and figures do illustrate how difficult it is to accurately equate any given case with another. The unique mixture of circumstances often determined the outcome. With this full contextual array in mind, we will first review a few additional short summaries of the circumstances, victims, and offenders compiled from interviews, clemency letters, and personal recollec-

Table 3.3. *Percentage Distribution of Offense and Victim Variables in Rape Cases That Resulted in Death Sentences,1924–1972*

Variables	%
Weapon	
Gun	42.0
Knife	29.2
Club	14.3
Hands	12.5
Other	2.0
Codefendants	
Yes	26.1
No	73.9
Location of rape	
Home	39.3
Auto	12.1
Isolated area	33.6
Street	15.0
Excessive violence	
Yes	15.5
No	84.5
Crime spree	
Yes	6.2
No	93.8
Number of victims	
Single	91.4
Multiple	8.6
Sex of victim	
Female	97.4
Male	0.9
Both	1.7
Race of victim	
Anglo	95.6
African-American	2.6
Hispanic	1.8
Victim/offender relationship	
Stranger	75.9
Acquaintance	22.3
Lover/other family	1.8
Age of victim	
1–19	53.0
20–29	19.3
30–39	9.6
40–49	4.8
Over 50	13.3

tions, and then return to the statistics to examine how rape cases that produced death sentences might have differed from cases that resulted in a prison sentence.

We have seen that in the majority of cases the victim and offender were strangers. While the nature of the offense generally allowed identification of the offender, in many cases there was some question in the mind of the victim concerning the exact details.

According to Earnest McCarty one IC, age about 45 or 50, was attacked and raped about 7:30 o'clock in the evening of May 10, 1936. It was alleged by the victim that she was returning to her home from a nearby school on the evening in question, when a "Mexican-looking Negro," about five and one-half feet tall, of about 140 pounds in weight, approached her and asked her how to find a certain Fort Worth street. It was further alleged that this man threw the victim's own coat over her head, threatened her, and had sexual intercourse with her. The woman stated that she scratched the attacker's face and pulled his hair, and she described his hair at first as long and straight, but later she said that she was sure the hair was short and stubby.
[*From the file of Earnest McCarty, #181, who was executed on July 9, 1937.*]

In other cases, the evidence appeared to be compelling, but the manner in which it was gathered would today raise serious constitutional issues.

On the night of January 7, 1937, Virgil Terrill, colored, raped Mrs. BW, who was the wife of a substantial and honorable worker in the oil fields, with a regular job. Prior to the alleged offense, Virgil Terrill did not know Mrs. BW, but evidently saw her for the first time as she undressed to go to bed on this night while he was standing outside the house. Mrs. BW, immediately after the alleged offense which occurred in the early hours of the morning, made outcry to her nearest neighbor, who immediately called the officers. Word was immediately flashed over the radio for the Kilgore police to arrest all negroes they could find up in the Kilgore negro section at that time. Without knowing anything about the circumstances of the case or how an entrance had been effected into the home of Mrs. BW, the Defendant Virgil Terrill, and several others were arrested and taken to jail in Kilgore on suspicion. When arrested and searched, two hinge pins were found in the pocket of Virgil Terrill, the Defendant. After he claimed the hinge pins which were found on him and admitted ownership of them, he was immediately undressed, and blood was found on his underclothes. Virgil Terrill's shoes also fitted perfectly the tracks made in the backyard of Mrs. BW, by her attacker, the tracks were by reason of recent rains, deeply

■ ■ ■ 49

embedded in the soil and plainly visible. The testimony showed that Mrs. W at the time of the alleged attack was menstruating, which accounted for the blood on the Defendant's underclothes.
[*From the file of Virgil Terrill, #189, who was executed on April 1, 1938.*]

Many offenses involved charges in addition to rape. In the late 1930s two brothers were charged with accosting a young couple on an isolated stretch of road in northeast Texas. The couple was robbed and kidnapped and the woman was raped. Both brothers were sentenced to death and eventually executed, one being the youngest offender to die in Texas' electric chair.

On the night of August 21, 1937 Mr. R and his wife Mrs. R, two young white people (husband and wife), left their home in Longview, Texas, to go to Arkansas on a visit to relatives. As Mr. R. worked until about midnight, they left Longview about 2:00 A.M. and R was driving a new automobile with a governor on it to retard its speed while the machine was properly broken in. After they crossed the county line between Harrison and Gregg counties, these white people were pursued for some two or three miles by this defendant and his brother, the negroes partially disguised through the use of sheets. A shot from the negroes car went through the fender of the R automobile. The R machine was forced to the edge of the highway and stopped, this defendant drew a pistol and presented same to R, while his brother Roscoe [#195] rifled Mr. R's pocket, taking all his money and also his watch. Then the two young white people were forced to accompany the negroes to an isolated spot several miles off the main highway, where this defendant brutally raped Mrs. R, asking her "Have you ever fucked a negro?" and otherwise grossly insulting her. [T]hen the two negroes took them to the point on the highway they had left their stolen automobile, and permitted them to go on their way. Masterful detective work on the part of Gregg County officers resulted in the arrest of these two negroes on the 28th of August, near Elmo, Texas.
[*From the file of Henderson Young, #196, who was executed, along with his brother, on May 6, 1938.*]

Approximately a decade later, in another northeastern Texas town, not far from the Texas-Arkansas border, a case involving a young teenage girl resulted not only in the capture, conviction, and eventual execution of the alleged offender, but also allegations of a coerced confession.

I was in town, at New Boston, Texas, [in the Northeast corner of the state] in April 1948 and they picked me up and put me in jail. When I was arrested I asked them what they were picking me up for and they told me I would find out. They carried me to the house of some white people. I was shown to a 13 year old white girl, they asked her if I was the one, and she told them no. They asked her several times if I was the one and each time she told them no. On the way to the house they asked me if I raped a 13 year old, white girl. I was carried to New Boston, Texas, and placed in jail. They came and got me about sundown and carried me to Linden, Texas, and placed me in jail there. The next day a man, who was a policeman, came to the jail at Linden, I was carried down into the office at the jail, he asked me if I had raped the girl. I told him that I had not, he got mad, told me that I was telling a damn lie, and he then hit me with his fist and kicked me. The sheriff of Bowie county then told me that he was not running for re-election anyway and that he had just as soon see them beat me to death as not. They wrote out a statement, which stated that I had raped the girl, and I signed it.

[From the file of Cleo Smith, #308, who was executed on August 24, 1948.]

While the majority of death-sentence rape cases involved strangers, some involved family members. In these cases the offense generally had a longer and more complicated history.

In June 1949 I was living with my wife and four of my children at George West, Live Oak County, Texas [about fifty miles northwest of Corpus Christi]. We were living in four rooms (two bedrooms and kitchen and bath). I had one daughter and a niece who were attending business college at San Antonio, Texas. My daughter, M aged 16, was at home and she wanted to go to San Antonio and stay with my other daughter and niece. A short time before she and I had an argument about her going on blind dates. She wanted to go to San Antonio to be with her sister and my niece and too she was unhappy over our argument because of the fact that I was opposed to her having blind dates. While I was sleeping one day her mother allowed her to go to San Antonio with my sister. She was supposed to return that night. She did not return that night and I went to San Antonio to hunt her. I remained there for four days but could not find her. Finally I called my wife and told her that I could not find M. We had an argument in our telephone conversation, as we had argued a thousand times previously, and I told her that I was through with her once and for all. That was on the morning of 6-4-49. I was arrested that same morning at a hotel at San Antonio, Texas. I was transferred to Live Oak County Jail, and I was later transferred to the Bee County Jail. At first, I was charged

with both rape and incest. My wife had filed charges against me, charging that I had committed rape and incest on my daughter M.
[*From the file of Felix Lewis, #328, who was executed on June 21, 1950.*]

While most files of those on death row for rape convictions reveal evidence of substantial community outrage at the offense, some included letters from citizens stating that they found it hard to believe that the person charged had actually committed the offense. These letters were generally written on behalf of the alleged offender in support of clemency consideration.

I will say that this is a sad surprise to me and others that know Morris Norman #208 is charged with rape, this negro boy has worked for me at different times around my home with my wife and daughter at home and I being away from home lots of times all day, we know nothing against him and have at all times found him a well behaved humble negro boy sincerely hoping that this boy gets a fair deal, I am at hand to help you and this boy in any just way.
[*Letter seeking clemency in file of Morris Norman, #208, who was executed on December 16, 1938.*]

I was very much shocked to learn that James Ervin #217 had been accused of this crime, as I had thought he was the best yard man and most trustworthy darkey I had ever had around me. He also did painting for me and various kinds of house work. He was a hard working boy and always had all the work he could do and had no need to rob anyone. He was always humble and polite and I never saw anything wrong in his behavior, and if he ever drank I never heard of it, or saw any indication of his having done so. He seemed perfectly honest and while I live entirely alone most of the time I never had any cause to fear James in any way. We people who he worked for have felt very keenly about his sentence and do hope something can be done to save his life.
[*Letter seeking clemency in file of James Ervin, #217, who was executed on May 19, 1939.*]

From these incomplete, and no doubt in many ways biased, summaries the range of forces shaping the crime and sentencing process begins to emerge. Some victims were more vulnerable than others. The accused could be portrayed alternatively as vicious, mistreated, or trustworthy. Some victims knew their assailant, others did not. Some assaults took place in public locations, others in the victim's home. In some cases the evidence was rock-solid, in others possibly contrived. Permeating these swirling sets of facts were the fears and prejudices of the prosecutors, jurors, victims, and defendants. Class differences between victim and offender appeared to make a difference—race even more so. Our task now becomes one of disentangling these considerations with rather crude statistical instruments.

Pre-*Furman* Research on Rape, Racial Discrimination, and Capital Punishment

Over the years it has been repeatedly suggested that the southern concentration of executions for rape was interwoven with the castelike boundaries between blacks and whites. The above accounts lend further credence to this generally accepted explanation. When it came to sexual relationships between black males and white females taboos could be obsessively absolute. Such was the case in the abolition movement before the Civil War, in Reconstruction efforts thereafter, and in the continuing antilynching debate immediately preceding the implementation of the Texas capital punishment statute in the 1920s.

By the mid-1930s, the leader of the Association of Southern Women for the Prevention of Lynching (ASWPL), Jessie Daniel Ames, a native of the East Texas area where many of these cases originated, was repeatedly speaking out against this "peculiarly construed chivalry," noting on one occasion that if the belief in racial superiority was to be maintained all white women must be placed "in a category characterized by physical frailty, goodness, purity, and chastity, and all Negro men in a category characterized by brutish build and sex perversion."[8] A similar case was made with numbing regularity by others:

> To get at the ultimate secret of the Southern rape complex, we need to turn back and recall the central status that Southern women had long taken up in Southern emotion—her identification with the very notion of the South itself. . . . Such, I think, was the ultimate content of the Southerner's rape complex. . . . Such is the explanation of the fact that, from the beginning, they justified—and sincerely justified—violence toward the Negro as demanded in defense of woman, and though the offenses of by far the greater number of the victims had nothing immediately to do with sex. . . . here once more it was the Negro who was the obviously appointed scapegoat.[9]

By the late 1950s, four years after *Brown v. Board of Education* had set up a benchmark turning point in the civil rights movement, death row prisoner John Mack had resigned himself to this system of seemingly unequal treatment.

> I have no worries—I'm just in trouble—and I can't avoid that. I'm a colored man and the white laws just won't accept the truth. Then after the

jury was picked it was said in the courtroom by one of the prosecutor's assistants "This is one nigger we've got to burn." They say we make an example out of him and the rest of the Niggers will stop and think before they do anything amongst their own color, much less our white women. [*From the file of John Mack, #406, who was executed on March 6, 1958.*]

Thus, the tradition of this peculiarly construed chivalry, lamented since the days of the abolitionists, remained firmly in place as the civil rights movement gained momentum in the 1950s and found substance in an increasingly aware and sympathetic Supreme Court. As Bowers eventually noted,

> It is by now no secret that blacks have been the primary target of executions for rape. . . . More than 85 percent of those executed for rape by the states were black. It is not, therefore, premature to suggest that the reluctance to abandon executions for rape in the South may reflect something more than a desire for protection against this particular crime. It may also reflect a desire to maintain a social system that depends upon a social distance between the races. Perhaps this increased proportion of executions for rape was a response in the South that the requisite social distance was not being maintained in recent years.[10]

While executions for rape, whether legal or illegal, functioned symbolically and practically to reinforce rigid racial boundaries, there is evidence that fluctuations occurred over time. The fact that African-American males were sentenced to death and executed for rape is not by itself evidence of a "peculiar chivalry." Their *relative* chances, in comparison with the chances of counterpart white offenders, of receiving the death sentence for rape does constitute such evidence.

In particular, as reflected in Figure 3.2, the probability that black offenders would be sentenced to death for rape remained between five and ten times the probability for white offenders, and reached a sharp peak during the stress-filled years of the 1930s depression. In some of these years blacks were twenty times more likely to be sentenced to death than white offenders for the crime of rape. This, of course, is consistent with the idea that social boundaries are most ambiguous, and therefore in greatest need of reinforcement, in times of economic turmoil.[11]

In related research, Elmer Johnson analyzed offenders sentenced to death for rape in North Carolina from 1909 to 1954, and found the anticipated link between race and the probability of receiving the death sentence.[12] Similar findings were reported by Partington, by Koeninger, and by Wolfgang and Reidel.[13] In a review and reanalysis of these and other studies Hagan, as well as Kleck, reconfirmed the basic conclusions.[14] At the risk of appearing to

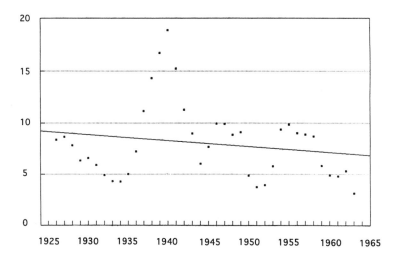

Figure 3.2. Ratio of probability of death-sentencing of African-Americans convicted of rape to probability for Anglos (five-year moving average).

document a well-established fact, we present data that are in many ways more complete than information previously available on pre-*Furman* capital rape cases in Texas compared with cases in which the outcome was a prison sentence.

Some information was retrievable on the total number (2,190) of convicted rapists sentenced to prison between 1923 and 1971. These data are compared with parallel information on death-sentenced inmates for this same time frame in Table 3.4. In addition, more complete information was available on offenders incarcerated for rape between 1942 and 1971 ($n = 1,526$). We drew a random sample of these inmates ($n = 84$) for more complete comparative purposes with the death-sentenced inmates ($n = 74$) in the same period.[15] These data are presented in Tables 3.5 and 3.6.

Over the full five decades, convicted black rapists constituted 76 percent of the death-sentenced rapists and only 31 percent of those sentenced to prison. Both Hispanics and those categorized as Anglos were underrepresented in comparative terms on death row. Death-sentenced inmates tended to be younger than their prison counterparts across all racial or ethnic groups. Finally, reflecting in all likelihood the regional distribution of historical traditions discussed in the first chapter, the eastern region of the state with its slave-plantation traditions was the most likely to sentence persons to death following a conviction of rape. As we will see in the next chapter, this same regional pattern did not appear in the case of capital murder, further confirming the special link between this "peculiar chivalry" and the legacy of slavery.

Table 3.4. *Distribution of Death-sentenced and Term-sentenced Convicted Rapists by Race, Age, and Region of Conviction, 1923–1971*

Variable	Death (n = 118)	Term (n = 2,190)	Difference
Race of offender			
Anglo	17.8%	50.2%	− 32.4%
African-American	76.3	30.9	+ 45.4
Hispanic	5.9	18.8	− 12.0
Mean age			
All	28.1 years	31.4 years	− 3.3 years
Anglo	31.4	33.1	− 1.7
African-American	27.3	30.1	− 2.8
Hispanic	27.7	27.9	− 0.2
Region of conviction			
East Texas	46.6%	35.1%	+ 11.5%
North Texas	30.5	25.1	+ 5.4
Central Texas	9.3	12.6	− 3.3
South Texas	6.0	13.5	− 7.6
West Texas	7.6	13.7	+ .06

While the slightly greater than two-to-one ratio for blacks on death row compared with prison for rape convictions is important, there is more to the story. From the more complete information gleaned from a sampling of cases for the period 1942 through 1971, we note in Table 3.5 that, in terms of education, death-sentenced inmates were much like those sentenced to prison. In both instances, at least 97 percent had not graduated from high school. In terms of prior arrests, the death-sentenced inmates were more likely to have had some offense-related contact with the police; that is, 53 percent compared with 37 percent had been arrested three or more times. The use of some kind of weapon, a gun or knife most often, increased the chances of a death sentence, as did the location of the rape in an isolated area such as the woods or a back alley. If the victim and offender were strangers, and most importantly if the victim was white, chances of a death sentence rose dramatically.

Without question, the most powerful predictor of a death sentence in rape cases during these years was the combination of the racial or ethnic characteristics of the victim and the offender. There were only two combinations of racial-ethnic characteristics that were more likely to yield a death sentence than a term in the state penitentiary. When males from an African-American background raped an Anglo female, the case was approximately thirty-five times more likely to result in capital punishment than a prison sentence. If an

Table 3.5. *Demographic, Offense, and Victim Information for Death-sentenced and Term-sentenced Convicted Rapists, 1942–1971*

Variables	Death (n = 74)	Term (n = 84)	Difference
Offender demographics			
Mean age			
All	29 years	31 years	− 2.0 years
Anglo	31	33	− 2.0
African-American	28	30	− 2.0
Hispanic	31	25	+ 6.0
Race/ethnicity			
Anglo	21.6%	57.4%	− 35.8%
African-American	72.9	25.2	+ 47.7
Hispanic	5.4	17.2	− 11.8
Education			
None	4.2%	5.1%	− 0.9%
Less than 6th grade	28.2	26.9	+ 1.3
6th grade or more	64.8	67.9	− 3.1
Graduated	2.8	0.0	+ 2.8
Occupation			
Skilled	8.0%	7.0%	+ 1.0%
Unskilled	92.0	93.0	+ 1.0
Prior arrests			
None	19.2%	37.9%	− 18.7%
1 or 2	27.4	25.3	+ 2.1
3 or more	53.4	36.8	+ 16.6
Offense information			
Weapon involved			
Yes	32.0%	9.2%	+ 22.8%
No	67.6	90.8	− 23.8
Weapons used by race (% yes)			
Anglo	16.0%	50.0%	− 34.0%
African-American	84.0	50.0	+ 34.0
Hispanic	0.0	0.0	0.0
Location of rape			
Home	40.8%	46.5%	5.7%
Auto	4.1	26.7	− 22.6
Isolated (woods, alley, etc.)	45.1	26.7	+ 18.4
Victim information			
Age of victim			
Less than 18 years	48.3%	57.9%	− 9.6%
18 years or more	51.7	42.1	+ 9.6
Race of victim			
Anglo	95.9%	61.6%	+ 34.3%
African-American	1.3	24.4	− 23.1
Hispanic	2.7	13.9	− 11.2
Victim/offender relationship			
Stranger	69.9%	44.8%	+ 25.1%
Acquaintance	30.1	55.2	− 25.1

Table 3.6. *Percentage of Death-sentenced and Term-sentenced Convicted Rapists by Offender/Victim Combinations of Race/Ethnicity, 1942–1971*

Variables	Death (n = 74)	Term (n = 84)
Anglo rapes Anglo	21.60	56.9
Anglo rapes African-American	0.00	1.1
Anglo rapes Hispanic	0.00	0.0
African-American rapes Anglo	70.2	2.3
African-American rapes African-American	1.30	22.0
African-American rapes Hispanic	1.30	0.0
Hispanic rapes Anglo	4.00	2.3
Hispanic rapes African-American	0.00	1.1
Hispanic rapes Hispanic	1.30	13.9

Hispanic male raped an Anglo female, the comparable chances were about two to one. In only one case did the rape of a black female result in a death sentence and actual execution. Roscoe Gibson (#440), a black male, was sentenced to death in June 1962 for raping a nine-year-old black girl in Houston. He was executed on October 6, 1962.

Grounds for Appeal

In 1972 this stark pattern, found throughout the southern states, would become an important ingredient in the Supreme Court's conclusion in *Furman v. Georgia* that capital punishment, as then administered, was arbitrary and capricious. In this and other cases the appellate process was increasingly guided by testimony and evidence presented and compiled by social scientists on a broad range of civil rights issues.[16] Between the 1920s and *Furman*, however, such refinements in the law remained a remote, hoped-for goal among legal reformers and organizations such as the NAACP's Legal Defense Fund. Likewise, the Warren Court decisions of the 1960s, which were eventually much maligned for handcuffing the police, favoring the rights of the defendant, and contributing to an ever-escalating crime rate, were on the distant legal horizon. Closer at hand were what today would be considered rather loose police practices and courtroom procedures.

Evidence is found throughout the death row records. Keeping in mind that much of this evidence and many of these accusations were obviously self-serving, the following vignettes, if true, illustrate what today would routinely be called police brutality.

I was arrested February 25, 1948 at my home by four officers from Harris County. On the way to Houston they drove out in the country and started beating me up. They kept beating and kicking me and wanted me to say I was guilty of the rape charge, but I would not admit something I was not guilty of. One of them grabbed my privates and started squeezing them, so then I told them that I would admit anything because I could not stand the pain any longer. They read me something off a sheet of paper to the effect that I had raped a white girl and tied her boyfriend up. They called the sheriff of Harris County and told him to meet us at South Main at the underpass. When we arrived at the underpass, the sheriff was there and I told him I was real glad to see him because they had been beating me up something awful. He said I wouldn't be glad to see him unless I told him what he wanted to hear, so I asked what that was. He told me that I had raped a white girl and tied her boyfriend up, and I told him I had not. He then hit me in the mouth, and put me in his car and carried me out in the country again. It was then that they started beating me up and squeezing my privates again, so I told them everything was just like they said. . . . So I signed a piece of paper.
[*From the file of Wilson Moore, #310, who was executed on February 1, 1949.*]

I was arrested about midnight on May 30, 1948 by the city police in Houston, Texas. After my arrest I was carried to the city jail and put in a room where I was placed in a corner and beat unmercifully as I refused to sign a statement they had written out. The men would come into the room two at a time and after about 36 hours of this beating, questioning, and no sleep, I signed the statement since I knew they would not stop.
[*From the file of William Wilson, #317, who was executed on February 5, 1950.*]

I was arrested July 2, 1950 and taken to the police station. As they were placing me in the cell one officer drew back a black jack to hit me. I grabbed it and wrestled it from his hand, got in the cell and locked the door myself and gave it back to him. The next day two plainclothesmen came in and took me out of the cell, and began questioning me. Every time I started to say something to explain, they hit me. One hit me in the stomach and one stood behind me and hit me on the head and face. They hit me four or five more times, and I started screaming because it hurt so much. They stopped hitting me then, I think the screams were arousing the neighborhood. I tried to sleep, but every time that I would try to sleep, some one would wake me up, and state that I had no right to sleep. Every time that I tried to tell what happened, I was beaten, and called a liar, so I stopped saying anything. They then moved me to the Harris

County Jail. They then prepared a statement for me. I was told to sign it. However, I was afraid, and I signed it.
[*From the file of Allen Matthews, #347, who was executed on September 5, 1951.*]

I was arrested on October 11, 1954. I was carried about six miles out in the country by the officers. They clamped the handcuffs very tight around my wrists. One officer kicked me and said "get in that car nigger, do you want these white people to hang you?" They wanted me to give them a confession I told them how could I when I don't know anything about this trouble. Then they hit me some more. I was carried to three separate jails in different counties namely: Fort Bend and Wharton a mob of people was around the jail. I was scared beyond description. I signed the confession under this condition after having been beaten by the officers and through fear and under threats that they'd turn me over to the mob if I didn't sign the statement.
[*From the file of Junior Lee Williams, #400, who was executed on March 5, 1960.*]

Far less information was contained in the inmate summaries of events that took place during trial. We found no defendant who prepared his own defense. With few exceptions, files did not contain information to estimate the quality of counsel or the vigor of the defense (e.g., number of objections or motions made, number of witnesses called). One indication that defense efforts were less than they might have been comes from a letter written to the creator of Perry Mason novels, Erle Stanley Gardner, from Jimmy Richardson.

Mr. Earl Stanley Gardner,
Court of Last Resort
New York City, NY

Dear Mr. Gardner:
My name is Jimmie Richardson and I am in desperate need of help, I have heard of your kindness and helpfulness in cases where legal aid was insufficient to support a client such as me. My trouble began the 15th day of July 1952 and I was first tried the 2nd day of September 1952.
I was very much abused in my trial and was denied my right to testify on my own behalf and was not allowed to supena [*sic*] not even one defense witness. I won't go into great detail at this time, but there is much more I could say if I could talk to someone. My case was tried in Palestine, Texas and later my new trial was tried in Fairfield, Texas, where I had the judge's brother for a court appointed attorney. I pled not guilty on a

charge of statutory rape. I am now on Death Row awaiting execution or for the hand of God to move to save me.
[*From the file of Jimmy Richardson, #375.*]

We found no indication of whether the famous author offered assistance to Richardson. What we do know is that the case was appealed to the Texas Court of Criminal Appeals on the basis of the following remarks made by the prosecutor during trial.

If you [the jury] turn a deaf ear to the thousands of mothers who have daughters of her age [the victim was 15] haven't you formed a league with Death and a covenant with hell? This negro is a lustful animal, without anything to transform to any kind of valuable citizen, because he lacks the very fundamental elements of mankind. You cannot gather dates from thorns nor can you get figs from thistles; you cannot get a nightingale from a goose egg, nor can you make a gentleman out of a jackass. If I might recount the particulars of this terrible crime that has been perpetrated by this imperfect being, the shame and sorrows and suffering, even the most inferior sob-sisters would cry out that Jimmy Richardson be instantly electrocuted.[17]

The appeals court reversed the verdict and granted Richardson a new trial. Once again he was convicted. Following a failed appeal of this second outcome, he was put to death for rape on June 24, 1954.

Another example of procedural irregularities involved a two-year appeals process in which the quality of evidence was questioned, and charges of police brutality and prosecutorial bad faith were made. The case involved the prisoner Bob White.

The subject was arrested for rape August 10, 1937. He states that prior to the alleged rape he had been in the field picking two watermelons which he brought back to the front porch of his mother's house. One of the watermelons was eaten, and after this the crowd of negroes who were on the porch began singing. While the negroes were singing they saw the sheriff drive by. The subject states he went to bed, and the next morning was at work in the field when EC drove by and told him to be near the highway when he came back by. When C came by the subject got on the running board of C's car and was taken to the house of LC. There the subject found eighteen other negroes on the lawn. Shortly after he arrived a man named WW called him aside and told him that he was suspected of raping Mrs. C and asked him what he knew about it. The subject denied any guilt, and W asked him who might have done it and the subject replied that he did not know. He was next questioned by the sheriff and gave the same answer. After about 30 minutes, the fingerprints that had been taken from the bedroom arrived and all the negroes were fingerprinted. Subject states his fingerprints did not match those of the rapist. Casts of footprints were also taken from tracks outside the victim's window. Subject claims these did not match his. The subject was then taken to jail and that [sic] Mrs. C had also stated that the subject was the rapist. The subject denied his guilt. That night and the three nights following the subject was taken into the woods near Livingston and beaten senseless. On the fourth night, he was suspended from the limbs of trees by chains tied around his wrists until he fainted. This treatment was administered for the purpose of obtaining a confession. The subject states that he never did confess. On the sixth night, August 15, 1937, the subject was taken to Beaumont, Texas where the District Attorney dictated a confession of the rape which the subject, when originally interviewed on June 7, 1939, denied having signed, claiming that an "X" was made on the signature line by the District Attorney. However, when interviewed on December 27, 1939, the subject admitted taking the pen in his hand and signing under duress. He states that he was then tried in Livingston and found guilty. His case was appealed and the decision was reversed and he was granted a new trial. [*From the file of Bob White, #220.*]

On June 12, 1941, during jury selection for the third trial, White was shot and killed by the victim's husband, W. S. Cochran. Cochran, a large landowner in Livingston, was immediately arrested, charged with murder, and released on $500 bond. He stood trial for the killing of White, but was acquitted a week later, on June 19, 1941. The following newspaper account describes the town "mood" after the killing.

General satisfaction over the killing of Bob White was apparent in the business district of Conroe which is practically all within one block of the courthouse. No expression of race hatred was heard. The attitude of the people seemed based on the belief that the guilty person was justly disposed of. Shortly after the shooting it was observed that a number of negroes were loitering in the courthouse corridors and a normal number were on the streets. A normal calm prevailed.[18]

While normal calm may have prevailed on the streets and in the corridors of the courthouse, the district attorney received the following threat, reprinted in the local newspaper:

If you ever visit Chicago South Side 200,000 negroes will send your body back to Texas in 1 inch parts, and I assure you when Hitler takes the United States that the Northern Negroes will join him just to crush the Southern peckawoods like you and Cochran. I hope a thousand misfortunes happen to your family.

P.S. don't take this letter as the work of a crank, because we are holding mass meetings and at a given time every negro north of the Mason Dixon line is going to swoop down on all parts of the South and kill every white cracker we come upon.

This is not a warning nor a threat, just something to look forward to and I personally hope that every curse conceivably will fall on you and your family for a hundred generations.[19]

Whatever the issues in capital rape cases, whatever the local response, appeals were not generally successful. It was not until twenty years after electrocutions were introduced in Texas, and after ninety-one persons had been executed for rape, that the first death-sentenced rapist avoided execution in 1945. By comparison, there were six death-sentenced murderers who avoided execution during 1925 and 1926 alone. The first commuted rape case involved a white male (Louis Klander, #270), convicted of raping four young white girls at knifepoint in a field. All the victims were strangers to their assailant. Klander was eventually released from prison on parole twenty years later in August 1966. The next non-executed rapists included two Hispanics and four Anglo offenders in the late 1940s and 1950s. It was not until 1960 that the first African-American convicted of capital rape avoided execution. The last two convicted capital rapists in Texas received clemency, one in 1962 and the other as a direct result of the *Furman* decision in 1972.

While not generally successful, appeals across all types of capital cases did become increasingly frequent over the five-decade period. This trend is evident in Figure 3.3, in which the length of time from arrival on death row to eventual execution is plotted. During the late 1920s and early 1930s persons were generally executed within a month following their routine thirty-day stay of execution. Thereafter, a steady increase is evident until, in the 1950s, occasional longer appeals stretched the average at a faster rate until late in the decade, when a more steady increase continued. In subsequent chapters we will see that this reluctance to execute convicted capital offenders continued with increased impact in the post-*Furman* years.

Conclusion

A recurrent theme in research on rape convictions prior to 1972 involves racial discrimination, and what was once labeled "a peculiarly construed chiv-

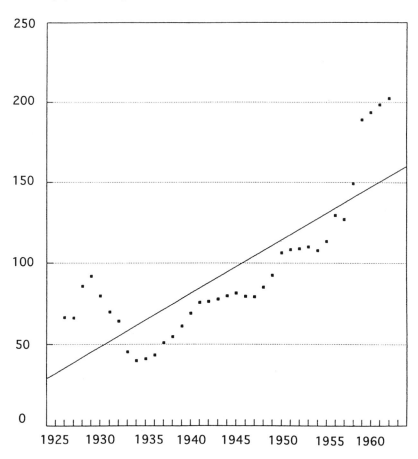

Figure 3.3. Time (days) from arrival on death row to execution for inmates convicted of rape, 1926–1964 (five-year moving average).

alry." Nationwide, the vast majority of executions for rape occurred in former Confederate states and the vast majority of those executed were black men who had raped white women. This point routinely has been cited as proof of arbitrariness in capital sentencing during the pre-*Furman* era.

Between 1923 and 1971, prison records reveal, 2,308 persons were convicted of rape in the state of Texas. Among these offenders, only 5 percent (118) received the death penalty; the rest served a prison sentence. Ninety-nine of those sentenced to death were eventually electrocuted. Thus, approximately 4 percent of all convicted rape offenders were put to death.

We have examined the backgrounds, offense information, and legal history of the 118 death-sentenced rapists. The majority of offenders were uneducated, young African-American males without lengthy records of property or violent crime convictions. Most had no prior prison record in Texas. The victims in these cases were almost entirely white women; most victims were strangers to their attackers. Only one offender who attacked a black victim ended up on death row; he too was black.

We pursued this basic pattern more precisely by comparing a group of capital rapists to a sample control group of imprisoned rapists between 1942 and 1971. We found that one dominating factor in the punishment decision involved the race of the victim. The victims of 95 percent of the death-sentenced offenders were Anglo women, compared with 62 percent among the prison-sentenced cases. Even more dramatically, when a black offender was convicted of raping a white woman, he was virtually assured of a death sentence. Postconviction appeals did little to change this pattern.

In this sense, "the peculiar chivalry," which originated in the mores of the plantation South and was designed to control castelike relations between black males and white females, remained an enduring legacy of slavery well into the latter half of the twentieth century. On the other hand, there is evidence of a convergence in the differential in sentencing patterns over these years as the legal system became substantially more reluctant to execute offenders for the charge of rape. The convergence in sentencing that reflected that reluctance to execute would continue to gain momentum in subsequent decades.

CHAPTER 4

CAPITAL MURDER AND MIDNIGHT APPEALS

■ ■ ■

He was attempting to shoot his estranged wife June 12, 1953, when his daughter was fatally shot. The two women, terrified, were huddled behind a door at the home of another of Meyer's daughters. His wife's claim in a divorce petition that he hit her with a rock was untrue, Meyer said. To a claim that he struck her with a chair, he said "I don't remember that, but I did slap her a little." "I was married 43 years, I had hell for 42 of them." [1]
[From the file of Henry Meyer, #384, who was executed for murder on June 8, 1955.]

During the five decades of the 1923–1972 period, 378 convicted murderers received the death sentence in Texas. Over these same years, prison records indicate, 7,771 persons were convicted in courts throughout the state and sent to the Texas Department of Corrections to begin prison terms for first-degree murder. Thus, as with the charge and conviction for rape, capital punishment was reserved for a small fraction (about 4 percent) of all first-degree murder convictions. This chapter examines the general sentencing patterns over time, the backgrounds of those convicted of capital murder as well as their victims, the specific nature of their crimes (e.g., location, weapon used), and whether there were any significant differences along these lines between death-sentence and prison-term cases. The final section will deal with the appeals process.

General Sentencing Patterns

We saw in Chapter 2 that the peak for death sentences came in the 1930s, with a relatively steady decline thereafter. Much of this trend was built around a decreased tendency to rely on capital punishment as opposed to a prison sentence for first-degree murder. This is reflected in Figure 4.1, where death-sentence and prison-sentence verdicts are compared across persons convicted of first-degree murder. Plotted across time, the rate of death sentences (per 100 prison sentences) for first-degree murder was in a relatively steady decline. The question arises whether the decreased chances of capital punishment for first-degree murder stemmed from an increasingly inclusive view of life—a legal and cultural climate in which the exclusion of persons in this ultimate sense was done with greater reluctance, perhaps reflecting an extension of antilynching and civil rights reforms.

Part of the answer lies in whether there is any evidence of a differential tendency to impose a death sentence on those most closely identified with a former slave status and whether this tendency, if present, changed over time. We have already seen that during the first year of its application, 1924, death by state-sanctioned electrocution claimed the lives of twelve African-American men and one Hispanic. Unless these persons were the only ones guilty of a potential capital offense, a very unlikely possibility considering that there were 103 persons sentenced to prison for first-degree murder during this same

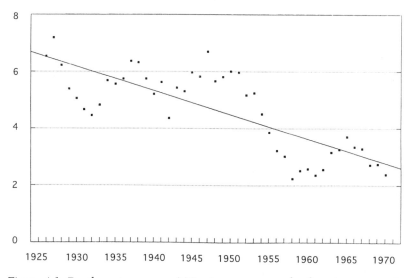

Figure 4.1. Death sentences per 100 prison sentences for first-degree murder, 1924–1971 (five-year moving average).

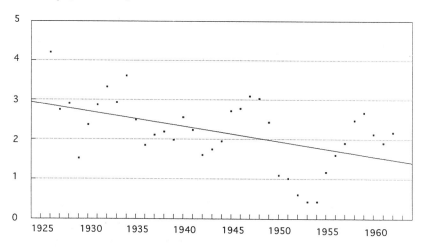

Figure 4.2. Ratio of probability of death-sentencing of African-Americans convicted of murder to probability for Anglos (five-year moving average): 1.0 indicates equal chance; >1.0 = greater chance for African-Americans; <1.0 = greater chance for Anglos.

year (32 of whom were white), this evidence strongly suggests racial bias in the newly centralized capital punishment procedures during the first year of implementation. The question now becomes whether this bias changed over time.

Figure 4.2 suggests that it did. Across the four decades included in these data, the chances that blacks would be sentenced to death following a conviction for first-degree murder, compared with the same probability for whites, decreased. A ratio of 1.0 indicates an equal chance; a ratio larger than 1 indicates a greater chance for blacks, less than 1 a greater chance for whites. For example, a ratio of 3.0 would indicate that blacks were three times more likely than whites to be sentenced to death after a conviction for first-degree murder. Looking at the general trend, from the 1920s and 1930s, blacks were about two and one-half to three times more likely to be sentenced to death. By the late 1940s and early 1950s there was a clear movement toward greater convergence. While there was a noticeable upward swing in the latter years of this four-decade period, the overall trend was in a downward direction, with white offenders actually having a greater chance of receiving the death penalty during the early 1950s. It is interesting to note in passing that when these data are compared with those in the previous chapter, we find a substantially heightened racial differential in sentencing patterns in the case of rape, thus providing further confirmation of the continuing role played by the "peculiar chivalry" tradition in state-sanctioned executions during these years.

On the other hand, looking at the percentage of persons sentenced to death for murder who were eventually executed (Figs. 4.3 and 4.4), we find that the proportion of death-sentenced blacks remained at a relatively constant level, fluctuating for the most part around 85 to 95 percent. There was a slight decrease during the early depression years and then a fairly constant decline beginning in the 1950s, perhaps in anticipation of the statewide moratorium on executions declared after 1964. Over this forty-one year pre-*Furman* period, the average yearly proportion of blacks sentenced to die who were eventually executed was 84 percent. By comparison, sixty-eight percent of the death-sentenced whites were eventually executed over the same four-decade period. A dramatic dip in the proportion of whites executed came in the 1940s when, for two years immediately following World War II, no death-sentenced whites were executed.

Thus, in cases of homicide, while the ratio of *death sentences* of African-Americans to those of Anglo defendants was following a downward trend, the rate of *execution* for death-sentenced blacks remained almost twenty percentage points higher than for whites. The shifts that did occur in execution patterns appear to have been related to specific events, such as the depression, and the post–World War II years when the civil rights movement was gaining momentum, as evidenced first by U.S. Supreme Court decisions dealing with equal access to public education (*Brown v. Board of Education*) and then in cases dealing with the rights of defendants in criminal proceedings (e.g., *Miranda v. Arizona*). The offender's race or ethnicity is, of course, only one characteristic of first-degree murder cases that might be taken into account by the agents in the courtroom charged with assessing punishment. Prosecutors, jurors, and judges were no doubt also reacting to characteristics of the victim along with the circumstances surrounding the homicide. For example, death sentences involving the additional charge of rape were more likely to result in an eventual execution than were death sentences involving any other type of additional felony charge (Fig. 4.5). Thus, as always, it is important to consider a range of victim, offense and offender characteristics when assessing the operation of death penalty practices.

Background of the Offenders

Once an offender was sentenced to death and a death warrant signed, the offender was transported to the death house in Huntsville to await execution. Table 4.1 presents the background characteristics of those persons admitted to death row following a conviction for murder.

A majority of persons convicted of capital murder between 1923 and 1972 were from a non-urban setting. The offender was typically a young (less than thirty years old), minority male who was, in two-thirds of the cases, single or

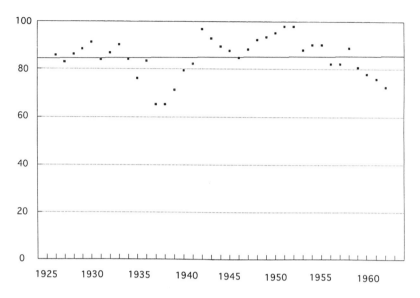

Figure 4.3. Percentage of African-Americans convicted of murder eventually executed, 1924–1971 (five-year moving average).

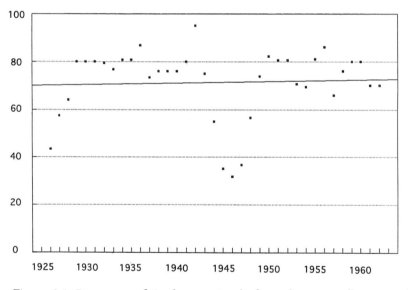

Figure 4.4. Percentage of Anglos convicted of murder eventually executed, 1924–1971 (five-year moving average).

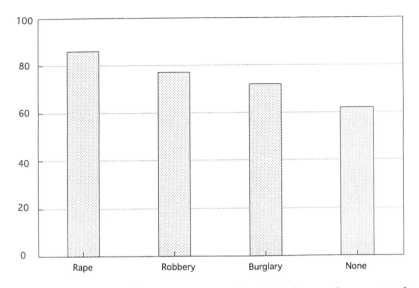

Figure 4.5. Percentage of convicts sentenced to death for murder associated with a second felony offense who were eventually executed, by second offense.

divorced at the time of the offense. Eight of those sentenced to death were less than eighteen years old when they committed murder.

Five offenders were older than sixty at the time of the crime. The oldest man to be electrocuted for murder was Clemens Matura (#182). Matura was sixty-five when a friend promised him "that he could have all the beer and whiskey he wanted" if he did "something" for him, which included going into a nearby elderly woman's house to "knock the shit out of that old bitch" with a hammer.[2] Matura killed the woman, was arrested and convicted, sentenced to death, and executed on July 2, 1937, at the age of 67. Matura had a lengthy violent criminal history, including a manslaughter conviction in 1897, a prior murder in 1923, and three periods of incarceration in the Texas prison system preceding his execution.

The employment history of the death-sentenced offenders indicated that most were unskilled laborers with lengthy histories of job instability. A majority (51 percent) were functionally illiterate, many with marginal intelligence. For example, the Stanford-Binet intelligence test was administered to Abbie Mouton (#339) following his arrival on death row. His IQ was rated at 46, with a mental age of five years. The psychologist who examined Mouton concluded his report with the statement "Reality has eluded this person com-

Table 4.1. *Percentage Distribution of Death-sentenced Murderers by Personal Variables, 1923–1972*

Variables	%
County of conviction	
Bexar (San Antonio)	5.5
Dallas/Tarrant (Ft. Worth)	15.1
El Paso	2.1
Harris (Houston)	18.3
McLennan (Waco)	2.9
Travis (Austin)	2.4
All others	53.7
Age at arrest	
14–19	9.0
20–29	47.2
30–39	26.3
40–49	11.1
50 and over	6.4
Race/ethnicity	
African-American	50.5
Anglo	38.7
Hispanic	10.8
Marital status	
Married/common-law	42.4
Divorced/separated/widowed	20.7
Single	36.9
Occupation	
Skilled laborer	17.5
Unskilled laborer	82.5
Years of education	
0	9.5
1–6	10.7
7–8	21.7
9–12	24.4
Attended college	3.4
Previous violent crime convictions	
0	77.9
1–2	20.7
3 or more	1.4
Murder conviction	
Yes	5.5
No	94.5
Property crime convictions	
0	66.6
1–2	24.6
3 or more	8.8
Prior adult prison sentences	
0	64.6
1–2	28.2
3 or more	7.2

pletely."[3] Mouton was executed on December 8, 1951, for the murder of a friend during an argument in a local tavern. The victim had made disparaging remarks about Mouton's young daughter.

To assess involvement in past criminal activities, these many years later, we are left with available criminal records. These are no doubt incomplete. As we shall see in later chapters this less than ideal data set accounts in large measure for noted changes in criminal records over the years. Keeping in mind the partial nature of these records, we note that the vast majority (77.9 percent) of the death-sentenced murderers in these decades had no recorded prior convictions for violent crimes. However, twenty-one of them had been convicted of a prior murder. Dwight Beard (#179), for example, was arrested in November 1933 and eventually sentenced to death for a murder in North Carolina. His death sentence, however, was commuted in March 1935 to life imprisonment. He escaped from the North Carolina State Penitentiary in August 1935. Two years later Beard had made his way to Dallas, where he was convicted of a murder-robbery. He was executed on June 4, 1937.

Porter Henderson (#329) was first arrested for murder in January 1929. He stated that he killed his first wife because "I caught a negro man [Henderson was also an African-American] in the bed with her."[4] He was sentenced to 99 years in the Texas prison system and was paroled in April 1945. He remarried and moved to Houston. In February 1949 Henderson's second wife left him for another man. He searched for his wife, found her and her new lover at a bus stop, where he shot her as she boarded the bus. He was executed on June 14, 1950, at the age of forty-seven.

Their criminal history information also indicates that two-thirds of the murderers had no recorded convictions for property crimes. Where such records were present, these death row inmates appeared to have been petty rather than professional thieves. No doubt reflecting their rural background and generally poor economic condition, several had been convicted of cattle, turkey, hog, or chicken theft. Furthermore, 64 percent of the death-sentenced killers had no record of incarceration in Texas. Again it should be noted that, while interesting, these records are no doubt incomplete and should be viewed as such.

The following four vignettes, taken from social summaries in inmate files, portray in greater detail the background and experiences of those sentenced to death for capital murder between 1923 and 1971.

General Kerzee [#318] was born in November 1895. His criminal record began about 1912 and he was first institutionalized at the State Juvenile Training School, Gatesville, Texas, where he served a 2-year sentence for house theft in Dallas. He has served 7 previous terms (once for horse theft and once for chicken theft) in the Texas Penitentiary, the first time being in 1916. From that date to the present [1949] he has served approximately 18 and a half years in the Texas Penitentiary. He was punished 12 times during his first commitment and maintained a clear conduct record during the remaining 6 times and was made a State Approved Trusty 4 of the 6 times. He could not remember the number of times he has served jail sentences since they are so numerous. He states he has legally been married two times and he was still married to his first wife when she died. He was married to his second wife only 10 or 11 months before they divorced. He admits having lived with other women in common law relationships. He has been residentially unstable since boyhood with the exception of time put up in prison and states he has never attended school. His employment history is of little significance since he has had short jobs only as common laborer, swamper on a truck, dishwasher, yard boy, fry cook, and farm laborer while in the Texas prison system. [*Kerzee was executed on August 10, 1949, for the murder of a female he apparently did not know.*]

Juan Gutierrez [#255] was born in June 1901 in Nuevo Leon, Mexico. He moved to the United States in 1914 at Laredo, Texas. He claimed at the time of the Classification Interview that he had never attended school. He has always lived on farms. As far as his employment history, Gutierrez was a common laborer, mostly cotton picking, fruit picking, sharecropping, and odd jobbing. From 1934–1936 in San Marcos, he was on W.P.A. No misconducts, no arrests, or court actions. [*Gutierrez was executed on May 2, 1944, for the murder of two male police officers.*]

Wisie Ellison [#180] was born in November 1900. His parents were sharecroppers. He had five brothers and sisters. Two of these died in infancy. He did not get to attend school regularly, as he had to help his people with farm labor in the community, and with gathering their cotton crop. He quit school while in the sixth grade. He was married to Mamie Ellison in 1922. They lived on two farms as sharecroppers, from 1922–1926, averaging approximately four and one-half bales of cotton per year. From 1925–1934, they had three girls and three boys. Ellison's admitted criminal history shows only two previous arrests. He states that he was not guilty of gambling, but that he was nevertheless fined in 1924 for this offense. During that same year, he was fined for operating a car without a license. [*Ellison was executed on June 4, 1937, for murdering his wife.*]

Robert Walker [#226] was born in May 1914. He was the youngest of eight children. Walker quit school in 1930 while still at the sixth-grade level. He quit to go to work to help his father. His attendance and grades were fairly good until his last year in school, and then his deportment, attendance and general average dropped considerably until he finally quit. He was married in December 1936 and had one child. They lived with her father. Walker was a truck driver. He stated that his only previous arrest was in June 1938, on a speeding charge, and in this instance he worked out a fine by working three days in the police office, returning to his home at night.

[*Walker was executed on April 19, 1940, for the murder of an acquaintance.*]

Murder with Additional Felony Charge

During the years when Texas was relying on electrocution as a means of execution, two thirds of all death-sentence convictions involved a felony in addition to the homicide. (see Table 4.2).

Forty percent of all killings were committed in the course of a robbery, 8 percent involved a rape, 7 percent the killing of a law enforcement official, 3 percent a burglary homicide, and 4 percent an attempt to escape from custody; and murder for some expected payment accounted for nearly 3 percent. These murders with an accompanying felony would eventually be incorporated into the post-*Furman* death-sentence statute in Texas. Killings motivated by jealousy or an argument, in connection with no additional crime, would be downgraded to noncapital offenses.

While the data are not reported in Table 4.2, we found on further analysis of the files that the defendants who were sentenced to death for charges involving murder along with an additional felony were primarily black and Hispanic (64 percent). Their victims were primarily males (76 percent), and typically Anglo (85 percent). Most of these offenders (80 percent) had had at least one prior arrest. Just under 50 percent had been previously incarcerated in an adult Texas prison. Among the felony-murderers, guns were used in nearly 70 percent of the killings.

The following vignettes, culled from the inmates' versions of the offenses contained in their prison files, illustrate the events that led up to and surrounded the eventual murders.

MURDER-ROBBERY. About three or four days before the 26th of February 1940 King [#242] left Odessa in a freight train and rode to Big Spring, where he went to a Mexican friend's house. King reported that this Mexican friend gave him four Prince Albert cans full of marijuana. He got off the train at Hillsboro and stole a sedan and bought himself a one half pint of whiskey. He reports that he drove the car to Alvarado, Texas where he stopped to get gasoline at a filling station where a Mr. ——, a white man,

Table 4.2. *Percentage Distribution of Offense and Victim Variables in Murder Cases That Resulted in Death Sentences, 1923–1972*

Variables	% (n = 378)
Offense information	
Type of homicide	
Robbery	40.3
Jealousy/lust/argument	33.2
Rape	7.8
Traffic stop/arrest	7.2
Escape from prison/jail	3.7
Burglary	3.2
Remuneration	2.6
Other felonies	2.0
Weapon involved	
Gun	63.9
Knife	10.6
Club	17.2
Hands/strangulation	7.5
Poison	0.8
Codefendants	
Yes	30.4
No	69.6
Location of homicide	
Home	36.1
Store	17.4
Isolated area	14.0
Street	12.9
Auto	11.8
Jail/prison	3.6
Bar/tavern	3.0
Motel	1.1
Excessive brutality/torture/mutilation	
Yes	22.1
No	77.9
Crime spree	
Yes	6.7
No	93.3
Victim information	
Number of victims	
Single	88.2
Multiple	11.8

Table 4.2. *Continued*

Variables	% ($n = 378$)
Sex of victim	
Male	63.2
Female	30.6
Both	6.2
Race/ethnicity of victim	
Anglo	75.0
African-American	17.7
Hispanic	6.0
Mixed	0.8
Other	0.5
Victim-offender relationship	
Stranger	48.9
Acquaintance	29.3
Lover/other family	21.8
Age of victim	
1–19	28.4
20–29	13.5
30–39	16.2
40–49	14.8
Over 50	27.1

was the proprietor. He reports that he and the proprietor got to talking and that he discovered the man was a bootlegger. He reports that he bought one pint of (unbonded) whiskey from the man. The subject reports that he was smoking marijuana at the time and that he and the man had drank [sic] some whiskey together. The subject reports that some kind of an argument started, but the subject was unable to remember what the argument was about. He states that when he started to the car, the man got between him and the car, and pulled a knife on the subject. The subject reports that he then pulled a .45 calibre pistol that he always carried for protection while hoboing, and told the man to move aside. King reports that the man kept coming at him and then [King] shot him once in the left arm and twice in the stomach. He drove away, wrecked the car near Dallas, and was arrested while walking on the highway. [*King was executed on March 22, 1942.*]

On July 26, 1958 the deceased owned and operated his store and defendant Jessie Smith [#413] parked his car nearby, got out, went into the

grocery store, picked up some groceries. When he reached the checking out stand at the counter, deceased was there. As the deceased started to check the defendant's groceries, the defendant demanded the deceased's money, hit him twice, and then shot him [and] as he was fleeing, shot him some more; the defendant was arrested a number of days later in some other hijackings.
[*Smith was executed on August 4, 1959.*]

MURDER OF A POLICE OFFICER. The subject offender [J. W. Richman, #224] went on a drunken spree of about a day and a half, during which time the subject states he smoked about eight or nine marijuana cigarettes. He hailed a taxi and ordered the man to take the subject north on the McKinney highway. Subject states he didn't know where he was going, but since he was drunk he was feeling in a spirit of bravado and just wanted to go somewhere. The cab passed through McKinney, Texas, about 8:00 P.M. on March 2, 1938. When the cab driver stopped the car for a traffic light, the subject states that a traffic cop drove by them on a motorcycle, and when the cab got to the north edge of town the policeman stopped them for questioning. The subject states that the policeman talked with the cab driver about four or five minutes, opened the back door where the subject was sitting, drew his gun, and ordered the subject to get out. The subject's answer was to fire eight shots into the side of the policeman, about breast high.
[*Richman was executed on March 18, 1940.*]

MURDER FOR REMUNERATION. The offender [Leslie Webb, #397] was convicted of murder with malice of JR, a 71 year old white male. The subject states that JR was killed on February 26, 1954, having been shot several times with a .22 rifle and then being burned beyond recognition. Offender states that he was living with his mother and father on a tenant farm about three miles from Gilmer, Texas. He states that he was working for his father and that he did not own an automobile, but that he did use his father's truck whenever he wanted to. He states that he was "practically raised by Mr. Jim and I have known him all my life. His place joined the place that we lived on." "Mr. Jim was always very nice to me and everyone else in my family." The subject states that on a Tuesday he went to see Mr. Jim that Mr. Jim was not home but Mrs. R. was. Mrs. R had been married to Mr. Jim about two years. She was about 20 years younger that Mr. Jim.

That morning at their house, offender reports, "Mrs. R. asked me what I was doing there and I told her I wanted to see about a job hauling pulp

wood during the slack season. She told me she knew of a job that was not hard to do but would pay me a lot more than hauling pulp wood. I asked her what she was talking about and she told me that she would pay me to kill Mr. Jim. I told her that I could not ever do that and then she told me that she would give me $1,000 if I would let her use my rifle so she could kill him. I told her I would think about it and I went back home. I didn't see Mrs. R and Mr. Jim again until about Friday when my daddy and I went by there after we had been wild hog hunting. Mrs. R. called me around to the back of the house and asked me if I had my rifle. I said I did and she said that she wanted to use it and told me that Mr. Jim was in the field behind the house. When I gave her the rifle, she asked me to come with her and I walked to the field with her but Mr. Jim was not there so we walked down to the bottom and just after we topped the knoll, Mrs. R. said, 'There he is' and started shooting. Mr. Jim fell and Mrs. R. ran up to him and he was dead. She took out his billfold and gave me three $10.00 bills and told me to get rid of the billfold and to take the gun and go on home." Subject was arrested a short time later.
[*Webb was executed in January 4, 1957.*]

Passion Murders

Approximately one third of the offenders eventually sentenced to death killed their victims in situations that we subjectively labeled "Jealousy/Lust/Arguments." Additional analysis of these data (not reported in Table 4.2) revealed several differences between these offenses and homicides that involved an additional felony. Nearly 90 percent of these "passion" homicides involved family members, friends, or acquaintances in arguments over debt, spite, or jealousy. The majority of the offenders were, again, either black or Hispanic, accounting for 54 percent of the cases, a smaller percentage than in felony-murder cases. In passion murder cases 51 percent of the victims were women; 57 percent were Anglo. Approximately one-quarter of these offenders had incarceration records in an adult prison. The majority of these passion murder offenses (67 percent), substantially more than in other types of cases, occurred in either a home or a tavern. Guns were involved in approximately 60 percent of the cases.

The following vignettes are again based on the offenders' accounts of the offenses and are taken from the inmate files constructed after the offenders had arrived on death row.

The homicide occurred on the 25th of April, 1938. Appellant [Ladell Rhodes, #218] and deceased had gone together for several months. Two

or three days prior to the killing they had a difficulty which resulted in the arrest of Rhodes upon the charge of simple assault upon the deceased. At the time of the difficulty to which [sic] Rhodes said to the deceased: "Willie Mae, you have run off for the last time. When I get you to the grave yard I will cut your G—d neck off and mine too." On the day of the homicide, Rhodes was released from jail about 3 P.M. Shortly after 8 P.M. the deceased, her sister and a friend were sitting in deceased's house talking when Rhodes knocked on the back door. Someone asked who was knocking and Rhodes replied: "The big bad wolf." Rhodes entered the house and the deceased ran from the house. The deceased's sister ran and called the police. Deceased begged Rhodes not to hurt her. No one saw Rhodes stab the deceased. However, when the officers responded and came to the scene of the homicide they found the deceased and Rhodes [who had attempted suicide by cutting his own throat] lying on the ground forty yards from the house of the deceased. The throat of the deceased had been cut "from ear to ear."
[*Rhodes was executed on June 26, 1939.*]

The subject [Harvey Nealy, #211] stated that he had been having trouble with his foster father (the victim) since before 1935. Five months prior to the commission of the present offense the subject had been traveling as a fighter with a carnival show. On the night of December 13, 1937, he returned from Fort Worth on a freight train to his home in Dallas to see his foster parents, arriving at the house about 2:00 A.M. He found his foster parents arguing, and after remonstrating with them, became involved in the argument himself. He began leaving the house when his foster father came toward him with an axe. After dodging a swing from the axe, the subject grabbed the axe from his foster father. Upon knocking his foster father down with the axe twice, the subject hit him across the back of the head with the sharp edge of the axe. About two blocks from the house, the subject flagged down a police car to explain the incident.
[*Nealy was executed on April 10, 1939.*]

The subject [Fred Leath, #429] states that after he had just gotten out of the Texas prison system for assault with intent to murder in September 1958 his depression began. He returned to Fort Worth to work as a window designer. In about two months he met a 15 year old boy at a YMCA. A homosexual relationship began. He and the deceased lived together for four months and nineteen days. The deceased did not work and Leath stated that he supported them both. Leath states that one day he and the deceased got into an argument and the deceased jerked the arm off a rocker and was threatening him and demanding his wallet and car keys.

Subject states that he reached back on a shelf for the keys and instead picked up a little .25 caliber automatic pistol and shot the boy. [*Leath was executed on November 9, 1961.*]

Without doubt, there are discrepancies between what the offenders recounted in their interviews on death row and what actually took place. At the same time, the above vignettes provide some glimpse of the variation in types of homicides that must have come into play when prosecutors, judges, and jurors were assessing the appropriate sanctions. In some cases victims and offenders were strangers. In other cases they were long-time friends or acquaintances. Alcohol or other mind-altering substances were influential in some cases. Intentional brutality was sometimes involved, while in other cases the killing seemed to be almost accidental.

Racial Bias in Death-Sentence Murder Cases

You probably recall the case of the old negro Elijah Johnson who killed another negro over a woman. The case seemed to be just an ordinary "run of the mill" negro killing. The state did not feel they had a case calling for severe punishment and let Johnson have several continuances. He was put to trial and everyone was astonished when the jury said "life imprisonment." The old negro however understood the situation better than us white folks. When the deputy sheriff was conveying him back to jail he said "Elijah, I am sure sorry that jury gave you such a jolt." The old negro replied, "That's alright Mr. —— I guess you white folks knows what you all is doing, its just my hard luck to be tried at the wrong time."[5]

The above account has several stark and troubling themes. To begin with, there is the distinction—by implication widely understood—drawn between "run-of-the-mill" negro killings and other homicides. In the former punishment expectations were light; in the latter less so. That the eventual severity of Elijah Johnson's sentence elicited surprise and regret raises the question why did he get life and not death? Was it because he had killed a member of a devalued class? What if he had killed a white person? Conversely, what if a white defendant had been charged with killing a black victim? Perhaps most troubling of all is that the "common sense" answers come all too readily once these questions are posed.

As noted, just over 50 percent of the offenders sentenced to death for murder between 1923 and 1971 were of African-American descent. This is far in excess of their proportion in the population. While important, this disproportionate representation among death-sentenced first-degree murderers by itself does not indicate discriminatory sentencing practices. Nor does it reflect any changes that might have been taking place across time. More compelling evidence comes from Figure 4.2. Two things are evident: First, we see that in Texas the odds that African-American offenders would be sentenced to death for first-degree murder were higher than for Anglos. Second, it is evident that over time this disparity was decreasing. Such evidence does suggest that defendant-based racial discrimination in the capital sentencing process remained a lingering expression of the not so distant legacy of slavery. Still, alternative explanations have been offered.[6]

A Brief Review of Early Sentencing Research

As part of a broader effort to assess race relations in the United States, systematic analysis of racial discrimination in capital sentencing began in the early 1940s. For example, Charles Mangum examined sentencing patterns in nine southern and border states, and found that among those sentenced to death, whites were less likely than blacks to be ultimately executed.[7] Guy Johnson, in 1941, analyzed the relationship between the race of the victim and that of the offender in murder cases in selected jurisdictions in Virginia, North Carolina, and Georgia.[8] He found that death sentences were imposed disproportionately when the victim was white and the defendant black. In what is now considered a classic study of racial discrimination, Harold Garfinkel, in 1949, obtained data from death certificates and Superior Court records of ten North Carolina counties during an eleven-year period.[9] He concluded that blacks were more likely to be charged with, prosecuted for, and convicted of first-degree murder than white defendants.

Further evidence of continuing racial discrimination surfaced in the 1950s as the post–World War II civil rights movement gained momentum, but researchers, armed with somewhat strengthened statistical tools, also began to pursue other correlates. Elmer Johnson published a study in 1957 that examined the backgrounds of offenders incarcerated on death row between 1909 and 1954 in North Carolina (Central Prison, Raleigh).[10] He found that these inmates had a lower education level than convicts who received prison sentences, that 52.9 percent had no previous prison sentence of six months or more, and that approximately half were unskilled laborers. He concluded that social class, not race, accounted for the differences between those who got death over imprisonment. Marvin Wolfgang, researching similar questions, found that when a black offender killed a white victim, courts tended to maximize punishment to ensure that "justice would be done."[11] He also recognized, however, that "it is not easy to evaluate race differentials of conviction without some knowledge of the circumstances involved in the whole homicide situation." Age and sex of the victim were critical, as were the location and circumstances of the homicide. Until these and other factors could be explored, doubts would remain concerning the influence of race on the sentencing process.

As research accumulated, there was also growing awareness of differences at successive points in the criminal justice process. One study in Ohio examined discrimination at the presentencing stage by comparing charge, trial, and conviction patterns, while looking at all defendants charged with committing a felony homicide in one county between 1947 and 1953. Of 353 blacks charged with murder, 33 killed whites. Of these, 27 were charged with first-degree murder and 15 were eventually convicted of this offense. By comparison, while 6 whites killed blacks, 2 were charged with first-degree murder; the remaining offenders were tried for lesser homicide charges. Although these data suggested some disparate treatment of blacks, the limited number of cases involving white offenders and black victims prevented statistically firm conclusions.[12]

In Texas, Henry Bullock studied convicted murderers and found that whites received longer prison sentences than blacks for similar crimes. He explained this apparent anomaly by noting that most of the victims in these white-offender cases were also white, thereby anticipating results and conclusions drawn more consistently in the post-*Furman* decades. And Rupert Koeninger, also focusing on proceedings in Texas, examined death sentencing patterns between 1946 and 1967 and concluded that minority offenders were disproportionately sentenced to death.[13] In the same vein, Franklin Williams, after an analysis of the relationship between race and sentencing, summarized attitudes toward interracial murder with the statement: "If a Negro kills a white man, it is murder. If a white man kills a Negro, it is unfortunate."[14]

On the West Coast, Charles Judson and his colleagues investigated the imposition of the death sentence upon convicted first-degree murderers in California during the years 1958 through 1966. Although they found that blacks were disproportionately sentenced to death, they concluded, with self-imposed caution, that the race of the victim and offender did not correlate with the execution decision. Instead these researchers concluded that the offender's social class was a more compelling explanation of the apparent racial difference in sentencing.[15]

Back on the East Coast, in a former Confederate state, Murchison and Schwab conducted a study of convicts executed in Virginia from 1908 through 1962 and found that 80 percent of those executed were black. They concluded, however, that this figure was not totally attributable to racial discrimination.[16] Farrell and Swigert selected a 50 percent random sample of all murders that resulted in arrests in the northeastern United States between 1955 and 1973. They concluded that "contrary to earlier studies, there are no significant differences in legal treatment in terms of the racial combination of the offender-victim pair." They did, however, find a correlation between offender and victim status and the severity of sentence.[17]

Thus, between the 1940s and the 1960s research results were mixed, owing in part to different research methodologies and in part to regional differences. The results may also reflect changes over time. Some of the variation during this period may have come from varying degrees of statistical sophistication. For example, the lack of control variables in the early, simple cross-tabular analysis and a reliance on limited data emerge as primary methodological problems. In five of the eleven studies conducted before 1972, no factors were included as control variables. Four other inquiries controlled for only the degree of homicide: felony and nonfelony murders. Two studies controlled for additional variables. However, one found discrimination against black offenders, while the second uncovered evidence of discrimination against white offenders. In a nearly exhaustive review of this research, Kleck surmised, "the evidence considered as a whole indicates no racial discrimination in use of the death penalty for murder outside the South, and even for the South empirical support for the discrimination hypothesis is weak."[18] Thus, notwithstanding the easy and common sense answers to the questions posed in Elijah Johnson's case, questions remain.

Death versus Life Sentences in Texas Murders, 1923–1971

The research reported in the next section avoids many of the methodological problems evident in prior research. Our data are based on a two-group design: murderers sentenced to death and those given prison terms for first-degree murder. The analysis controls for such extraneous variables as the type of homicide, presence of codefendants, region or location of the homicide, weapon used, education level, occupation, and prior criminal history, in addition to race, age, and sex of offender and victim.

We begin with a general description of the differences between the death-sentenced (n = 375) and imprisoned killers (n = 7,371) during the period 1923–1971. We then focus on all 186 male murderers sentenced to death and a sample comparison group of 260 male murderers sentenced to a prison term in the Texas Department of Corrections during the period 1942–1971.[19]

Table 4.3 presents data on the race, age, and region of the state where a conviction was obtained for all offenders sentenced to death or prison for first-degree murder between 1923 and 1971. These comparisons provide a broad picture of several variables that affected general sentencing patterns.

Over the full five decades, black offenders appear to have been sentenced to both prison and death disproportionately, considering that blacks constituted only 13 percent of the state population during this time. However, in

Table 4.3. *Distribution of Death-sentenced and Term-sentenced Convicted Murderers by Race, Age, and Region of Conviction, 1923–1971* [a]

Variables	Death (n = 375)	Term (n = 7,771)	Difference
Race of offender			
Anglo	38.5%	33.7%	+4.8%
African-American	50.5	48.9	+1.6
Hispanic	11.0	17.5	−6.5
Mean age			
All	30.5 years	34.1 years	−3.4* years
Anglo	32.3	37.0	−4.7*
African-American	29.4	33.6	−4.2*
Hispanic	27.5	30.0	−2.5
Region of conviction			
East Texas	36.8%	36.9%	−0.1%
West Texas	12.3	12.8	−0.5
North Texas	22.4	20.4	+2.0
South Texas	11.7	15.3	−3.6
Central Texas	16.8	14.6	+2.2

[a] For the purposes of statistical comparison, we combined both the death-sentenced and term inmates into one group of murderers. Then, for purposes of statistical tests, we treated the death-sentenced inmates as a sample from the total group of killers.
* Significant at the .01 level.

respect to the ratio of the total percentage of blacks sentenced to prison for murder to the percentage who receive death, the claim of racial discrimination is reduced. The proportion of those convicted who found themselves on death row was greater than that of Anglo offenders, but the difference is not great. It is a difference that could, at least potentially, be explained by other characteristics of the cases to be explored shortly. It is important in this context to note that Hispanic offenders were more likely to be sentenced to the penitentiary than to death row for first-degree murder.

One possibly important consideration for prosecutors, judges, and jurors involves the offender's age. In the pre-*Furman* era, there is some hint that executed blacks were often significantly younger at the time of conviction than their white counterparts (pre-*Furman* data did not separate Anglos and Hispanics)—especially in the South. Citing these sparse studies, Bowers offered his data as further evidence of racial discrimination.[20] The data presented in Table 4.3 raise questions regarding this argument. While minority group members sentenced to death were younger than Anglos, the same is true for the imprisoned murderers. Those sentenced to death were significantly younger at conviction than the imprisoned murderers. Rather than systematically sentencing younger minorities to death, murderers of all racial categories who received death tended to be younger than the larger pool of imprisoned convicted murderers—although the difference in age between Hispanics sentenced to death or those imprisoned was not statistically significant. The gap in age is in fact greatest among Anglos. Age, then, does appear to have made some difference in the sentencing decision, but not a difference strongly linked to variation across racial or ethnic categories.

Texas is a large and geographically, economically, and culturally diverse state. Distinct regions reflect almost unique settlement patterns. For example, East Texas was settled in the 1840s and 1850s by groups of white farmers from other Southern states. This area, prior to the Civil War, was economically tied to cotton and was the site of many plantations and a large slave population. In the early 1920s, this area also had much Ku Klux Klan and lynching activity.[21] Because of this history, and because of the information on the overrepresentation of death-sentenced rape cases from East Texas discussed in Chapter 3, we hypothesized that in this region blacks would receive harsher sentences than whites for the crime of first-degree murder.

Overall, the data in Table 4.3 clearly show our expectations were wrong. Regional differences, as related to this former slave-holding area of the state, seem to be restricted to rape and what Jessie Daniel Ames called a peculiar form of chivalry. No significant regional differences associated with former plantation counties appeared in the proportion of murderers sentenced to death versus those imprisoned. However, in South Texas, a region with a rich Hispanic heritage, prison sentences were somewhat more likely than capital punishment. When analyzing regional effects, we also controlled for the offender's race and ethnicity. In this analysis, too, no significant differences emerged across the five regions. Nonwhites in the East and South Texas regions were no more likely to receive death than in the other regions. The question now becomes what other factors might be at work.

To gather information for this more detailed question, we drew a sample of murderers sentenced to prison ($n = 260$) and compared them with all ($n = 186$) murderers sentenced to death between 1942 and 1971. Table 4.4 contains the relevant data on a variety of variables.

As was the case over the full five decades, the offender's age did not strongly affect the likelihood of receiving the death penalty for murder. Two offender characteristics that were associated with variation in sentencing were years of education and occupation. While offenders with eight years of education or less constituted the majority of both the term- and the death-sentenced groups, they received the death penalty proportionately *less* often than those with a higher level of education once convicted of first-degree murder. In related fashion, offenders whose occupation was classified as professional

Table 4.4. *Percentage Distribution of Death-sentenced and Term-sentenced Convicted Murderers by Offender, Offense, and Victim Variables, 1942–1971*

Variables	Death % ($n = 186$)	Term % ($n = 260$)	Association[a]
Offender variables			
Age			.005
16–21	19.2	16.3	
22–49	73.7	72.2	
50 and over	7.1	11.5	
Occupation			.011*
Nonprofessional	90.7	96.5	
Professional	9.3	3.5	
Education			.014*
0–8 years	59.9	73.2	
9 years or more	40.1	26.8	
Criminal History			.00
Arrested			
No	20.4	21.5	
Yes	79.6	78.5	
Violent arrests			.005
No	67.7	75.0	
Yes	32.3	25.0	
Violent convictions			.001
No	76.3	80.0	
Yes	23.7	20.0	
Property convictions			.034*
No	53.8	74.6	
Yes	46.2	25.4	
Prison			.034*
No	58.1	78.1	
Yes	41.9	21.9	
Offense information			
Weapon			.001
Gun	61.2	64.1	
Other	38.8	35.9	
Codefendants			.033*
No	73.2	89.0	
Yes	26.8	11.0	
Felony murder			.234*
No	40.5	88.8	
Yes	59.5	11.2	

Table 4.4. *Continued*

Variables	Death % (n = 186)	Term % (n = 260)	Association[a]
Victim variables			
Number of victims			.042*
Single victim	87.0	98.5	
Multiple victims	13.0	1.5	
Gender of victim			.017*
Male	59.9	74.2	
Female	40.1	25.8	
Age of victim			.000
0–21	29.1	10.3	
22–49	35.9	69.8	
50 and over	35.0	19.8	
Relationship			.033*
Primary	24.3	24.2	
Acquaintance	28.2	60.0	
Stranger	37.6	14.6	
Law enforcer	9.9	1.2	

[a]Uncertainty coefficient was employed for every category except age of offender, age of victim, and relationship for which Somer's D^2 is reported.
* Significant at the .01 level, using likelihood ratio chi-square.

were the distinct minority in both the death row and the prison groups, but once convicted of murder their chances of receiving a death sentence were slightly higher. The latter finding should be viewed with some caution given the limited number (only twenty-five cases) of persons in the professional classification, but it may represent an important departure from conclusions generally drawn in earlier research regarding class-related differences in death-sentencing practices, which was carried out without reference to comparisons across sentence categories.

The offender's criminal history was divided into five categories: prior arrests, prior violent arrests, prior violent convictions, prior property convictions, and prior prison commitments. Prior arrests, prior violent arrests, and prior violent convictions were not significantly associated with sentence outcomes. On the other hand, prison commitments were. Offenders with histories of imprisonment were overrepresented in the death-sentenced group. These offenders were certified repeaters and perhaps perceived by prosecutors, judges, and jurors as hard-core criminals more deserving of the full weight of the law.

In addition, the following offense characteristics were examined: type of weapon used, the presence of codefendants, and the type of homicide. The percentage of offenders who used guns to kill their victims did not differ statistically across the two groups. The data do suggest, however, that the murder situations that involve codefendants increased the offenders' chances of being sentenced to death. It may be that this reflects a judgment among those who were distributing justice that these offenses were on the whole more serious than single-offender homicides. A more likely explanation, based on our reading of the cases, is the fact that codefendants were often used to supply information in the course of a plea bargain. In this sense, prosecutors had stronger evidence to present to jurors in homicides with codefendants. Our best guess is that this enhancement of evidence accounts for the noted increase in death sentences among cases involving codefendants.

The greatest single offense-defining factor associated with death sentencing in these three decades preceding *Furman* was whether the homicide occurred in the course of another felony. Of all offenders who committed felony murder ($n = 139$), 79 percent received the death penalty.

Several victim characteristics were associated with the likelihood of receiving a death sentence for murder. First, if the offense involved more than one victim, chances rose substantially. While single victim offenses constituted the vast majority of cases among both those sentenced to death and those imprisoned for murder, the death sentence cases were composed of 13 percent multiple-victim cases, compared with just over 1 percent among the prison term cases. The gender of the victim also made a difference. In the death-sentence cases, 40 percent of the cases involved a female victim, whereas in prison-sentence cases it was roughly 25 percent.

This apparent bias in respect to female victims may, in part, be due to a general sympathy for more vulnerable victims. It may also reflect the finding that the female-victim category includes the homicide cases that constituted the vast majority of offenses most likely to end up on death row: rape-homicides; this emphasizes again the importance of considering the influence of offense and victim characteristics as they occur in reality—simultaneously.

An additional victim characteristic that reflected a concern for vulnerable victims is age. Here the finding is that cases involving victims under twenty-one years of age and cases involving victims over fifty were more likely to result in a death sentence. As is the case for female-victim homicides, this may reflect a tendency on the part of prosecutors, jurors, and judges to react more severely when victims are, for whatever reason, perceived to be less able to protect themselves.

A fourth characteristic related to sentence outcome is the relationship between the victim and the offender. Cases involving offenders who were strangers to their victims are more likely to be treated severely than cases involving intimate or acquaintance relationships. Approximately 40 percent of

Table 4.5. *Percentage Distribution of Death-sentenced and Term-sentenced Convicted Murderers by Race Variables, 1942–1971*

Race Variables	Death (n = 186) %	Term (n = 260) %	Association
Race of offender			.019*
Anglo	46.2	30.4	
Non-Anglo	53.8	69.6	
Race of victim			.145*
Anglo	78.5	34.5	
Non-Anglo	21.5	65.5	
Non-Anglo kills Anglo			.079*
Yes	31.8	6.6	
No	68.2	93.4	
Victim-offender combinations			
African-American kills Anglo	26.8	4.7	
African-American kills African-American	15.1	49.4	
African-American kills Hispanic	1.1	0.4	
Anglo kills Anglo	47.5	28.0	
Anglo kills African-American	0.0	0.8	
Anglo kills Hispanic	0.6	1.9	
Hispanic kills Anglo	5.0	1.6	
Hispanic kills African-American	1.7	0.4	
Hispanic kills Hispanic	2.2	12.8	

*Significant at the .01 level.

the death-sentence cases involved offenders who were strangers to their victim, compared with roughly 15 percent of those cases that resulted in a prison sentence.

In Table 4.5, the race of the offender, the race of the victim, and various related combinations are presented for separate analysis. As in the total five-decade period, white offenders are overrepresented on death row in comparison with their numbers serving terms. As can be readily seen, the race of the victim is also an important correlate of whether a case resulted in a death or prison sentence. Nearly 80 percent of the death-sentence cases involved a white victim, compared with approximately 35 percent of the prison-sentence cases. The idea that what mattered was not the race of the victim or offender alone but the combination of victim-offender characteristics is supported in the third panel of Table 4.5. Cases involving murder of an Anglo victim by a non-Anglo offender (either Hispanic or black) were more likely to result in a death sentence. Slightly more than 32 percent of the death-sentence cases, compared with approximately 7 percent of the prison-sentence cases, involved this combination.

The final panel in Table 4.5 reveals further detail. Although cases involving African-American offenders and Anglo victims were much more likely to result in a death rather than a prison sentence, it is also clear that it is the Anglo victim that is being protected as much as the minority offender who is being punished, in that cases involving murder of an Anglo victim by an Anglo offender were also more likely to result in a death sentence. A small number of cases involving African-American offenders and Hispanic victims or Hispanic offenders and black victims make further analysis difficult. Nevertheless, in these cases also, when the victim and offender were of different ethnic backgrounds, there was a slight tendency toward a death-sentence outcome.

The latter finding suggests something that may have already occurred to the reader. The racial and ethnic combination of victims and offenders is in all likelihood related to a number of additional characteristics of the offense. For example, interracial cases may be more likely to involve strangers. Also, given economic opportunities during these years, Anglos were most likely to be the proprietors of businesses. This being true, homicide cases in which robbery was also involved would have been more likely to involve an Anglo victim. What these and other possibilities suggest is that more detailed analysis needs to be done.

To accomplish this analysis, statistical techniques that are perhaps less widely familiar come into play.[22] When employing these tools, it is important to note that there were statistically significant correlations among several of the characteristics we were able to code. For example, homicide cases involving another felony were more likely to involve offenders with prison records, codefendants, strangers, and white victims. What is suggested by these and other linkages among offense characteristics (e.g., that even non-second-felony cases with white victims were more likely to involve strangers) is that we need to control for more than one variable at a time if we are to understand more precisely the mixture of offender, victim, and offense combinations most likely to produce a heightened probability of a death sentence. Unfortunately, reality does not yield easily to such statistical precision.

Numerous modeling equations were explored to develop the most useful and parsimonious set of conditions for predicting sentence outcome. In the end, seven variables were included simultaneously.[23] Four of these variables stand out as strongly related to a heightened probability of a death sentence when other conditions of the offense, offender and victim are statistically controlled: (1) whether an additional felony was connected with the homicide; (2) whether the victim was Anglo; (3) whether the victim was female; and (4) whether the victim was Anglo and the offender was African-American. Just as important is the finding that when the broader array of characteristics was included for simultaneous controls, the offender's prison record, the presence of codefendants, and whether the victim and offender were strangers diminished in predictive importance to a level of statistical insignificance.

In the end, then, the first impressions left by Elijah Johnson's case remain. Even after controlling for a range of other explanations, the devalued status of persons of an African-American heritage and the related concern with maintaining social distinctions continued to greatly influence the capital punishment process. The question for subsequent chapters is whether there was any noticeable change in this pattern of discrimination as we moved into the latter quarter of the twentieth century. First, it is important to examine one more stage in the process.

Appellate Review

One of the least-researched areas of the capital sentencing process in the time frame covered in this chapter is the legal history of the offender's case following a death sentence. Currently the most comprehensive and relevant set of data is contained in Appendix A of William Bowers's *Legal Homicide: Death as Punishment, 1864–1982*. Even this listing is not exhaustive and lacks several critical variables (e.g., plea, type of counsel, confessions). Building on a rather sparse research base, death penalty scholars have asserted that minorities have been discriminated against because of harsher postsentencing.[24] This harshness, it is argued, stems from a lack of resources, inadequate counsel, and/or ignorance of the legal system. Whatever the reasons, data summarized in Figures 4.2 and 4.3 clearly suggest that African-American offenders, once sentenced to death, were more likely to be eventually executed throughout the four decades between the 1920s and the 1960s, when all executions came to a temporary halt.

In Texas, the appellate process is funneled through the Texas Court of Criminal Appeals, the state's highest appellate court in criminal cases. While review of capital cases was not legally automatic during these years, we found that in practice it almost was. The Court of Criminal Appeals reviewed just over 91 percent of the capital murder cases during this era. Anglo-offender cases were appealed 96 percent of the time, while cases involving African-American and Hispanic offenders were reviewed 89 percent of the time.

There is evidence that some offenders were cajoled or pressured into not appealing their cases by those involved in the trial. This informal persuasion seemed to be more frequent during the 1920s and 1930s than in subsequent years. For example, Booker T. Williams (#008) was convinced to forgo his appeals because of the threat (not unrealistic given events reviewed in Chapter 1) that a lynch mob might storm the jail if he waited there for a ruling by the Court of Criminal Appeals. Williams was arrested for robbing and murdering a white sawmill commissary manager in the East Texas community of Lufkin on February 27, 1924. Four days later he was found guilty of the crime and sentenced to death. The jury deliberated thirteen minutes. When townspeople, bent on a lynching, tried to storm the jail, the Texas National Guard was called in for protection. Williams did not appeal his case and was executed on April 4, 1924, five weeks following his arrest.

In further exploration of the evidence related to the appeals process, we examined the offenders' files for any type of "confession." We simply wanted to know whether the offender admitted the crime or not. Therefore a confession was coded "yes" whenever it occurred at the time of arrest, in custody, during the trial stage, or the classification interview on death row. Confessions were of two varieties: written or oral. Seventy-five percent of the files had no record of admission of guilt. Further analysis revealed evidence of alleged coercion in approximately a quarter of the cases. This alleged coercion was present in approximately 10 percent of the white offender cases and about 16 percent of the minorities' cases. Following are some examples derived from inmate files, of these allegations:

Webster Lyons [#227] states that on December 11, 1938 while standing on a street corner in San Antonio, Texas he was arrested and taken to the San Antonio jail. He stayed there only an hour or so, after which he was taken to Seguin, Texas where two police officers allegedly tortured him until he confessed to the murder. Lyons states that part of the torture consisted of a severe beating in the stomach and wrapping of a cord about the scrotum and twisting the scrotum and testicles.
[*Lyons was executed on April 28, 1940.*]

I [F.M. McClendon, #319] was arrested in my home in Houston on July 9, 1948 at about 6:30 p.m. I was arrested by four city policemen (plainclothes) or city detectives, and one Texas Ranger. Two of the men hit me and kicked me while we were in my house. The officers put me in the auto and started driving toward the police station. At about 6:50 PM the officers stopped the car along Buffalo Bayou. The Ranger hit me several times in the stomach. He also kicked me in the groin and in the stomach. One of the other officers slapped me in the face. I told the officers that I was the one who killed the man because I was afraid they would beat me to death. We arrived at the Rangers' headquarters at about 7:30 PM. I signed the confession of the murder because I was afraid they would beat me to death.
[*McClendon was executed on August 14, 1949.*]

I [Darious Goleman, #360] was arrested on June 27, 1949. I was not allowed to see my wife or anything. I was then driven to the prison system so they [police officers] could dig up my old prison record. I was then taken back to the Kountz jail. Around 3:00 A.M. an officer came in and got me. I was questioned for a few minutes and beat some. We were making too much noise, so the police officers took me out in the Big Thicket [an area northeast of Houston, Texas] that was supposed to be the scene of the crime. I had my hands handcuffed behind me. I was laid across a log and they took turns beating me in the stomach and choking me. They told me that they would hang me in the jail and then tell the newspapers that I had committed suicide if I didn't sign a statement. I took this punishment until about daylight. I finally agreed to sign a statement.
[*Goleman was executed on February 4, 1953.*]

In other cases there were allegations of ineffective counsel, for example, in a letter written to the Board of Pardons and Paroles by a title company owner, the lack of adequate defense and failure to appeal in the case of Delores Quiroz (#254), convicted of killing a Hispanic maid, after having intercourse with and robbing her.

I did not represent this boy at trial. His people are very poor and they scraped up a small sum and employed an old lawyer but he utterly failed to make any effort to defend the boy at all; he knew about the boy being insane since he was kicked in the head by a mule about seven years ago, but he did not interpose the plea of insanity in his defense; he interposed no pleas of any kind as a defense for the boy at trial; he refused to file a motion for a new trial for him, although it was a death case; and thereby, of course, failed and refused to give notice of appeal for him, and therefore, the boy lost his chance of appeal to and review by the Court of Criminal Appeals.
[*Quiroz was executed on October 29, 1943.*]

Variations in the appeals process on these and other grounds are reflected in the finding that minorities were "processed" more quickly than whites. Less than one-fourth of the minority killers, compared with over one-third of the Anglos, received any reprieve beyond the customary thirty days given since the 1930s. The average length of time spent on death row was just under eighty days. However, there is clear evidence that this changed over time. As we have seen in the preceding chapter, there is evidence that the time from conviction to execution lengthened during the pre-*Furman* years for convicted capital rapists. Figure 4.6 establishes that the same was true for those con-

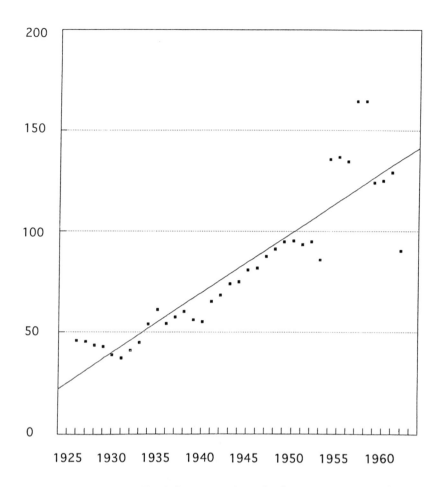

Figure 4.6. Mean time (days) from arrival on death row to execution for inmates convicted of murder, 1926–1962 (five-year moving average).

victed of capital murder. The time from admission on death row to execution lengthened from something close to a month and a half in the 1930s to a period closer to five months in the late 1950s. This shift was approximately the same for all categories of offenders.

What about appeals beyond the state level? Blacks and Hispanics consistently filed federal appeals less often. Appeals were filed in the United States Supreme Court in 11 percent of the cases involving either Hispanic or African-American offenders, compared with 17 percent of the Anglo-offender cases.

Harry Lacy (#222) was the first murderer to appeal to the Supreme Court. Justice Hugo Black granted Lacy a stay of execution on August 4, 1939. According to a newspaper account of the case:

The negro, Harry Lacy, was sentenced to die in the electric chair on August 17 for the slaying [argument over a stolen hog] of Edgar Womack, Trinity county rancher. J. S. Bracewell, Houston attorney, who represented the negro, applied to the supreme court for the stay of execution, contending racial prejudice entered the trial.

The negro was tried originally in Grimes county and given the death penalty. The case was reversed and he was tried again, with the same result. Again there was an appeal and again a new trial was ordered.

The third trial was held in Conroe, and the death penalty this time upheld by the court of criminal appeals. Mr. Bracewell applied to the Supreme Court for a writ of certiorari [in 1939]. The Supreme Court is not in session, but Justice Black granted the stay until it meets in October [1939].

[Lacy was executed on December 19, 1939.]

Of all the murder defendants on death row, only 6 percent were granted new trials—4 percent Anglos and 2 percent African-American or Hispanic defendants. Ultimately the decision whether to appeal made little difference. Trials and related procedures were upheld in just over 90 percent of the appealed cases.

Conclusion

During the 1920s through the early 1970s the majority of death-sentenced murderers were minority males in their middle twenties, with little or no formal education and a sporadic employment history. The majority were not married at the time of the offense. During the early years of this five-decade period they came primarily from rural or small town Texas. In later years, as the state's population shifted to urban settings, so did the origins of the offenders. They did not have lengthy recorded histories of violent or predatory crime, although spotty record-keeping practices make this finding an underestimation of the true picture. The majority of the murderers had no prior record of conviction for a violent crime, though some 35 percent had spent time in an adult state penitentiary. The majority of these offenders knew their victims as family members, lovers, friends, or acquaintances. White males were the most common victims. Offenses were not, as a rule, part of a crime spree. In general, offenses did not involve excessive brutality or torture.

Research on capital sentencing for murder prior to 1972 revolved around the question of racial bias. Previous research reveals ambiguous and mixed findings largely stemming from different research designs and analytic techniques. To ascertain whether race or ethnicity disproportionately affected punishment, net of other considerations, we compared a group of capital murderers with a control group of imprisoned murderers between 1942 and 1971, controlling for a number of factors.

In terms of sheer numbers, blacks constituted the majority in the death row population and a near majority in the prison group. In contrast to findings for rape cases, examined in Chapter 3, region of the state did not appear to affect the sentencing decisions. The death-sentenced group was more likely to have a record of prior felony convictions and their cases were more likely to involve codefendants. Another important factor that led to a greater likelihood that an offender would receive a death sentence was the involvement of more than one victim. Murders associated with an additional felony were five times more likely to result in a death sentence.

The single most dominant factor in the punishment decision involved the race of the victim. Nearly 80 percent of the death-sentence cases involved white victims, compared with 35 percent of the prison-sentence cases. Ferreting out all the factors that might account for this stark pattern involves rather sophisticated statistical procedures. Once applied, these procedures suggest that the punishment decisions reflected a mixture of both legal and extralegal variables. In the final analysis, death sentences in the pre-*Furman* era for murder were driven not so much by the offender's race as they were by the victim's race and by involvement of persons of different ethnic backgrounds. Quite clearly these differences were a residual expression of the legacy of slavery.

However, not everyone sentenced to death during these decades was actually executed. A number of offenders received some form of clemency, the subject of the next chapter.

CHAPTER 5

SPARED THE CHAIR
AND SENTENCED TO LIFE

■ ■ ■

The Governor shall have the authority to commute the punishment in every case of capital felony, by changing the penalty of death into that of imprisonment for life, or for a term of years, either with or without hard labor.[1]

Lisen, this is Albert's mother writen to you kind harted men [Board of Pardons and Parole] beggin you plese sir don't kill my child, plese sir give him a chance like they did those other boys [two codefendants received life sentences] fore he hasn't kill any one. I can't harly rest at nite. . . . he is all i have to depend on, he haven't ben in any thing before.[2]

Reducing punishment through some form of executive action has ancient roots in Mosaic, Vedic, Greek, Roman, Germanic, and English laws. Indeed, clemency, in one form or another, has been characterized as a living fossil, revealing the structure of justice when patriarchs, oligarchs or monarchs distributed punishment or mercy with substantial independence guided by personal whim or compassion and estimates of political gain.[3] As this tradition evolved through the closing years of the eighteenth century in Europe, it was, as Charles Dickens wrote, the best of times and the worst of times. Revolutionaries were fueling the "Terror" in France, a collection of former British

colonies were struggling to form a more perfect union, and houses of detention were being filled beyond capacity in England, where the number of capital offenses rose to more than two hundred.

For offenders in cities such as London, this meant that rather petty offenders were confronted with a death sentence, often without regard to mitigating
factors such as age, gender, or life circumstances. It also meant that justice in
England was increasingly tempered by discretionary mercy. According to one
count, in the last decade of the eighteenth century royal clemency in England
was extended to four-fifths of all convicted capital offenders. For many, the
law in its mercy substituted a trip to the Australian penal colony for a death
sentence.[4]

American colonists brought the English doctrine of clemency with them.
Clemency was to be a discretionary executive act of mercy, unconstrained by
the formal and more rigid procedures of the courtroom and aimed at reducing
the finality and harshness of capital or other sentences. However, in the ensuing legislative debates many legislators were convinced that discretionary
executive clemency, in practice, would be politically abused. Distrusting centralized power and corrupted political influence, lawmakers buffered executive discretion with pardon councils or boards. Together, governors and
boards shaped the clemency process in the newly emerging nation, until today
some twenty-nine states vest clemency power in the governor's hands, guided
by non-binding recommendations from variously defined advisory boards. In
sixteen additional states (including Texas) clemency powers are shared by an
administrative panel or board and the governor. In the remaining five states
the principal authority resides in an administrative panel, usually appointed
by the governor.[5]

The Clemency Process in Texas

By 1857, on the eve of the Civil War, Texas legislators were still arguing over
the legal contours of their recently formed state. Meeting for the sixth time,
they took as one task modification of the existing penal code. Among its numerous provisions this code provided that slaves were not punishable by fine
or imprisonment in the penitentiary or house of correction. Instead, slaves
were subject to death, branding, standing in the pillory, and whipping. Death
could accompany the offenses of murder, insurrection, arson, or rape. Branding might follow burglary and robbery, as well as assaults with intent to commit murder, rape, or robbery. Whipping, either public or private, was reserved for "all offenses not specially enumerated."

The penal code, as revised, went on to specify punishments for free persons
of color. In a final section the governor received his clemency powers:

The Governor shall have the authority to commute the punishment in every case of capital felony, by changing the penalty of death into that of imprisonment for life, or for a term of years, either with or without hard labor, which may be done by his warrant to the proper Sheriff, commanding him not to execute the penalty of death, and directing him to convey the prisoner to the penitentiary, stating therein the time for which and the manner in which the defendant is to be confined, which warrant shall be sufficient authority to the Sheriff to deliver, and to the proper officers of the Penitentiary to receive the convict.[6]

This power to reduce sentences, along with the related power to grant total pardons, gave the governor substantial discretion to modify sanctions according to his or her personal beliefs about the nature of the crime, any doubt about guilt or the fairness of the trial, mitigating circumstances such as the age, mental or physical condition of the defendant, or the potential for rehabilitation. For the most part, governors used pardons as a release valve to control the prisoner population throughout much of the late nineteenth and early twentieth centuries.

The clemency process was initiated when inmates or their lawyers, family, or friends applied for clemency. It was not unusual for a governor to receive hundreds of such requests during the year. To aid the governor in disposal of these applications the Twenty-third Texas Legislature in 1893 created the Board of Pardon Advisors. A two-member board was appointed by the governor to serve 100 days per year.

The new board consisted of two political appointees whose duty it was to review and investigate all pardon and commutation applications. Most importantly, the board was to judge the merits of each individual case and then make recommendations to the governor. All actions by the board were to be recorded, and the governor was to file his reasons for clemency in the office of the secretary of state.[7] Eventually, all noncapital offenders could directly petition the board for a review. Capital offenses required that the three main trial officers (district attorney, judge, county sheriff) apply to the board. However, in practice this did not stop friends or relatives from petitioning the board for clemency, and on occasion the board would pursue the issue with the trial officers involved.

While there was some legal formality in the application process, there was also ample room for personal prejudice and political and financial gain. Some fifty years after the Civil War, amid charges of corruption and personal bias, between 1915 and 1917 Governor James E. "Pa" Ferguson granted just under 1,800 pardons. His wife, Miriam "Ma" Ferguson, honored some 3,600 requests for early termination of sentence. While justifications for these actions in terms of crowded cellblocks and strained state resources could easily be developed, for many lawmakers these massive releases represented indiscriminate and possibly corrupt abuse of executive privilege.[8]

The commutation process was streamlined further in 1936, when the legislature replaced the Board of Pardon Advisors with the Board of Pardons and Parole (BPP). The new board was expanded to three members who served staggered terms to avoid complete domination by any one governor.[9] Although the BPP's duties remained basically the same, members were instructed to obtain a social history of those seeking clemency. In March 1936 the governor asked the newly formed Bureau of Classification in the Texas prison system to assist in this effort.[10] Prison classification officers interviewed the condemned, collected additional materials such as letters from family and friends, and then forwarded the material to the BPP, which in turn reviewed the information and with the concurrence of trial officials made a clemency recommendation to the governor.

Reasons for Commutation

The clemency process stipulated that the Board of Pardons and Parole would make a recommendation to the governor to commute a condemned person's sentence. Governors were then left to their own discretion. Between 1923 and 1972, 147 (29 percent) of the 510 offenders admitted to death row escaped their date with the chair. Their death sentences were commuted, and in most cases they subsequently received a life sentence in the state penitentiary. Two inmates, Bob White, #220, and James Graves, #455, died prior to their execution; White was killed during his second retrial, and Graves died of unrecorded causes on death row.[11]

In most instances the governor provided at least a brief justification for his or her decision. Some consisted of a single paragraph; others extended to several pages of detailed narrative outlining the facts, findings, and personal feelings about the case. The following proclamation, issued in July 1948, is illustrative of the more extended sort:

Ernest Williams, [#305] was convicted in the District Court of Caldwell County, Texas, and on May 10, 1948, he was sentenced to DEATH for the crime of MURDER.

In a report dated July 21, 1948, the Board of Pardons and Paroles recommends the commutation of his death sentence to life imprisonment in the Texas Penitentiary. May 21, 1948, the subject was granted a Constitutional reprieve of Thirty Days and Order That Execution be Stayed for Thirty Days, from June 28, 1948, to July 28, 1948. In a letter to the Board, dated May 20, 1948, Judge J. R. Fuchs, New Braunfels, Texas, states that he is very definitely of the opinion that this case deserves commutation of death sentence to a life sentence. Honorable William George Richards, Representative, Caldwell and Hays Counties, has written a letter in behalf of the subject. Honorable C. H. Richards, Attorney and County Parole Officer, Lockhart, Texas, has urged clemency in behalf of the subject. Mr. Richards states that he has never known or heard of him being in any trouble before. The records of the Department of Public Safety, Austin, Texas fail to reveal a past criminal record as far as this subject is concerned. On file are letters and petitions signed by numerous citizens of Caldwell County requesting a commutation of the Death sentence.

Acting upon and because of the recommendations of the Board,

NOW, THEREFORE, I, BEAUFORD H. JESTER, Governor of the state of Texas, by virtue of authority vested in me under the Constitution and laws of this State, upon the recommendation herein above cited and for reasons herein set out now on file in the office of the Secretary of State, do hereby grant unto the said,

ERNEST WILLIAMS, the
COMMUTATION OF HIS DEATH SENTENCE TO LIFE
IMPRISONMENT IN THE PENITENTIARY.
[*Official commutation letter from inmate file.*]

These recorded justifications, along with supporting documents, reveal that governors often justified clemency in part on their assessment of the offender's personal background or state of mind at the time of the offense. These considerations came in various forms. In at least ten cases sentences were commuted with the simple rationale that the offender had an otherwise good record or that he came from a family with a good reputation. An additional fifteen clemency decisions were justified on the basis of mental deficiency. Four more were granted when the governor noted that the offender was intoxicated at the time of the offense and thus not in total control of his faculties. Advanced age (one case) and comparative youthfulness (seven cases) were also mentioned. Nationality or ethnic heritage was referenced in four cases, in which Mexican diplomatic efforts were cited (two cases) and sympathy was generated by the impression that the offender was a simple "ignorant Mexican."

Numerous clemency cases also contained references to offense-specific mitigating circumstances. In some eighteen cases the governor cited his or her opinion that although the court had found otherwise, there appeared to have been a lack of premeditation on the part of the offender. In some six cases the governor was convinced that there had been enough provocation by the victim to warrant mercy. In another six, the governor made reference to a simple "miscarriage of justice," citing such circumstances as the fact that the death-sentenced offender had not actually been the "trigger man."

The largest single category of commutation rationales over these five decades (some thirty cases) had to do with trial-related issues—questions about the evidence, confessions, and accomplices. In ten cases persons were spared the electric chair when the governors noted that accomplices had received lesser sentences. In some twenty cases the governors concluded that there had been enough conflicting or otherwise faulty evidence (e.g., coerced confessions), conclusions at trial notwithstanding, to warrant a commutation of the death sentence.

Many of the condemned inmates' files contained letters written by friends, relatives, and acquaintances seeking clemency that reflected the same range of considerations. There were also contrary letters from those incensed by the crime and any consideration of clemency. These letters often contained rich descriptions of the offender's character, personal habits, outlook on life, idiosyncrasies, personality flaws, home life, and mental capacity. They reflect the notions of the Jim Crow era in which they were written, with all its stereotypes and gross simplifications, tainted with paternalism, in the description of the accused, their upbringing, and their life histories.

One letter writer who "would suffer her right arm cut off" before uttering one word in defense of a negro nevertheless trusted this "poor boy" and pled for clemency.

Just a line in regard to the character of J.E., the colored man who was recently sent to prison in Huntsville.

I have known J. five or six years. He did so much work for several of my close friends and neighbors, Mrs. T.B. and my daughter (a beautiful girl) are the dearest of friends and they have ridden to the Lake many, many times with J. and the three of them worked together in and around the camp all day. *Two lovely women* with their beautiful diamonds and lovely car completely at the mercy of the poor boy had he been a mean negro. I was born and reared in the South, have dealt with and been accustomed to Negroes all my life, and I will say for J. I have never known a *cleaner,* more *courteous hardworking* boy than J. was, and I believe him incapable of the atrocious crime [rape] they accused him of. I have prayed that he might be spared the execution and in time the public would realize he was an innocent boy. I am a woman of 73 years—a church member, also an O.E.S. [Order of the Eastern Star] member, and would suffer my right arm cut off before I would utter one word in defense of a negro—or any one I thought guilty of the nature he has been accused.

I pray God you may be able to help him and many of us will feel very

grateful to the Pardon Board for their interest and consideration in this matter.
[*Letter in inmate's file written March 31, 1939, for James Ervin, #217, who was executed for the crime of rape a month and a half later, May 19, 1939.*]

Another sympathetic letter writer simply noted the mitigating circumstances of an offender's childhood.

In reply you are advised that this boy spent several years of his childhood here [Milford, Texas], living with his mother, CK who later married MV. Other than juvenile delinquencies of a minor character, we know of no serious trouble he was in until the crime [murder] he was convicted of the past year. However, the writer had lost track of him for several months just before he was arrested and I am not prepared to make a report covering his life for the past four or five years.

About all that I know that could be said in his favor would be that he grew up in the usual atmosphere of negro domestic conflict having to do with divorce, probably of his mother and father and the usual immoral influences surrounding many negro homes.
[*Letter in inmate's file written February 2, 1942, for Rogers Lee King, #242, who was executed for the crime of murder a month and a half later, March 22, 1942.*]

In another case the local sheriff suggested that the killing had really been an accident.

I [sheriff of Brazoria County] was in attendance upon his trial, and I have talked to various persons, white citizens as well as Negroes in the community in which he lives, and I am quite thoroughly convinced that John, and V.J., the State's principal witness, were intimate and had been intimate for some time prior to the killing. I am convinced in my own mind that John Banks and V.J. were tussling over the gun and that the gun was accidentally discharged and shot the little girl. John is weak minded but has always been a hard-working, humble little Negro, and as far as my investigation shows, has never been in any trouble before whatsoever. It would please me very much to see you exercise clemency in this case.
[*Letter in inmate's file written March 31, 1938, for Johnnie Banks, #191, who was executed for the crime of murder one month later, April 29, 1938.*]

Paternalism, regret for not coming forward sooner, and a belief in the man's innocence motivated yet another plea for mercy on behalf of a man convicted of murder.

Things have developed now—that I am very sorry that we did not render him any assistance and not make further investigations, if you have had long experience with negroes, other than behind bars you do know that they depend much on "their white folks" and to think of him being electricuted [sic] for a crime that I DO NOT BELIEVE HE PARTICIPATED IN, is a burden on my heart. I beg of you to study this case closely and I hope that you can conscientiously recommend clemency before it is TOO LATE.
[*Letter in inmate's file written July 16, 1938, for Sam Cash, #202, whose death sentence for murder was commuted to life four months later, November 16, 1938.*]

While mainly ineffectual, these letters reflect beliefs that in many cases the system of justice was not being tempered by a measure of mercy. Clemency provided a remedy. Many other letters advocated quite the contrary. Offenders were, in the minds of these concerned citizens, richly deserving of the punishment they were about to receive.

I have known Harry Lacy since his early childhood, and have known him intimately. His father worked for me ahead of Harry and I have had close contact with Harry Lacy up to the time he committed the murder for which he received his sentence.

He has always had a questionable reputation, and readily was considered a negro that would bear watching by white people, and especially when he had a few drinks and the advantage.

Harry Lacy has had meted out to him what I consider a just verdict, as he has been tried twice, given every right accorded him under the law, and should pay the penalty, for he justly owes it to society.

I am endeavoring to view his case just as I would had I not been a close relative of the person that he murdered. I have known him all his life, have carefully observed his characteristics and behavior through life, and feel that he is reaping his just reward, and that society will be rid of a dangerous character when he is electrocuted.
[*Letter in inmate's file written on June 29, 1939, in regard to Harry Lacy, #222, who was executed for the crime of murder five and a half months later, December 19, 1939.*]

I have known him [the condemned] since he was a little boy. His mother did house work and washing for me for about 15 years. She was a good old woman and I thought a lots of her as an old Mexican woman. The boy caused her a lots of trouble. He was just a gambelar and a rober and as you know a murdera. He would not work, and had no means of support only by living off of others. I think he got what he deserved when he got the chair. I do not think he deserves any consideration.

The man he killed was of no relation of mine but was a nite watchman and constable here. I was paying him to watch my places of business at the time he was killed. It mite be true that he was a little hard on people when they got out of line but with this Mexican he needed what the officer gave him.

I hope that you do not think I am narrow and do not think of the other fellow, for before writing you I thought of both side and put my self in the Mexican place, And I still think he got justis.

[*Letter in inmate's file written February 24, 1939, in regard to Genaro Lugo, #213, who was executed for the crime of murder two months later, April 23, 1939.*]

Given the level of personal discretion allowed in the clemency proceedings, the precise effect of such letters was not always clear. Nearly every commutation document signed by the governors mentioned petitions and letters from sympathetic prominent local citizens. These letters clearly carried great weight. For example, in the case of J. F. Hogan, a man sentenced to death for murder, 511 citizens of Hidalgo County and adjoining regions in South Texas, including nine members of the original trial jury, signed a petition for clemency. This petition was honored five days before Christmas in the midst of the depression in 1934, when death sentences were being carried out at record rates. As was the case elsewhere in the United States, to judge from evidence from other states examined in more recent years,[12] the clemency process during the pre-*Furman* period in Texas was guided by what amounted to community petition drives. This is not to say that petitions signed by a lengthy list of "prominent citizens" automatically resulted in clemency. Many of those put to death had similar documents compiled in their behalf to no avail.

Governors Who Issued Commutations

Between 1924 and 1972, governors intervened in 100, or approximately one out of five cases. These 100 cases do not include the 47 Texas inmates on death row at the end of June 1972, who received commutations because of the historic *Furman v. Georgia*[13] decision, which invalidated the death sentences of some 620 death row prisoners nationwide. The cases of the 47 *Furman* commutees who resided on death row at the time of the decision will be examined in a later section.

The frequency and rationale for commutation in pre-*Furman* Texas was not unlike practices found in other states such as Pennsylvania, California, Oregon, and Florida, in roughly the same period.[14] The proportion of commutations is comparable, as are the reasons given. As in these other states, questions about guilt and punishment handed out to codefendants, posttrial testimonials about the offender's character, and calculations of political costs or advantages all appeared to affect the outcome. Governor Miriam "Ma" Ferguson holds the record for the most commutations (sixteen cases) during two terms, having granted commutations in seven out of twenty-two cases during her first term of office and in nine out of thirty cases in her second term. The fewest commutations (two cases) was granted by the two-term governor W. Lee O'Daniel between 1939 and 1942.

The rate of commutation, however, reveals some interesting variations among the governors. On the basis of rates alone, Governor John Connally had the highest commutation rate—nearly one commutation per execution. However, as an indicator of personal leanings, this rate may be misleading in that Governor Connally's administration extended into the general moratorium on executions that began in July 1964. No further executions occurred in Texas until 1982. Connally commuted four capital offenders after 1964. Preston Smith, Connally's successor, commuted ten sentences between 1969 and 1972. If we exclude Connally and Smith from the analysis because of the moratorium, Governor "Ma" Ferguson again emerges as the clear leader. In addition, during her second administration, Ferguson freed (through pardons and furloughs) some 2,000 state prisoners convicted for lesser offenses in less than two years. In these cases, Miriam acknowledged that her husband, former governor Jim "Pa" Ferguson, appointed to the powerful Texas Highway Commission, made the actual release decisions, while she simply signed the documents.

Women on Death Row

Between 1924 and 1972, only three women, Emma Oliver (#340), Maggie Morgan (#427), and Carolyn Lima (#443), were sentenced to death. All had their sentences commuted to life. Emma Oliver had a lengthy criminal history (beginning in May 1934), replete with charges of vagrancy, prostitution, and acts of violence, including four arrests for murder, seven for aggravated assault, and one for attempted murder. She was convicted of one murder in February 1947. She served one and one-half years in the penitentiary before her release. During the first year following her release she was arrested three times for aggravated assault. Then, in February 1949, she was charged with murder with malice and sentenced to die for killing a forty-year-old black male acquaintance in San Antonio in an apparent dispute over three dollars. According to testimony taken in court, after discovering the body of the victim, the police officer went across the street and found the accused, Emma who reportedly yelled, "Here I am, ____[deleted in the original], I killed him."

After her trial, she became the first woman in Texas to be sentenced to death by electrocution some twenty-five years after the statute was put in place.

One ground for her appeal was that "no member of the Negro race was appointed on the jury commission that selected the grand jurors, nor on the grand jury that indicted appellant." In addition, the appeals claimed that the trial had been biased when the district attorney stated in court "That the colored man in the recent war fought alongside the white soldiers, bleeding and dying and offering his all, and that a dead Negro's rights in the courts were to be protected the same as a white person's." Hearing this statement, the audience "composed largely of Negroes, said, 'Amen, Amen.'" Finding no proof of discrimination, nor even any statement from Emma Oliver's lawyers establishing the fact that she herself was of African-American descent, the Court of Criminal Appeals denied the significance of these claims.[15]

Once Emma Oliver was admitted to death row, a psychological report (documented in the inmate file) was compiled, which read in part:

> The test pattern presented here is indicative of a definite psychosis. There are signs of rather severe organic brain damage, and the Wechsler points up a deterioration of 33% or greater. . . . It can be definitely stated that this individual is psychotic and in only limited contact with reality. . . . A delusional pattern is evidenced especially in the religious area. The emotions are confused and not in keeping with the situation. . . . Word-salad and inappropriatenesses occur often enough to give suspicion of it being caused by more than limited intellectual powers. The state of mental confusion and type of symptomology seem to indicate definite schizoid type of psychosis.

Governor Allan Shivers commuted Emma Oliver's death sentence to life imprisonment on June 29, 1951. The reason given was simply, "On file are letters and petitions signed by numerous citizens of Bexar County requesting a commutation of the Death sentence in this case." Emma Oliver died in prison of cancer, some twelve years later, in February 1963.

Maggie Morgan was sentenced to death in May 1961 for the murder of a forty-eight-year-old white female (stranger) in Houston. Morgan (who was African-American) worked at a massage parlor and a patron asked her if she would "do a job" to "get rid of somebody" for him for $1,600 cash. The "somebody" was the patron's wife. Morgan and the victim's husband were convicted of the murder and Morgan was sentenced to death, though strongly denying her guilt, claiming she had only a minor part in the crime. The victim's husband received a life sentence.

After interviewing Maggie Morgan a couple of weeks after her conviction, a prison doctor summarized his impressions:

This is a 48 year old married colored female, somewhat obese who looks her approximate age. . . . Most of her adult life has been spent in Houston where she came in 1930 and has done mostly church work, directing music, teaching voice and piano. She has been married, once in 1934 to a husband thirty years her senior and the fruit of this marriage was a male child who is now twenty four years old, living and well. . . . She was divorced in 1938. Her second marriage was consummated in 1940 to her present husband who is fifty six years of age, works for Sheffield Steel Company and they have two girls ages thirteen and six years who are both living and well.

During the interview the patient speaks spontaneously, freely and is polite and cooperative. . . . She states that she does not think that her trial was conducted quite to her liking and that she was not allowed to take the stand in her own behalf. . . . She is good humored and has a sense of humor and her affect is normal. . . . She smiles frequently during the interview but not inappropriately. She denies sadness, depression and suicidal thoughts which brings on another quasi-religious lecture. She prays alot. . . . She also states "I put myself in Jonah's place—I was another Jonah—That's the way I picture myself. It's not for what I have done because I have not done anything—It's just to show me the power of God." She is here speaking of her recent trials and tribulations and the fact that she is awaiting execution. Throughout the interview she maintains quite steadfastly that she was "framed."

. . . . She doubts the competence of her lawyer but "was dependent on the Lord." When asked to discuss her thoughts about the fact that (her codefendant) got a change of venue when she did not, of this she says "The whole thing was a paid deal to get him off the electric chair."
[*From the file of Maggie Morgan, #427.*]

Letters recommending clemency were written by various trial officials in part because the codefendant was sentenced to life imprisonment. Governor Price Daniel commuted Maggie Morgan's death sentence to life imprisonment on July 25, 1961. She died in prison nine years later, on September 12, 1970.

Carolyn Lima was sentenced to death in January 1963 (along with codefendant Leslie Ashley [#442]), for the 1961 slaying of a forty-five-year-old male acquaintance in Houston. Lima, a prostitute, had a lengthy sexual relationship with the victim. In February 1961, Lima, accompanied by Ashley (reportedly a male prostitute), went to the victim's office, where the victim suggested that Ashley take part in a three-way sexual act. Ashley refused. Shortly thereafter, a scuffle occurred between Lima and the victim. Ashley took a gun from Lima's purse and shot the victim once. The victim brandished a "bayonet" at Lima, who then grabbed the pistol and shot the victim five more times.

Ashley and Lima took the body to an open field, doused it with gasoline, and set it ablaze. They fled Texas and were later apprehended in New York

City. While on death row, Lima received six reprieves. Her sentence was finally commuted to five years' imprisonment in April 1965, on the rationale that the offense was in part precipitated by the victim and thus a matter of self-defense. Lima was discharged from prison the same day of her commutation. Her codefendant's sentence was commuted to a fifteen-year sentence on January 14, 1966.

Could They Be Innocent?

The most troubling issue permeating the capital punishment debate is that irrevocable punishments are imposed by fallible human beings. Indeed, it is precisely this issue that undergirds much of the rationale for clemency. In 1964 Hugo Bedau published an account of the best-known potential miscarriages of justice involving homicide since 1893. He concluded that eight of these high-profile cases had resulted in wrongful executions. Twenty-three years later, in 1987, a more thorough follow-up to this study was published in the *Stanford Law Review*,[16] in part to correct misrepresentations of the earlier research that suggested that the chances of mistaken executions were virtually zero. To the contrary, Bedau and Radelet concluded in their update that "The publication of the present research shows the reality of such mistakes to be a virtual certainty." And more particularly, "[A close] inspection of the annual distribution of our cases shows that in virtually every year in this century . . . at least one person has been under death sentence who was later proved to be innocent."[17] In support of these claims Bedau and Radelet identified twenty-two "close calls" and twenty-three persons actually executed in error during the period of study.

While the evidence in some of these cases can be disputed and one might quarrel with the precise figures, there can be little doubt that mistakes have been and will continue to be made. In recent years in Texas the widely publicized cases of Randall Adams (#602), chronicled in the film *The Thin Blue Line,* and Clarence Brandley (#680), documented in detail in *White Lies,* by Nick Davies,[18] come most readily to mind. Both cases are discussed in greater detail in Chapter 8. Given the much shorter time between conviction and execution in the pre-*Furman* years, it is not surprising to find parallel cases in these earlier decades.

Perhaps the first "close call" during the electrocution period in Texas came two years after the death row in Huntsville was opened. The case involved the murder of a woman on August 21, 1926, in Bexar County just outside San Antonio. Anastacio Vargas (#46) was convicted of the crime and initially sentenced to life imprisonment. On appeal, the conviction was reversed and a retrial ordered. After his second trial Vargas was once again convicted. Ironically, this time he was sentenced to die by electrocution on November 2, 1927. He was transferred to the death house in Huntsville three days later with an execution date set one month later, on December 16, 1927.

The trial record established that the victim had died from a number of blows about the face and head with a blunt instrument. A neighbor testified that on the night of the offense she had seen two persons on horseback near the home of the victim and that one of them was Vargas. The victim's husband testified that on the night of the assault he had been called out of his house by two persons who claimed to be lost. While talking with these men he was hit on the head and knocked unconscious for several hours. He claimed to have recognized one of his assailants as Anastacio Vargas. When he regained consciousness, he went back into his house, where he found his wife. She told him, according to his trial testimony, that she had been attacked by two men, one of whom was Vargas, who had been an employee previous to the assault. The wife died from her injuries some ten days later. While the husband's testimony was initially convincing, eventually questions were raised about its veracity.

A second reprieve set Vargas's final execution date for March 16, 1928. On March 9, 1928, a week before the scheduled execution, Governor Dan Moody commuted the death sentence to life imprisonment, noting that the reason was Vargas's innocence. Vargas had been the victim of misidentification that had resulted from questionable prosecutorial and witness behavior. He was released from prison on October 21, 1929, with a full pardon. In 1965, at the age of seventy-three years, he sued the state for damages and was eventually awarded $20,000.

At least five additional inmates had their sentences commuted because of expressed doubts regarding their guilt: Percy Howard (#64), Jessie Charles (#69), Sam Cash (#202), Willie Caesar (#204), and Gordon Morris (#382).

In September 1920, Percy Howard and an accomplice allegedly robbed and murdered a male short-time acquaintance near El Paso, Texas. Howard and his accomplice then allegedly stole the deceased's auto and were eventually arrested in California sometime in 1923. At trial, on the basis of testimony from Howard's accomplice, it was established that the two had gone to El Paso looking for work. They registered at the Hotel Grand and the Tri-State Hotel on the nights just prior to the murder—hotel registers corroborated this portion of the testimony. Unable to find work, they decided to return to Big Spring in a Ford touring car, driven by the eventual victim, whom they had hired. Two days later the three men arrived in Pecos, where they spent the night. The next morning, just outside town, Howard asked that the victim stop the car, whereupon, according to the accomplice's testimony, Howard shot the victim twice. Falling to his knees, the victim begged for his life.

Instead, the accomplice reported, Howard took a shovel and struck the victim over the head. Both men then buried the body and continued their trip back to Big Spring. The body was discovered a little less than a month later.

Howard was eventually arrested and sentenced to death. The codefendant, who was the state's principal witness, received a twenty-year prison term. Howard protested his innocence and blamed the killing on the codefendant. Howard's sentence was commuted to life in May 1930 on the grounds that it was never clearly established that he was the actual triggerman. He was released from prison on parole four years later.

In a similar case Jessie Charles was convicted and sentenced to death in June 1929 for allegedly shooting to death a young victim, according to the summary in the appellate decision, "because the deceased, a white boy [Jessie Charles was black], was in what was commonly called the negro part of town." As in the case of Percy Howard, this conviction was based on the testimony of an accomplice, though in this instance there was evidence offered that Charles had admitted the shooting. On a second motion for a rehearing, the appellate court, acknowledging their own confusion regarding the facts surrounding the confession, noted:

In our original opinion we said the officer who arrested appellant testified that "appellant told him that he did the shooting." In the motion for rehearing appellant calls our attention to the inaccuracy of this statement. The confusion in the mind of the writer of the opinion evidently arose from the fact that when the sheriff went to arrest appellant he took with him [an accomplice], who had told the sheriff he knew appellant and knew who did the shooting. The sheriff did testify that when they got to appellant's house and flashed the light through the screen door and saw appellant's clothes that Cole told him (the sheriff) that appellant was the man who did the shooting.[19]

Having found some discrepancy in the record regarding who had confessed to what act, the appellate court nevertheless overruled the motion for a rehearing. Charles continued to maintain his innocence and his sentence was eventually commuted to life seven months after the above appeal was denied. The reason given was once again the question of guilt in the mind of Governor Dan Moody. Nine years later Jessie Charles escaped from prison, in December 1938. We found no record of his being subsequently caught.

Sam Cash was a twenty-one-year-old black man with seven years of formal education and "laborer" as his designated occupation at the time of the offense for which he was sentenced to die. He—along with a codefendant, Fobie Grays, of "negro tenant parentage," who had attended school through the

fourth grade—was convicted and sentenced to death in May 1938 for a murder-robbery of a prominent local businessman.

Grays had lived in the community all his life and had built up a "fairly
regular employment history." In addition, writing in a sympathetic though
quite paternalistic tone, the official conducting the interview on death row
reported how he had talked with Gray's father, who was reported "to be an
humble, peaceful negro of the better tenant farmer group." In contrast, a letter
signed jointly by the local constable and justice of the peace related how Grays
"at one time attacked Mr. P., a prominent farm manager of this locality. Mr. P.
on this occasion defended himself with a pistol. We consider [Grays] to be
one of the worst young negroes of this locality. He would attack a white man
just as quick as he would another negro. He has been a town loafer for the
past several years. In our opinion, the verdict of the jury should stand."

Sam Cash, for his part, maintained his complete innocence of the crime.
Several persons eventually wrote on his behalf. In one such letter included in
the inmate's file, written by the owner of a local hardware and farm machinery
business, Sam Cash's case for clemency was supported, again in terms that
clearly reflected the racial climate, social structure, and understandings of
the time:

> . . . Sam has always been willing to work and help his mother but is a
> negro that does not in my opinion have the average negro intelligence—
> and I do believe that he is entitled to some clemency, for I have known
> negroes all my life and have been working them—and my ancestors for
> generations past have done the same thing. . . .

Moreover, prior to his execution on July 20, 1938, Fobie Grays wrote letters
to the Board of Pardons and Paroles, requesting clemency for Cash and ad-
mitting full responsibility for the murder. Sam Cash's sentence was commuted
to life in November the same year. He was finally paroled from prison on
February 23, 1953, after serving fifteen years.

As Sam Cash's case was being resolved, Willie Caesar and six other codefendants were convicted in June 1938 for a murder in El Campo, Texas, just
southwest of Houston. Caesar was sentenced to die, while his codefendants
received prison terms. The incident revolved around a disturbance outside a
dance hall. Information contained in letters from an assistant district attorney,
summaries taken from the death row records, and Willie Caesar's own account
of the events yield the following picture.

Caesar was indicted jointly with several defendants for the murder of a
sometime "special officer" in the City of El Campo. The victim was white and
all the defendants were black. The altercation took place at a "negro dance
hall," where a party was in progress to mark what was referred to as "bonus

celebration." The victim had stopped to chat in front of the dance hall, where he had served as a security guard on other occasions. While he was talking, a disturbance broke out inside the dance hall and the victim went in to see if he could help stop the fight. The assistant district attorney summarized his understanding of the subsequent killing as follows:

> A negro woman, one of the joint defendants in this case, was engaged in a fight with another negro, who was trying to escort her from the dance hall. The State's testimony showed that the deceased attempted to escort this woman from the dance hall and succeeded in getting her out of the hall and on the front steps. . . . At this point a fight ensued between the woman and the deceased. . . . [the woman] had a knife and the deceased had a pistol, and during the fight he struck the woman over the head with his pistol.
>
> [At this point, several of the bystanders] became incensed over the fight and crowded around the deceased, uttering threats. The deceased backed away from the negroes and fired his pistol into the air two or three times, seemingly to scare the negroes from him. He continued to back down the street and was finally thrown off of his feet and there suffered injuries from knife wounds which caused his death.
> [*From the file of Willie Caesar, #204.*]

Willie Caesar's version of his involvement in the events on the night of the "bonus celebration" were recorded during his interview with a death row officer. He had been inside the dance hall when the first shots were fired. Hearing the shots, persons including himself began a "stampede" to the door. By the time he got outside the victim was lying on the ground, stabbed to death. It was Caesar's belief that testimony against him had come from a person who had been his enemy for some time. The mutual animosity stemmed from jealousy arising from trying "to go with the same girl." He explained his signed confession by noting that it had been coerced after spending forty-eight hours without food or drink in the Houston jail.

The interviewing officer noted: "His general manner is that of the average negro laborer, and his manner during the interview was on a relatively simple and sincere plane." Supporting letters compiled by a caseworker contained statements such as "He has patronized my store and I consider him honest. . . . He was sometimes a week or two in arrears, but he always came in and paid his bills when he could." Caesar's brothers reported that "Willie had obtained very little education as his father believed in training them for hard work, and he was kept in the field instead of going to school." His ex-wife reported that he "had always been good to her."

When everything was considered, the assistant district attorney in charge of the case concluded, "The evidence in this case is weak. . . . There are no other cases pending against him, and the trial failed to develop that he had been in any trouble of any kind prior thereto." The death sentence was commuted to life in July 1938. Seventeen years later, on July 6, 1955, at the age of fifty-eight, Willie Caesar was released on parole.

Gordon Morris (#382) was a white man who had been arrested four times in the 1940s for various petty crimes. He was sent to the Texas prison system in 1945 for a burglary conviction and was discharged two years later, in August 1947. He returned to Houston and moved in with Ruby Lee Smith that same month. One year later Smith married another man, who in 1950 was sent to the Texas prison system. Morris and Smith once again took up a common-law marriage that lasted several years. On July 11, 1953, several friends of Morris came by his house to visit and drink. They continued drinking all day and eventually went to the house of one of the friends. According to Morris, Ruby Smith passed out, while he and his friends continued to drink. Early the next morning Morris reported that he was picked up by an acquaintance; they drove around, drank more whiskey, and eventually returned to the residence where they had left Ruby sleeping.

As they drove up to the house, they were confronted by the police and Morris was arrested for the murder of Ruby Smith, who had been kicked and beaten to death. Morris maintained his innocence, but was sentenced to death for the crime on November 26, 1954. The trial, from impaneling of the jury to the assessment of punishment, took one day. Subsequent investigation by Morris's brother of the circumstances surrounding the crime revealed mistaken eyewitness testimony. When informed, former jurors urged a pardon. Three days before Morris's scheduled execution Governor Allan Shivers commuted the death sentence to life imprisonment.[20] Fourteen years later Morris was paroled, but was returned to prison after a parole violation in 1973. He was reparoled in 1976.

The Commuted and Executed Populations

A common element in the above cases is the involvement of one or more codefendants. In these cases the question of guilt, that is, of who actually did the killing, was difficult to assess. To obtain convictions prosecutors were compelled to rely on evidence gained from participants in the crime. In this sense, many death penalty cases represent real-life variations on the classic prisoner's dilemma, so often the subject of game theory experiments.[21] In the prototypical prisoner's dilemma the police admit that they do not have enough evidence to secure a conviction. Each prisoner knows that if he implicates the other, he is less likely himself to receive the maximum punishment. On the other hand, if both remain silent any punishment becomes less likely. As Edgar Allan Poe put the problem, "Each [person], so placed, is not so much greedy of reward, or anxious for escape, as fearful of betrayal. He betrays eagerly and early that he may not himself be betrayed."[22]

Drawing on the inherent strain of this choice situation, police and prosecutors strike plea bargains. The question becomes whether this makes any difference in the eventual sentencing outcome. When the 100 commuted cases are analyzed separately, some 36 percent are seen to involve codefendants. By contrast, 27 percent in the total pool of death-sentence homicide cases, discussed in the last chapter, involved codefendants; the discrepancy indicates that codefendant testimony did influence the commutation process in a moderate, but important way.

Other apparent influences on the commutation process are summarized in Table 5.1. These data reveal some rather interesting differences between persons who received a commutation of their sentence and those eventually executed. First, the type of offense sets the stage for subsequent decisions. In the five decades prior to *Furman* persons could be and were sentenced to death for robbery by firearms. Arguably this was the least serious of the capital offenses. It was in these cases that justice was most likely to be tempered by the governor's mercy. From looking a bit beneath the figures in Table 5.1, it also becomes clear that juries and governors became more reluctant to impose the death sentence in robbery cases as the years passed, though this tempering of justice was quicker in coming for white than for black offenders.

Of the first three armed robbers sentenced to die in the 1920s two were Anglos (one executed, one commuted) and one was African-American (executed). Of the five firearm robbers sentenced to die in the 1930s, four were white and one black. All four white offenders had their sentences commuted. The black offender was executed on May 6, 1938. The lone offender sentenced to die for robbery in the 1950s was black and he was executed on June 11, 1958. The last offender to be executed for robbery with a firearm, on May 15, 1962, was a twenty-one-year-old African-American. The final two death sentences for armed robbery were commuted as part of a general moratorium on executions—one black and one white offender. Thus, of the five persons executed for robbery by firearms four were black offenders. The single execution of a white offender for armed robbery was carried out on September 5, 1929.

Figures such as these, while derived from a small number of data, suggest quite strongly a point we and many others have noted a number of times: that race, in combination with the type of offense charged, was a dominating influence on the commutation process. Indeed, the data for the full time period across all types of offenses show that 63 percent of those executed were black offenders, reflecting the pattern noted in Chapter 2. Whereas 61 percent of the white condemned offenders were executed, 82 percent of African-American offenders met the same fate. Across time and place the executive's

Table 5.1. *Distribution of Commuted and Executed Capital Offenders by Offender, Offense, and Victim Variables*

Variables	Commuted (n = 100)	Executed (n = 361)	% Commuted
Offense variables*			
Murder	82	257	24
Rape	11	99	10
Robbery by firearms	7	5	58
Offender variables			
Race/ethnicity*			
African-American	37	229	14
Hispanic	19	25	43
Anglo	44	107	29
Mean age (years)	32.4	29.1	
Gender			
Male	97	361	21
Female	3	0	100
Prior criminal history			
Violent crime convictions[a]			
0	84	266	24
1–2	15	73	17
3 or more	0	6	0
Property crime convictions[b]			
0	73	226	24
1–2	15	73	17
3 or more	0	6	0
Prior adult prison			
0	72	220	25
1–2	23	98	19
3 or more	5	27	16
Victim variables			
Relationship to offender			
Acquaintance	43	79	35
Primary/family member	25	50	33
Law enforcement	9	43	17
Stranger	23	175	12
Race of victim			
Anglo	68	291	20
African-American	21	43	33
Hispanic	11	11	50
Gender of victim			
Male	63	179	26
Female	39	195	17
Both	2	20	9
Number of victims			
1	95	314	23
2 or more	5	40	11

[a] Violent crimes consist of murder, rape, and aggravated assault.
[b] Property crimes consist of theft, burglary, auto theft, and arson.
* Statistically significant at the .01 level.

clemency power has allowed justice to be tempered by mercy, but it has also opened the door for personal prejudice. At the same time, it is also important to note the more complex interweaving of considerations that influenced the outcome of cases.

Table 5.1 suggests that rape was the offense least likely to result in a commuted sentence. We saw in Chapter 3 that much of this reluctance can be traced to what has been called a "peculiar chivalry," closely linked to the long-standing castelike boundaries in sexual matters. It was not until the civil rights movement had gained substantial momentum in the post–World War II era that, in 1960, the first black convicted of rape was not executed. Two years later a second convicted black rapist had his sentence commuted. The third was a direct result of the *Furman* decision. Thus, of the eleven commuted death sentences for rape during the pre-Furman years, eight were either Hispanic or Anglo offenders.

Taken as a whole, Table 5.1 indicates that among the three major ethnic/racial categories Hispanics were the most likely to have their sentences commuted. However, once these cases are spread across many more combinations of offense characteristics, we begin to run short of statistically reliable information. Hence, we are left with speculation. We saw in Chapter 4 that Hispanics were the least likely to receive a death sentence for murder. This may have been due to a higher proportion of "acquaintance" killings in this group of offenders.[23] In addition, there is some indication that Hispanic offenders may have been less likely to be convicted of capital rape. For example, whereas, Hispanic offenders constituted 6 percent of the rape cases that ended up on death row, they represented 11 percent of the death row murder cases. Since cases involving rape were the least likely to be commuted, this also may have contributed to the higher commutation rate among Hispanic offenders.

Beyond these rather simple mixtures of offense and offender characteristics, however, we are left on shaky statistical ground indeed. What we can say additionally is that an extensive criminal history also influenced the chances of receiving a commuted sentence. Persons with a record of three or more instances of involvement with the criminal law (whether measured in terms of violent or property crime convictions or of having been sentenced to a term in prison) were the least likely to have their sentences commuted. In addition, cases that involved single victims were more than twice as likely to result in the granting of clemency (23 percent), compared with crimes in which two or more persons were victimized (11 percent).

As we have seen in previous chapters, factors beyond the characteristics of the offender and type of crime influence the sanctioning process. In particular, the probability of gubernatorial clemency, like the severity of court imposed punishments, was distributed according to characteristics of the victim and the relationship between the victim and the offender. Hispanic-victim cases were the most likely to be commuted—50 percent (eleven of the twenty-two cases) resulted in commutation. Black-victim cases were the second most likely to result in commutation, 33 percent of such cases being commuted, compared with 19 percent of cases involving Anglo victims. This pattern further underscores what has been noted numerous times: Minority-victim cases were treated less severely than other offenses.

One dramatic difference among those granted clemency during the pre-*Furman* years and those eventually executed is how well the victim and offender knew one another. When the victim and offender were acquaintances or family members, just over one-third of the death sentences were eventually commuted. By contrast, about one in ten of the death sentences for crimes involving strangers resulted in commutation. With such evidence in hand, we are once again able to note, as have others who have investigated patterns in other places and times have done, that the greater the relational distance between victim and offender, the more severe the punishment.[24]

As with the racial and ethnic characteristics of the offender, it is clearly important to recognize that these victim-linked considerations did not operate in isolation. Cases involving Hispanic offenders were somewhat more likely to involve persons who knew one another. Thus, on this basis alone we would expect a heightened chance of commutation. It is also true that offenses involving Hispanics were more likely to take place in the southern and border regions of the state, where the heritage of Spanish land grants and migration patterns from Mexico is the strongest. It may be that these traditions, with their strong Roman Catholic influence, produced more reluctance to take the life of fellow community members, even when their crimes were extreme. Given the influence that local community members had on the commutation process, this heritage could easily have influenced gubernatorial decisions.[25]

In summary, during the five decades being analyzed the time from arrest to eventual execution was short (in the early decades a matter of months) compared with the lengthy proceedings in the post-*Furman* years. Still, the decision to commute involved some complexity. Appeals were heard, interviews conducted, letters composed, petitions signed, and all this material assembled and sent to the Board of Pardons and Paroles officials and then on to the governor. Twenty-nine percent of all those who arrived on death row between 1923 and 1972 were granted clemency. The data reveal that the decision to exercise clemency was not based solely on the legal facts as narrowly conceived. An offender's personal history and victim-related factors also shaped the decision, as did the governor's estimate of the political fallout of one decision or another. The very few women offenders clearly benefited from executive clemency in the form of mercy. In general, Anglo and Hispanic offenders benefited more than offenders whose ancestors could be traced to the shores of Africa. Offenders who harmed family members (and acquaintances) were more likely to obtain sentence reductions. Offenders who committed crimes against strangers (especially women in rape cases) had a very low probability of clemency.

The Subsequent Prison Records of Offenders Granted Commutation

Once a death sentence was commuted, prisoners faced prison sentences of various lengths. Among the one hundred offenders who had their death sentences commuted in the pre-*Furman* era, ninety-four were resentenced to ninety-nine years or "life" imprisonment, one offender to fifty years, two to thirty years, one to fifteen years, and one to five years. Once the sentence was commuted the inmate entered the general prisoner population.

Texas prison records contain social summaries, official commitment papers, and "travel cards." The latter, brief records for the subjects we studied, "traveled" with them as reassignments to different units within the prison system occurred. Since they contain a running record of an inmate's prison rule violations and punishments, by consulting these records, we reconstructed the former death row inmates' histories of serious rule violations once they reentered the general prison population. These violations include instances of murder, sexual assault, attacking prison officers, and escape. A common assumption about commuted capital offenders, particularly murderers, is that they represent a disproportionate threat to the lives and safety of other prisoners and staff members.[26] The institutional misconduct records of the 100 commutees enable us to test this widely held belief.

Eighty of the one hundred commutees committed no violent offenses over the course of their average stay of twelve years in the general prison population. Incidents involving the twenty remaining inmates are summarized in Table 5.2. These twenty inmates were charged with thirty-nine infractions. The most frequent charge was escape or attempted escape. Most of these fifteen escape-related charges were connected with additional charges of violence.

Those Who Killed in Prison

Three former death row prisoners committed four prison killings. All three murderers were Anglo and had an average age at conviction of twenty-three years, whereas the mean age of the remaining ninety-seven was twenty-nine years. Much of their time in the general prison population was spent in solitary confinement for various less serious rule infractions. One was whipped (twenty lashes) on three different occasions in 1938 for refusing to work.

Clyde Thompson (#83) had his death sentence commuted in August 1931

Table 5.2. *Serious Institutional Rule Violations by the Twenty Pre-*Furman *Commutee Prisoners*

Rule Violation	Frequency
Inmate-inmate violations	
Murder	4
Aggravated assault with weapon	6
Aggravated assault	5
Sex by force	0
Inmate-officer violations	
Murder	0
Striking an officer	0
Weapon-related attack	0
Violation against prison order	
Escape/attempt to escape	15
Rioting	1
Participating/fomenting work strikes	8
Total violent cases	34
Number of inmates in violent cases	20

to five years' imprisonment. Leaving death row, he was transferred to the nearby Retrieve Unit. He was nineteen years old, the youngest person to be sentenced to death at that time. In January 1933, he and several other prisoners planned an escape. However, one of the coconspirators tipped off the guards. The would-be escapees, not knowing the guards were aware of their ill-fated plan, began to run from a work detail. One was immediately shot. The others were quickly rounded up. A few weeks later Thompson and another inmate killed the informer. Thompson would continue his trail of violence two and a half years later, in July 1935, when he killed another inmate, who Thompson claimed was attempting to homosexually rape him.[27] Twenty years later he was paroled and received a final release from supervision at the age of fifty-one in January 1963. During the final years of his confinement he became deeply involved with religion, teaching inmate Sunday school classes. After release, Thompson became a Church of Christ minister and established a ministry in Huntsville, Texas, where he worked with many prisoners after their release from prison.[28]

Louis Klander, convicted of rape, had his death sentence commuted to ninety-nine years (or life imprisonment) in July 1945, when he was twenty-five years old. In that same year, shortly after his release from death row, he and another inmate murdered a fellow prisoner at the Eastham Unit. It is not clear what motivated the killing. Klander testified against his partner and thereafter, for the next thirteen years, remained in protective lockup. He was paroled from prison in August 1966, but returned on a burglary conviction a year and a half later. After serving nine years for this burglary conviction he was paroled once more at the age of fifty-six in November 1976. We found no record of his having returned to the prison system in Texas following this release.

The third former death row resident found guilty of a murder while in prison after leaving death row was Claude Edwards (#481), a convicted murderer whose original death sentence was commuted to ninety-nine years in July 1969, when he was twenty-seven years old. Twelve years later, in October 1981, he killed another inmate, when, according to Edwards, the inmate "made a sexual pass" at him. As of mid-July 1992, Claude Edwards remains incarcerated in the Texas prison system.

Release Behavior of the "100"

Seventy-nine of the one hundred persons whose death sentences were commuted in the pre-*Furman* years eventually gained release from prison on parole. To estimate how these individuals did in terms of their later criminal activities, we combed, by hand and computer, through Texas prison admission records over the six-decade period between 1925 and 1988. This, of course, leaves the question of out-of-state offenses uninvestigated. The records of Texas reincarceration indicate that seven of the former death row inmates paroled during the pre-*Furman* years were convicted of later felonies and returned to prison; two returned on the charge of illegally possessing a firearm and one each for charges of rape, robbery, burglary, aggravated assault, and kidnapping. Another sixteen returned to prison for technical violations of their parole conditions (e.g., curfew, drinking, associating with known criminals), though it is not possible from the records to tell whether these "technical violations" also involved further criminal activities. Thus, over the time period covered, twenty-three (30 percent) of the seventy-nine released former death row inmates eventually returned to prison in Texas. Fifteen of the twenty-one who did not gain parole died in prison. Five were eventually discharged after serving out their sentence and one remains in prison as of this writing, without ever having been released. These data are quite consistent with other studies of former capital offenders on parole and not inconsistent with recidivism patterns of the general population.[29]

The *Furman*-Commuted Offenders: A Natural Experiment

In the early 1960s state-sanctioned executions in the United States came to a halt. This moratorium was encouraged by the increasingly mobilized civil rights movement and mounting evidence that there were systematic disparities in the way capital punishment was being administered. These findings and strengthened reform efforts became focused by a phalanx of well-trained lawyers who began an active challenge of capital sentencing statutes around the country.[30]

These efforts reached fruition when, in a 5–4 vote, justices on the United States Supreme Court in *Furman v. Georgia* decided that capital punishment as then practiced was unconstitutional.[31] The Court's majority concluded that jurors were not being given effective sentencing guidelines for their deliberations, resulting in a situation in which death was being "wantonly and freakishly" imposed.[32] The death penalty, as then administered, was therefore in violation of the Eighth Amendment and the due process clause of the Fourteenth Amendment. This landmark ruling invalidated death-sentencing schemes in thirty states and the District of Columbia and affected some 620 death row inmates nationwide.

Forty-seven inmates were physically present on the Texas death row on June 29, 1972, when the *Furman* decision was announced. Governor Price Daniel commuted all forty-seven inmates to life imprisonment or ninety-nine years between July 1972 and January 1973. Of these forty-seven, thirty-seven had been convicted of murder, seven of rape, and three of armed robbery. These were not the only cases affected.[33] Other offenders in various stages of processing, housed in local jails throughout Texas, were awaiting transfer to the death house or the final processing of their cases. Lacking some critical bits of information, we did not follow these additional post-*Furman* commutees. Once sentenced and having had their sentences commuted, they were processed, like all new inmates, through the prison system's diagnostic unit for admission to the general prison population.

Critics of the *Furman* ruling feared the public would be endangered by the former death row prisoners if they were ever released into the community. Others warned that the *Furman*-commuted inmates posed a more immediate and significant threat to the prisoner population. By tracking these forty-seven inmates from the time of their commutation until the end of 1988, we have been able to examine the extent to which these fears were realized. In a sense, mapping the behavior of the "*Furman* Forty-seven" represents a "natural experiment" of sorts to test whether these offenders did indeed constitute a distinct continuing menace to society and therefore whether there was a basis for justifying their execution.

It is important in any such study to view behavior in comparative terms. We compare the prison and postrelease behavior of the commuted inmates with that of a group of 156 male inmates all of whom were convicted of murder ($n = 128$), and rape ($n = 28$) and sentenced to life terms. Data on serious institutional misconduct were gathered from the inmates' prison records. Postinstitutional (recidivism) data for those paroled were obtained from the Texas Board of Pardons and Parole. This, of course, leaves the question of postrelease behavior in locations other than Texas open to question, and worthy of more complete analysis.

Demographic and Offense Characteristics

In most respects, the *Furman* Forty-seven and the control group are comparable in terms of their general characteristics. The mean age in 1973 for the *Furman* Forty-seven was thirty-two years, compared with thirty for the "lifers." Forty-six percent of the *Furman* inmates were of African-American heritage, compared with 49 percent of the life group. The life-sentence group had been convicted of committing proportionately more violent previous offenses than the *Furman* inmates, though the difference was not statistically significant. In total, both groups of prisoners had been convicted of committing seven prior murders, seven rapes, twenty-three robberies, and twenty-five aggravated assaults. The rates of prior adult incarceration for both groups were similar. For purposes of this analysis, the *Furman* group had spent nearly ten years in the general prisoner population. The life sentence group averaged just over eleven years. While this difference was statistically significant, it is not considered large enough to make a difference in expected behavior following release. On the basis of these basic similarities we would expect roughly the same level of prison rule violations and similar patterns of behavior while on parole. That indeed is what we found.

Institutional Behavior

Overall, 75 percent of the *Furman* and 70 percent of the comparison group inmates committed no serious infractions during their confinement in the general prison population, as of December 1988. In addition, 93 percent of the *Furman* group and 90 percent of the comparison group had no record of offenses classified by prison personnel as "aggravated assault" or "fighting with a weapon" (the two major categories of nonlethal violent offenses) while incarcerated in Texas prison units. Who, then, were the serious rule violators? It has long been noted that within a penitentiary, as in the outside community, a small number of individuals account for a disproportionate amount of the trouble.[34] This often-noted pattern is once again replicated.

Of the *Furman* group, twelve prisoners (nine murderers and three rapists) were responsible for 21 serious violent offenses. One inmate, a convicted murderer, committed 6 of these serious infractions. Among the comparison group, forty-seven inmates committed 116 offenses, one inmate committing 17 and another 14. The twelve former death row serious rule violators committed an

average of 14.3 disciplinary infractions (this figure includes less serious violations as well) per inmate. The forty-seven serious violators among the comparison group committed an identical average of 14.3 infractions per offender,
again suggesting little difference in the behavioral tendencies between those
who received the death sentence and those originally sentenced to life.[35] The
high-rate offenders in both groups were slightly younger than the other inmates. Among the *Furman* high-rate offenders, there were nine African-
Americans, two Hispanics, and one Anglo. Among the life-sentence comparison group, thirty-two (68 percent) were African-American, five were Hispanic,
and ten were Anglo.

These data suggest quite clearly that a small percentage of prisoners accounted for the bulk of serious disciplinary actions. None of these inmates
committed or were implicated in a prison homicide. The *Furman* inmates, as
compared with the life-sentence cohort, were not unusually disruptive or re-
bellious, nor did they pose a disproportionate threat to other inmates and staff,
as had been previously predicted by politicians, clinicians and administra-
tors.[36] The question now becomes whether the same can be said of the behavior outside of the prison system of the formerly death-sentenced inmates who
were eventually released into the community.

Conduct in the Free Community

Over the course of fourteen years, thirty-one (66 percent) of the forty-seven
Furman inmates were eventually released to the community; twenty-eight
were paroled, one was discharged, and one pardoned; one had his case dismissed after appeal. Of the thirty-one released (again evidence is limited to
that from Texas records) six had their parole revoked, three died, and twenty-
three are still living in the community (this includes one of the parolees who
had parole revoked but who has since been reparoled).[37] Sixteen inmates were
not released from prison—three died in prison and thirteen were still incarcerated as of 1988.

As for the comparison life-sentence group, 109 (70 percent) were released
and 18 were returned to prison. Of this 18 returned to prison, 6 had committed rape, 1 had committed robbery, and 4 had committed burglaries.

Excluding technical violations, data from the Texas prison system and the
Board of Pardons and Paroles indicate that 94 percent of the life sentence
inmates and 86 percent of the *Furman* releasees were not convicted of a new
felony while in the free community. As found in previous studies, the period
immediately following release was the most critical time.[38] In both the *Furman*
and the comparison groups the vast majority of persons who returned to
prison had done so within two years. While overall the recidivism rates for
both groups were comparatively low, one inmate in the *Furman* group com-

mitted another homicide while on parole. He murdered his girlfriend and then committed suicide. These acts, committed in 1985, occurred within 12 months of his release from prison. We found no record showing that anyone from the released sample of life-sentence inmates had been convicted of an additional murder and returned to prison in Texas.

In evaluating these findings, as always, strong caution should be observed. Our analysis is restricted to events and criminal cases in Texas. It is always possible that persons left the state and found themselves again behind bars in another jurisdiction. It is also possible that released inmates committed their crimes after our cutoff point or committed crimes that went undetected. In a comparison of death-sentenced and life-sentenced inmates, these shortcomings probably make little difference. One set of inmates would probably not be more likely to leave the state, nor is one group more likely to have engaged in criminal behavior after our cutoff point.

However, policy often turns on absolute rather than comparative assessments. Here the limitations of this research are more problematic. The case of Kenneth McDuff (#485) illustrates these concerns. McDuff was sentenced to die under the pre-*Furman* statute for a 1966 incident involving the killing of three teenagers (one female and two males). On September 18, 1972, approximately three months following the *Furman* decision, his death sentence was commuted to life. He first came up for parole consideration in 1976 and was turned down, as he was repeatedly over the next decade. However, twenty-three years after his conviction for the offense, three members of the Board of Pardons and Paroles, under some pressure from court orders to control the size of a bulging, overcrowded prison system, noted McDuff's clean prison record and eventually voted for his release on September 18, 1989.

McDuff was returned to jail for a brief period a year later, between September and December of 1990, under allegations of terrorist threats. However, no new charges were filed and he was released. Approximately two years later his face appeared on the national television show "America's Most Wanted" following allegations by a suspected accomplice that he had been involved in an abduction and murder in Austin. Following a tip from one of the show's viewers, McDuff was picked up in Kansas City, Missouri, where he was working as a garbage collector.[39] In 1993 he was convicted of capital murder and sentenced to death. He is currently back on death row, where he faces additional charges of capital murder.

This case, like numerous prior dramatic instances of "wrongful releases," has raised political pressure for life sentences without the possibility of parole. McDuff's release is also being used to further strengthen the argument for the death penalty. While evidence regarding deterrence of the general population may be questionable, it is clear, proponents of the death penalty are quick to point out, that had McDuff's death sentence been carried out, he, at least, would not have been free to kill again. These and other policy considerations will be discussed in greater detail in Chapter 8.

Conclusion

Between 1924 and 1972, the death sentences of 147 inmates were commuted, most to life imprisonment. Of those commuted prior to the *Furman* decision, we found some differences between the executed and the commuted populations. Clemency was more likely to have been bestowed on whites who killed other whites. Those who crossed racial lines to kill (especially blacks) were more likely to be dispatched in the electric chair. Rapists, again particularly blacks, were rarely granted clemency. On the other hand, all three women convicted of capital murder had their sentences commuted.

We tracked the prison and release behavior of the 147 commutees. Three commutees killed four other prisoners during the course of their confinement in the general inmate population. Although that is a small absolute number, if transformed into a rate, it would be higher than that for most other identifiable groups of inmates. Thus the propensity to violence was higher among these than other general prison population inmates. However, the large majority of those whose sentences were commuted to life were not involved in predatory crime against fellow inmates within the prison walls. Furthermore, most did not assault or attack correctional personnel. Hence the prediction that these death-sentenced individuals would massively threaten life and limb of persons inside prison proved to be false.

In regard to their behavior following their release, again the majority of commutees lived without a record of violence in the free community. There were, however, exceptions. Thus, while predictions of widespread future dangerousness rarely come true, exceptions open the door for substantial concern. Willingness to execute the many and thereby tolerate a large proportion of "false-positive" predictions so as to avoid even the possibility of a repetition of violence remains very much on the policy agenda. We will return to this topic during the post-*Furman* years in Chapter 7 as well as some final summary comments in Chapter 8.

CHAPTER 6

ADOPTION OF LETHAL INJECTION AND CONTEMPORARY DEATH RITUALS

■ ■ ■

The Texas sentencing statute occurs in a technical context newly weird and wonderful to me every time I look at it. . . .

What is wanted, and wanting, is an example, one single example in the whole range of civilized law outside of this one statute, that explicitly makes a person's cruel death depend on a prediction of that person's *future* conduct.[1]

Prediction of future criminal conduct is an essential element in many of the decisions rendered throughout our criminal justice system. The task that a Texas jury must perform in answering the statutory question in issue is thus basically no different from the tasks performed countless times each day throughout the American system of criminal justice.[2]

His head pointed up, his body lay flat and still for seconds. Then a harsh rasping began. His fingers trembled up and down, and the witnesses, standing near his midsection say that his stomach heaved. Quiet returned, and his head turned to the right, toward the black dividing rail. A second spasm of wheezing began. It was brief. Charlie's body moved no more.[3]

On June 29, 1972, in *Furman v. Georgia,* the U.S. Supreme Court, in a 5–4 split opinion, declared capital punishment, as then administered, unconstitutional. Relying on evidence much like the data reviewed in previous chapters, as well as more generally constructed arguments, the Court's majority concluded that in practice the death penalty was being applied in an arbitrary and capricious fashion. Where lies the fault? What to do in remedy? On these questions the Court was also split.

Two justices in the majority, Justices Brennan and Marshall, concluded that capital punishment was, under any circumstances or legislative scheme, cruel and unusual punishment and therefore in violation of the Eighth Amendment. The remedy was total abolition. The remaining three justices in the majority were less sweeping in their condemnation. Justice Douglas concluded that the statutes under review allowed juries too much discretion, resulting in discrimination against defendants on the basis of race and impoverished life circumstances. Consequently the statutes were in violation of the Eighth Amendment and the equal protection clause of the Fourteenth. Justice Stewart viewed the "capriciously selected random handful" of convicted capital offenders in less precise terms. It was as if these defendants were being struck by lightning. Like Justice Douglas, Stewart found the source of this "wanton" and "freakish" imposition of the death penalty in the standardless legislative schemes that allowed juries too loose a rein. For his argument, Justice White took a somewhat different tack. The death penalty would be constitutional if it advanced some legitimate punishment aim such as deterrence. As then practiced, the death penalty failed this test in that it was so infrequently imposed and in such an unpredictable manner that its deterrent influence was lost. Justice White found lengthy incarceration a more legitimate alternative for reasons of deterrence, incapacitation, and retribution. While divided in their rationale, these five justices were firm in their conclusion: jurors were given too much discretion. The remedy resided in more structured statutory guidelines.

State legislatures were quick to oblige. By 1976 new or revised capital punishment statutes had been passed in thirty-five states. Two roughly defined categories of sentencing guidelines emerged: statutes with mandatory provisions and statutes that provided guided discretion. Mandatory statutes took the Court's concern with standardless discretion to an extreme and eliminated all discretion in assessing punishment. Offenders convicted of homicide in specific circumstances (e.g., during the course of another felony; killing a police officer) received an automatic death sentence. Guided discretion statutes limited sentencing choices less absolutely, usually by listing aggravating and mitigating circumstances for jurors to consider.

When these statutes took effect they were immediately challenged as lawyers began guiding cases toward a hearing before the Supreme Court. Four years after *Furman,* on July 2, 1976, the Supreme Court announced its decision on cases from Louisiana, North Carolina, Florida, Georgia, and Texas.[4] The Court struck down mandatory statutes for being too rigid.[5] Other sentencing schemes fared better.[6] In their acceptance of the guided discretion statutes in Georgia, Florida, and Texas, as well as in subsequent cases, the Court began to clarify the implications of the splintered opinions in *Furman*. First, statutory guidance was acceptable when it defined a subclass of homicides—for example, homicides involving robbery, multiple homicides, and homicides accompanied by a set of aggravating circumstances, such as torture of the victim. Second, each of the statutes approved in the post-*Furman* era contained a set of explicit standards—for example, circumstances of the offense or proclivities of the offender—that constrained juries from developing a set of criteria totally on their own. Finally, each death penalty statute found acceptable by the Supreme Court contained provisions for *automatic* appellate review by a court of statewide jurisdiction.

Some six months after these decisions, on January 17, 1977, Gary Gilmore became the first person in the United States to be executed under the post-*Furman* statutes. It was not until five years later (December 7, 1982) that the first convicted felon would die under the new Texas statute. By mid-1992, a total of 177 persons had been executed nationwide following convictions for the deaths of 231 victims. Texas accounted for the largest single state total (50), followed by Florida (29), Louisiana (20), and Georgia (15).[7]

Texas and Its "Almost" Automatic Statute

Texas was one of the first states to fashion a new statute to meet *Furman*'s concerns. To limit the discretion deemed unconstitutional in *Furman*, the Sixty-Third Legislature in Texas passed House Bill 200, which became effective on June 14, 1973, eleven months after the *Furman* decision.[8] This new statute limited capital punishment to offenders who had knowingly and intentionally committed murder in one of five circumstances:

1. the person murdered a peace officer or fireman who was acting in the lawful discharge of an official duty and who the defendant knew was a peace officer or fireman;
2. the person intentionally committed the murder in the course of committing or attempting to commit kidnapping, burglary, robbery, forcible rape or arson;
3. the person committed the murder for remuneration or the promise of remuneration or employed another to commit the murder for remuneration or the promise of remuneration;
4. the person committed the murder while escaping or attempting to escape from a penal institution; or

5. the person, while incarcerated in a penal institution, murdered another who was employed in the operation of the penal institution.[9]

A sixth circumstance was added in 1985:

6. the person murdered more than one person: (a) during the same criminal transaction; or (b) during different criminal transactions but the murders are committed pursuant to the same scheme or course of conduct.[10]

When an offender is found guilty and at least one of these circumstances obtains, a punishment hearing is held. In the punishment stage of the bifurcated proceedings, the jury must address two or three questions (question 3 is asked only when the evidence warrants):

1. whether the conduct of the defendant that caused the death of the deceased was committed deliberately and with the reasonable expectation that the death of the deceased would result;
2. whether there is a probability that the defendant would commit criminal acts of violence that would constitute a continuing threat to society; and
3. if raised by the evidence, whether the conduct of the defendant in killing the deceased was unreasonable in response to the provocation, if any, by the deceased.[11]

Under this sentencing scheme, if the jury finds the defendant guilty and unanimously answers yes to all of the questions posed, the judge must impose a death sentence. A negative answer to any question by jurors (requiring agreement of ten jurors) results in an automatic sentence of life imprisonment. This Texas law also provides for a mandatory review of capital cases by the Court of Criminal Appeals.[12] Such rigidly defined procedures were fashioned to address precisely *Furman's* concern with eliminating arbitrary and capricious jury decisions, and led Justice Rehnquist in a subsequent case, *Adams v. Texas*, to conclude: "It is hard to imagine a system of capital sentencing that leaves less discretion in the hands of the jury while at the same time allowing them to consider the particular circumstances of each case—that is, to perform their assigned task at all."[13]

Other legal scholars have been far more skeptical. One is Charles Black, who in a 1977 update of his widely cited book, *Capital Punishment: The Inevitability of Caprice and Mistake*, presented a scathing attack on the new Texas statute, noting, "The Texas sentencing statute occurs in a technical context newly weird and wonderful to me every time I look at it. . . .

■ ■ ■ 131

"What is wanted, and wanting, is an example, one single example in the whole range of civilized law outside of this one statute, that explicitly and in terms makes a person's cruel death depend on a prediction of that person's *future* conduct."[14]

The first question posed to jurors in Texas, Black continued, is redundant in that it inquired "about the actual or constructive intent to kill, [when] without [such] an affirmative finding . . . nobody would have been convicted of first degree murder at all."[15] The third question, for Black, is likewise flawed by redundancy in that if unreasonable response were not supported by the evidence, a finding of murder without malice, or manslaughter, would result rather than first-degree murder. This leaves the second issue, which calls on the jury to base their decision on predictions of future conduct.

The U.S. Supreme Court upheld the new Texas statute in *Jurek v. Texas*, noting among other things that Texas had limited juror discretion by reducing the categories of murder punishable by death. Jurors in other states (e.g., Florida and Georgia) are explicitly instructed to consider sets of mitigating factors; in Texas they are asked to consider the offender's potential for future dangerousness. Deliberations surrounding this potential, the Court held, allow jurors to take any relevant mitigating or aggravating factors into consideration.[16] The empirical vagaries and accuracy of predictions of future behavior will be discussed in the next chapter.

Approximately one year after *Jurek*, on August 29, 1977, the method of execution in Texas changed from electrocution to lethal injection. The statute setting out the procedure was quite detailed. Preparations for the execution were to begin two weeks in advance with the gathering of a witness-to-the-execution list. The means of disposing of the inmate's property were specified, as were the categories of persons to be notified. "Practice sessions" were mandated, as were security measures, procedures for administering the lethal doses of drugs, and provisions for last-minute appeals, along with procedures for declaring the individual dead and for the disposition of the body (see Appendix C).

The legislative rationale for changing the means of execution resided in the belief that lethal injections were more humane than the physically traumatic and visually offensive electrocution. Clearly legislators in Texas were responding to Justice Brennan's assertion in *Furman* that "it appears that there is no method available that guarantees an immediate and painless death." In addition, a Dallas reporter had filed suit seeking permission to film executions, and state officials believed that, should the suit be successful, the injection procedure would be less unsightly and thus less susceptible to graphic journalistic descriptions that could elicit new charges of cruelty and inhumane punishment.

By January 1981 three states, Oklahoma, Idaho, and New Mexico, had followed the lead of Texas by enacting lethal injection statutes, though no one had yet been executed under the revised procedures. Two inmates held on the death rows in Oklahoma and Texas at the time petitioned the U.S. Department of Health and Human Services to ban the use of drugs for execution, claiming: "There is strong evidence to believe [that the use of drugs] may actually result in agonizingly slow and painful deaths that are far more barbaric than those caused by the more traditional means of execution." The petition continued, "The day is fast approaching when the final appeals of prisoners on death row in Texas, Oklahoma, Idaho or New Mexico will be exhausted. . . . Under an unsubstantiated medical veneer of humanity and decency, the first execution by means of a drug poses a real threat of leading to society's widespread but misguided acceptance of lethal injection as a cheap and deceptively palatable way of performing executions."[17]

Failing to stop the procedures through Department of Health and Human Services channels, lawyers for the inmates continued to press their cases before a federal district judge, asserting that the Food and Drug Administration had not approved the drugs for the stated purpose. While initially unsuccessful, a sympathetic hearing was eventually secured and reported in a 2–1 decision in the U.S. Court of Appeals in October 1983,[18] by which time Washington, Arkansas, Montana, Massachusetts, Nevada, New Jersey, Delaware, and North Carolina had been added to the list of states with lethal injection procedures.

Writing for the majority, Circuit Judge J. Skelly Wright wrote: "In a civilized society, if we assume as we must that the state may take the life of a person as punishment, decency demands that the life be taken without cruelty. . . . In this case FDA is clearly refusing to exercise enforcement discretion because it does not wish to become embroiled in an issue so morally and constitutionally troubling as the death penalty. Yet this action amounts to an abnegation of statutory responsibility by the very agency that Congress has charged with the task of ensuring that our people do not suffer harm from misbranded drugs."[19]

In dissent, Circuit Judge Antonin Scalia buttressed his legal argument first with references to Texas Governor Dolph Briscoe's statement, when signing the injection bill into law, that he hoped the bill would "provide some dignity with death" and then with references to a 1953 British report, *Royal Commission on Capital Punishment: 1949–53*, which concluded: "Intravenous injection, if practicable, would fulfill our three requisites [of humanity, certainty, and decency] better than any other method."[20] In March 1985 Scalia's position won out when the U.S. Supreme Court in a unanimous decision finally reversed the 1983 U.S. Circuit Court of Appeals decision, after some eight executions had been carried out by lethal injection.[21]

Painless or not, whether a continuing threat to human dignity or an affir-

Table 6.1. *Methods of Execution by State*[a]

State	Method	State	Method
Alabama	Electrocution	Montana	Hanging
Arizona	Gas chamber		Lethal injection
Arkansas	Lethal injection	Nebraska	Electrocution
	Electrocution	Nevada	Lethal injection
California	Gas chamber	New Hampshire	Lethal injection
Colorado	Lethal injection	New Jersey	Lethal injection
Connecticut	Electrocution	New Mexico	Lethal injection
Delaware	Lethal injection	North Carolina	Gas chamber
	Hanging		Lethal injection
Florida	Electrocution	Ohio	Electrocution
Georgia	Electrocution	Oklahoma	Lethal injection
Idaho	Lethal injection	Oregon	Lethal injection
	Firing squad	Pennsylvania	Lethal injection
Illinois	Lethal injection	South Carolina	Electrocution
Indiana	Electrocution	South Dakota	Lethal injection
Kentucky	Electrocution	Tennessee	Electrocution
Louisiana	Lethal injection	Texas	Lethal injection
Maryland	Gas chamber	Utah	Firing squad
Mississippi	Gas chamber		Lethal injection
	Lethal injection	Virginia	Electrocution
Missouri	Lethal injection	Washington	Lethal injection
		Wyoming	Lethal injection

[a]States with no death penalty: Alaska, Hawaii, Iowa, Kansas, Maine, Massachusetts, Michigan, Minnesota, New York, North Dakota, Rhode Island, Vermont, West Virginia, Wisconsin.

mation of moral principles and victims' rights, lethal injection procedures were eventually enacted a number of additional states. The state-by-state modes of execution as of mid-1992 are listed in Table 6.1.[22]

Sentencing Trends

Prior to 1965, death row inmates in Texas were housed in the Walls Unit in Huntsville, in the same building where executions took place. The death house consisted of eight 5-by-10-foot cells and a 45-foot corridor that led to the "little green door" enclosing the electric chair, executioner's booth, and witness viewing area. In the pre-*Furman* era few cells were necessary because of the short stay on death row. In the decades between the 1920s and the 1950s, death row inmates were typically electrocuted within a few months of their arrival on the row. The means of execution, "Old Sparky," remains on display in the Texas Prison Museum in downtown Huntsville.

During the late 1950s and early 1960s increased litigious resistance considerably lengthened the stay of death row inmates. At the same time prosecutors continued to secure death sentences each year. More arrivals and fewer departures meant strained facilities. In response, death row was moved to the Ellis Unit, a large, maximum security prison located twelve miles north of Huntsville. Electrocutions, however, were still carried out in the old execution chamber.

At the Ellis Unit, death row inmates were quartered in J-21 wing, a former high-security cellblock. John Devries (#507) was the first post-*Furman* inmate to receive a death sentence. He was convicted in Jefferson County, bordering Louisiana, of a murder-burglary, sentenced to death, and assigned a cell on death row in February 1974. Five months later he hanged himself in his cell. Eighteen years later, in July 1992, death row had expanded to include an entire section of the prison, housing some 350 death row inmates. The first post-*Furman* execution took place when Charlie Brooks (#592) was executed shortly after midnight on December 7, 1982, approximately four years following his conviction in Dallas for a murder-robbery/kidnapping.

Figure 6.1 depicts the number of death-sentence and life-imprisonment decisions for capital murder between 1974 and 1988. The number of offenders convicted of capital murder who received the death sentence was roughly three times the number who were sentenced to prison for life.[23] The annual number of death sentences peaked twice at forty-four, in 1978 and 1986.

Types of Offenders, Offenses, and Victims

Just under half of the 421 offenders sentenced to death between 1974 and 1988 were convicted in counties that define the six major metropolitan regions of the state. Nearly 60 percent of the capital murderers were in their twenties at the time of arrest. Six offenders were seventeen years old when arrested. The oldest, Margarito Bravo (#567), was fifty-five when arrested in 1976 for killing a police officer. Bravo's sentence was commuted to life imprisonment ten years after his conviction, in October 1986. At the age of seventy-one, he is still incarcerated as of this writing.

These post-*Furman* death-sentenced inmates were evenly split between Anglo (50 percent) and non-Anglo males (36 percent were African-American and 14 percent were Hispanic).[24] Two-thirds were single or divorced at the time they committed their offense. Like their predecessors in the pre-*Furman* years, residents on death row in the post-*Furman* years were primarily unskilled laborers (68 percent) or craftsmen (13 percent), with less than a high school education (just under 90 percent). Over half of the post-1972 offenders had one or more property crime convictions. Fifty-six percent had a prior violent crime conviction. Just over half of the offenders had been sentenced to prison

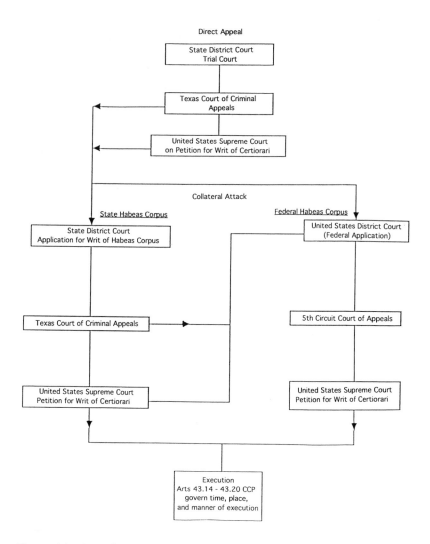

Figure 6.1. Capital case procedure (based on Robert S. Walt, *Criminal Law Update*, October 19, 1988, p. 3).

previously. While the latter figures are higher than those found among the pre-*Furman* residents of death row, in all likelihood the difference is due to better record keeping in more recent years.

What types of murders did these death row inmates commit? By a factor of almost three, murder in the course of a robbery constituted the largest category of capital offenses. Such cases accounted for 207 offenders sentenced to death, compared with 77 in the next most frequent category, rape-murder. One-third of the robbery-murder offenders came from the largest metropolitan area in the state—Houston. Approximately 10 percent of the death-sentenced offenders were convicted for burglary-murder, 7 percent for kidnapping-murder, 7 percent for killings of police, and 5 percent for killings for hire. This distribution of cases, along with offender and victim characteristics, are the subject of analysis in the next chapter.

The most frequent location of the capital murders that ended in a death sentence was the home (30 percent), followed closely by offenses in a place of business (27 percent). The majority (65 percent) of the victims in these cases were killed with a gun. Eighty percent involved a single victim. Half of these victims had not yet reached their thirtieth birthday. In two-thirds of the cases at least one of the victims was a female. In nearly 80 percent of the cases the victim was an Anglo, approximately 6 percent were African-American, and 10 percent were Hispanic.

While a majority of the death row offenders acted singly, a sizable percentage (47 percent) participated in the crime with codefendants. The idea that capital offenses involve a crime spree proved to be true in 20 percent of the cases, and evidence of excessive violence (e.g., torture, mutilation, burning of the body) was present in just over a third of the cases. In general, the victim(s) and the offender(s) were strangers—60 percent of the cases. In only 5 percent were they relatives. Reflecting the rise of the more impersonal world of the urban setting, as well as statutory changes that eliminated "passion killings" from the category of capital offenses, this dominance of killings of strangers increased vis à vis the pre-*Furman* era, as can be seen by comparison with data reviewed in previous chapters.

Execution and Commutation Information

Of the 421 offenders sentenced to death during the period of this analysis, approximately 300 are still on death row as of this writing. Fifty have been executed as of July 1992. After Charlie Brooks (#592) became the first person to be executed by lethal injection in 1982, two years passed before 3 persons were executed in 1984, followed by 6 in 1985, 10 in 1986, 6 in 1987, 3 in 1988, 4 in both 1989 and 1990, 5 in 1991, and 8 by July 1992.

Eight of the post-*Furman* inmates have died on death row, including three suicides, and one murder. Eighty death sentences have been commuted either through judicial or gubernatorial action. Over half of these commutations occurred during 1981–1983, mostly in response to *Adams v. Texas*[25] in 1980 and *Estelle v. Smith* in 1981.[26] Judicial commutations mainly resulted from appellate court action and the reluctance of district attorneys to retry these cases. Ten inmates had their cases dismissed by the courts.

As of the end of 1990, death-sentenced inmates had served an average of just over five years on death row. This figure, however, is misleading in that it includes persons recently arrived. Time spent on death row for many inmates has been longer. By the end of 1990, just over forty inmates had been on death row for a decade or more. One inmate, Excell White (#511), has been on death row since August 1974. Of those executed, the average time spent on death row was 7.55 years, and for those commuted just over four and one-half years. This, of course, is substantially longer than cases processed during the pre-*Furman* years. Indeed, the increased length of time between conviction and execution is perhaps the most dramatic difference between the pre- and post-*Furman* eras.

Life on Death Row

Death row inmates are kept physically separate from other inmates. They occupy cell blocks on one end of the prison, opposite the general prisoner population. In a sense, death row is actually a prison within a prison. A premium is placed on security. When first established in the post-*Furman* era, death row policies kept inmates locked in their cells twenty or more hours each day. Rolling plastic shields and 5 × 9 cells girded with thick wire mesh are in place to protect guards and inmates from being stabbed, spat upon, or doused with scalding water, urine, or feces when walking down the tiers or runs.

The psychological pressures of death row confinement under these conditions are many for both inmates and staff. In considering these pressures during the pre-*Furman* years Justice Felix Frankfurter had written of "the onset of insanity while awaiting execution of a death sentence," an assertion that Justice Brennan echoed in *Furman*, citing it as one of the reasons why he opposed capital punishment on the grounds that it did not "comport with human dignity." In recent years, such assertions regarding the impact of death row pressures have been the subject of some research.[27]

In post-*Furman* Texas, all the daily activities of inmates on the "row" reflect the dominance of security. With the exception of "work-capable" inmates (discussed below), death row prisoners are fed in their cells; guards slip trays of food through steel-covered slots in the cell doors. Whenever inmates are taken from their cells, whether for showers, recreation, visits, or psychiatric or medical care, strict custody procedures are followed. The following excerpt from the correctional officers' rulebook describes recreation procedures:

> Prior to placing any inmate in the recreation area, the dayroom and the recreation yard will be shaken down. Placing an inmate into the recreation area will be done by two officers approaching the inmate while he is confined in his cell, and give [*sic*] him the opportunity to recreate. If the inmate wants to recreate, the inmate must submit to a thorough strip search. The officers will shake down all clothing, shoes, etc. All clothing will be

retained by the officers except for his underwear, shower shoes or tennis shoes. Once the inmate puts his underwear and shoes on, the officer will order the inmate to back up to the cell door to be handcuffed. The inmate's back of hands will be facing each other with thumbs out. The restraints will be placed on the inmate, and the wing officer will tell the picket officer to open the designated cell. The inmate will be escorted down the run with one officer in front and one officer behind the inmate, both using a hand held shield if no rolling shield is present.

Once the inmate is in the recreation area, the restraints will be removed. Note: At no time shall no [sic] more than one inmate be escorted to the recreation area. While inmates are recreating, officers assigned to the wings will shake down the inmate's cell for contraband. Inmates can bring the following items to the recreation area: 1) rolled cigarettes, 2) a little coffee and cup. Inmates cannot bring the following items to the recreation area: 1) cans of tobacco, 2) cans of coffee, 3) large amount of legal work, books, or anything that contraband could be concealed in, radio, fans, etc.

Guards follow similarly strict and detailed procedures when transporting death row inmates to and from single, caged-in showers. Condemned prisoners who leave the death row wing are to be escorted by two prison officers. As they move through the prison the main corridor is cleared, often by the guards shouting, "Dead man comin' through."[28]

A consent decree signed in conjunction with *Ruiz v. Estelle*, one of the most complex and comprehensive prisoners' rights cases in U.S. correctional history,[29] changed the conditions on death row for some inmates. In this decree, prison officials agreed to classify death row prisoners into categories of "death row work-capable" and "death row segregation," as stipulated in the 1985 "Death Row Activity Plan." As a result of this agreement, some death row prisoners now have the right to recreation outside their cells five days a week. Inmates considered to be threats to institutional security are also allowed recreation, but in individual "recreation cages," outside areas adjacent to their cellblock.

The procedures outlined above for the recreation of inmates now apply to death row "segregation" inmates only. Prisoners classified as work-capable are allowed many more privileges and are subject to lessened security restrictions. Work-capable inmates, approximately one-third of the death row population, live in two-man cells without wire mesh. As a rule, they are not handcuffed, even outside their prison wing, nor are they strip-searched. They are fed from steam tables buffet-style and are allowed to eat either in their cells or in dayrooms. They take showers in the general prison population's bathhouse. These prisoners are also permitted to be out of their cells for fourteen hours a day on weekdays and ten hours a day on weekends; four of those hours may be spent outdoors. Overall, these death row residents are treated much like the general inmate population.

Some of these inmates are assigned as orderlies or janitors to take care of the cellblock. Most work in a garment factory built squarely behind the two wings that house the work-capable death row inmates. This factory began operation in July 1986 and now utilizes a variable number of death row inmates, depending on the availability of supervisors, during three four-hour shifts. Inmates are trained to work various machines to make sheets, aprons, towels, uniforms, and other products.

When the consent decree establishing the work program was signed, it was greeted with cynicism and guarded skepticism by staff and inmates alike. Some guards wondered aloud what all the fuss was about: These inmates are the dregs, the worst of the worst—why should we be terribly concerned with their comfort or job training? They are here for committing abominable acts to await death, not release to the work force. One inmate, from his equally cynical vantage point, stated: "Hell, this is slave labor. You know they're working us to get what they can for themselves. It's just like at Auschwitz. They'll get what they can from us before they kill us."[30] Other inmates complained of the lack of pay and the absence of a positive influence their work performance might have on the outcome of their appeals. All of the inmates interviewed, however, conceded that the program had distinct advantages. Even the most cynical admitted preference for the work program when confronted with the alternative of being locked down twenty hours a day.

Overall, the garment factory where death row inmates work has become a model of efficiency, frequently visited by numerous correctional officials from out of state. Sales of its products to state agencies totaled just over $1 million in its first full year of operation (1987) and $1.4 million in 1991.

What would prompt a "dead man" to work, for free, in a prison industry? The majority of inmates cited greater daily freedom and privileges. Others referred to the short-term psychological advantages of the program: "The work program gives me a reason to get up in the morning. If I were in segregation, I would probably sleep all day just trying to forget. It gives me a sense of dignity, doing something to completion." Other inmates discussed the potential long-term advantages, beyond death row: "If I get commuted, working here may show them [the parole board] that I can make it on the outside. It will show them that we aren't a continuing threat to society."[31]

The garment factory and the work-capable wings are clean and quiet, especially in comparison with the noise levels of the segregation wings. The prisoners seem to have much better attitudes, and the overall quality of cellblock life is higher. There is certainly less stress. Since the inception of the program, no serious violent incidents (e.g., stabbings, hostage situations, melees) have occurred in the living and work areas. The garment factory supervisor stated that disciplinary infractions are rare—less than one a month—and he recalled only one fistfight.[32] This represents strong testimony to the success of the classification system, to the security programs, and to the good behavior of these inmates, since the inmate-to-staff ratio in the factory is often ten to one.

Even with this work program in place, however, the ultimate agenda looms large. Jackson and Christian, writing before the work-capable program was put in place, best summarized the irony:

> Death row is deeded to the notion that these men, of all the criminals in the penitentiary, are special. They are the ones society has said are not capable or deserving of redemption or reform. . . . To give them schooling, training, or therapy would create an ambiguity the system is not ready to manage and which it has no desire to have become overt: It would ac-knowledge that residence on the Row is still tentative. In order to deal with the Row and what it means, the prison system adopts the posture of the inmate who says, "We're here for one thing: we're here to die."[33]

Execution Rituals

Figure 6.1 summarizes the appeals process. Once appeals are exhausted, or voluntarily ended, the preparation for execution begins. Two weeks prior to the scheduled execution date, condemned inmates decide what to do with their personal property and select persons they wish to witness the execution. One week prior to execution, law enforcement officers, who will be on hand outside the Walls Unit on the night of the execution for crowd control, are notified. At the same time, persons who will actually administer the lethal chemicals assemble to run through two practice sessions.

Three days prior to the execution, prison officials make arrangements for telephone contact with the governor's office on the night of execution. Family members agree to burial arrangements, either to claim the body or to have the prison system bury the inmate in the Joe Byrd Cemetery (named for the assis-tant warden involved in the execution of many prisoners in the pre-*Furman* era). A prison physician agrees to attend the execution and to certify the time of death.

Two days prior to the execution, the necessary papers to obtain the lethal injection chemicals are filed. Prison officials inspect the death chamber to ensure that all necessary equipment is in working order. They also notify a Huntsville funeral home to make arrangements for removal of the body. Around 4:00 P.M. of the day prior to execution morning, the prisoner is trans-ported from the death row cell block at Ellis I to the Walls Unit.

On December 7, 1982, Charlie Brooks (#592), a "three-time loser" from

Dallas, whose stated occupation was "professional criminal," became the first inmate to be executed by lethal injection. In states across the nation the media kept the public informed with more than the usual coverage. These accounts described both the offender and offense in graphic detail. Relying on the available record, as well as his own conversations with Charlie Brooks, a journalist in Texas described the night of the crime:

On cheap streets, Charlie swaggered too much. The knife and bullet scars on his belly were the price he had paid for bravado. He was too showy, as well. On the night of his last crime, he was plumed for memory: a factory-faded denim cap on his head, the kind with zippered pockets in the crown; a mustache that curved back to his sideburns; brown sunshades; one or two earrings, diamond or pearl; a slinky polyester print on his chest; yellow gloves on his hands; and, across his shoulders, a tan topcoat with shoplifter's "drop pockets" inside. Charlie Brooks was not a criminal of cautious taste or nondescript style. He was a pool hall rooster.[34]

Like some 40 percent of the cases of fellow death row residents, Charlie Brooks's offense had involved a codefendant and there was some question as to who had actually done the killing. There was less question regarding the surrounding events. A prostitute acquaintance had traded sexual favors for the use of a car and had asked Brooks and his codefendant to go for a ride with her. After going to a local motel and taking heroin, the three kept drinking and decided to drive around town. When the car broke down, Brooks walked to a nearby used car lot and asked for a "test drive." It was company policy that a customer testing out the car be accompanied by an employee. Sometime during the drive, Brooks and his codefendant turned on the employee, put him in the trunk, gagged and bound with adhesive tape and a clothes hanger wire. There was a single bullet found in the victim's head. It was for this offense that Charlie Brooks had been sentenced to die.

On execution night spectators, mainly students from the nearby university but also others including some seventy-five reporters, assembled outside the Walls Unit in Huntsville awaiting news of Brooks's death. On one side were those protesting capital punishment with a quiet candlelight vigil. On the other were spectators carrying signs reading "Kill him in vein" and "Bring back Old Sparky" and shouting slogans of derision at those in the anti-capital-punishment vigil. This circuslike atmosphere would be repeated again and again over the next few years as the number of executions accumulated, but eventually the public would all but totally lose interest in these middle-of-the-night events.[35]

Inside the Walls Unit the actual execution took place. At 7:30 P.M. Brooks was given his last meal, a T-bone steak, french fries, hot rolls, iced tea, and peach cobbler, after which he showered and donned "prison whites" and then waited in a cell adjoining the execution chamber, where the prison doctor checked his veins to ensure they would accommodate the needle. The lethal dosages of sodium pentathol, Pavulon, and potassium chloride were ready to be carried in tubes strung through a hole in a wall, arranged so that Brooks and his executioners would be in separate rooms. After Brooks was brought to the execution room and strapped to the gurney, a medical technician, supervised by a medical doctor, inserted the needle. Shortly after midnight the drugs began to flow.

In his closing thoughts a journalist reporting the event recalled an interview with Brooks when Brooks had admitted killing the victim. He had killed him, but had not meant to. The soon-to-be executed offender remembered being both "stoned and soused" and acting as if in a sleep-walking dream. While noting that neither the law nor common morality accepts dope and drunkenness as an excuse, the reporter reflected on both Brooks and his executioners: "When taking irreversible actions, we all develop qualms about what we do."[36]

Qualms or not, the basic ritual would be repeated again and again until some forty-nine additional offenders had been executed in Texas over the next decade. The following are accounts of how two of these additional death row inmates spent their final day. The first is from the file of Elliott Johnson, #739.

Ellis I Unit—6/23/87

12:27 A.M.	Sleeping in bunk
2:25 A.M.	Ate breakfast—biscuits, oatmeal & scrambled eggs. Did not eat figs, beef gravy or milk.
3:25 A.M.	Sleeping in bunk.
8:00 A.M.	Sitting on bunk watching T.V.
8:30 A.M.	Requested last meal: Cheeseburger and french fries.
9:30 A.M.	Sitting and lying on bunk watching T.V.
10:00 A.M.	Talking with Leon King, #624.
10:30 A.M.	Listening to stereo.
11:00 A.M.	Talking with Chaplain Alex Taylor.
12 noon	Talking with Wayne East, #720.
12:30 P.M.	Laying on bunk listening to radio.
1:00 P.M.	Started visit with his sister from Port Arthur. Also visited briefly with a friend.
2:57 P.M.	Visits with sister and friend ended and Johnson returned to the recreation room. Johnson refused a lunch of smoked links,

	macaroni & cheese, black-eyed peas, turnip greens, squash, grated cheese, rolls, peanut butter cookies, and cold beverage.
3:35 P.M.	Advised that his appeal had been denied, he said nothing. Advised that he was going to be transported to Huntsville.
3:36 P.M.	Removed from cell and searched.
3:37 P.M.	Placed in restraints.
3:41 P.M.	Removed from wing.
3:45 P.M.	Departed from Ellis I.
4:20 P.M.	Arrived at the Huntsville "Walls" Unit, taken to the death house where restraints removed, he was searched and placed in cell.
4:45 P.M.	Received a copy of the telefax from warden that Federal District Judge Howell Cobb denied appeal. His response was, "oh." Clothing to be worn: Light blue shirt and blue pants.
5:53–5:58 P.M.	Showered, shaved and dressed.
6:09 P.M.	Advised of 5th Circuit denial. No response.
6:30 P.M.	Ate all of his meal and drank some punch.
7:35 P.M.	Advised that the Supreme Court denied stay, he said, "Okay, thank you."
8:05 P.M.	Reading the Houston Post. Talked with his mother. She is an inmate at the Gatesville Unit. She is serving 6 years sentence for theft which began 5/1/87. His mood was calm as he visited on and off with Chaplain Pickett since his arrival at the Huntsville Unit.

Four hours later, the final procedure for execution began when the inmate was moved from his holding cell to the death chamber at 12:01 A.M. The death chamber houses only a gurney and the medical paraphernalia to administer the lethal combination of drugs. After he was strapped to the gurney, catheters were placed in each arm and a saline solution began flowing. Witnesses were brought into the death chamber, a room twelve by sixteen feet, according to provisions in Article 43.20 of the Code of Criminal Procedure:

The following persons may be present at the execution: the executioner and such persons as may be necessary to assist him in conducting the execution; the Board of Directors of the Department of Corrections, the county judge and sheriff of the county in which the Department of Corrections is situated, and any relatives or friends of the condemned person that he may request, not exceeding five in number, shall be admitted. No convict shall be permitted by the prison authorities to witness the execution.[37]

After the last witness had entered the room, the door to the death chamber was closed. The warden then asked the man for his last statement. He replied,

"I am very sorry for bringing all the pain and hurt to the family. I hope you find it in your heart to forgive me. Try not to worry too much about me. Remember one thing, Mother, I love you." After which the warden simply stated, "We are ready." Executioners, behind a one-way mirror, began the flow of drugs. Shortly thereafter, a Texas Department of Corrections physician confirmed that Johnson was dead. The time required for the execution procedure on this occasion was fifty-two minutes.

The following is an official account, from the inmate file, of how John Thompson, #610, spent his last hours prior to execution.

Ellis I Unit 7/7/87

12:00 midnight	Packing property
12:30 A.M.	Asleep
2:15 A.M.	Pill call; accepted nasal inhalant, and refused antibiotic
2:30 A.M.	Asleep
3:00 A.M.	Ate one biscuit with butter/peanut butter mixture, coffee and milk
3:30 A.M.	Laying in bunk smoking
4:00–4:30 A.M.	Property inventoried
5:00–6:00 A.M.	In dayroom
6:30–7:15 A.M.	Talking with Catholic chaplain Father Cornelius Ryan in dayroom
7:15 A.M.	Recreating in dayroom
8:50–10:15 A.M.	Visiting with father, mother, brother, and brother's girlfriend
11:00 A.M.	Visiting with fiancee, brother, sister and brother-in-law. Last meal requested: freshly squeezed orange juice
2:30 P.M.	Exited visiting room.
2:40 P.M.	Sitting in cell
3:00 P.M.	Sitting on bunk talking to Ricky Morrow, #753
3:30 P.M.	Still talking to Morrow
3:45 P.M.	Talking with Chaplain Alex Taylor
3:55 P.M.	Moved off wing; enroute to Huntsville
4:32 P.M.	Arrived at the Huntsville Unit
4:47 P.M.	Entered death house, searched and placed in holding cell. Mood is calm. Chaplain Pickett is with him.
5:30 P.M.	Last meal served
5:55 P.M.	Finished meal
5:59 P.M.	Showered and dressed in light blue pants, light blue shirt, and white socks
7:00 P.M.	Informed that Supreme Court denied stay. He stated he appreciated "Ya'll telling me so I didn't have to hear it on the news." He then requested a radio station be found so he could hear the news. Mood appears calm.

7:50 P.M.	Visiting with his attorney.
9:15 P.M.	Ended visit with attorney.
9:30 P.M.	Visiting with Father Cornelius Ryan.
10:00 P.M.	Ended visit with Father Ryan,
10:30 P.M.	Called his sister.
10:55 P.M.	Visiting with another attorney.
12:02 A.M.	Taken from holding cell.
12:04 A.M.	Strapped to gurney.
12:06 A.M.	Saline solution flowing in left arm.
12:08 A.M.	Saline solution flowing in right arm.
12:11 A.M.	No Last Statement.
12:11 A.M.	Lethal dose began.
12:13 A.M.	Lethal dose finished.
12:20 A.M.	Pronounced dead

Those present at the execution were:

OFFICIALS:
The Honorable Jim Mattox, Attorney General, State of Texas
Bill Zapalac, Attorney General's Office
James Gaston, Attorney General's Office
Darrell White, Sheriff, Walker County
Lloyd Roark, Justice of the Peace, Walker County
James A. Collins, Deputy Director of Operations
J. Kirk Brown, General Counsel
Charles Brown, Assistant Director of Public Information
David Nunnelee, Public Information Office
James Saffle, Warden, Oklahoma Department of Corrections
John Tillingast, Medical Director, Oklahoma Department of
    Corrections
Bobby Boone, Major, Oklahoma Department of Corrections

REPORTERS:
David Rodrick, KMOL-TV, San Antonio
Jeff Brown, Brazosport Facts
Mike Graczyk, Associated Press
Paula Dittrick, United Press International
Terry Scott Bertling, Huntsville Item

PERSONAL WITNESSES:
Brother-in-Law
Father
Brother
Friend
Attorney

In this last case the entire execution procedure took only eighteen minutes. On other occasions the process did not go as smoothly. When executions first resumed in Texas, condemned inmates were strapped to the gurney at 11:00 P.M. to await their execution at midnight. This procedure was changed after the second man to be executed, J. D. Autry, gained a last-minute postponement. On October 5, 1983, Autry was strapped to the gurney and the intravenous tubes were placed in his arms when Supreme Court Justice Byron White issued a last-minute stay while a legal issue raised by a California inmate was decided. Five months later, after the issue was resolved, Autry became the second man to be executed by lethal injection, on March 14, 1984.

On another occasion, a stay of execution temporarily rescued Robert Streetman after he had been strapped in the gurney shortly after midnight. He was taken off the gurney and returned to the holding cell while he, along with witnesses, officials, and executioners, awaited the outcome of a pending appeal. Just after 3:00 A.M. word arrived that the execution could go forward. Streetman was pronounced dead at 3:26 A.M.

Not all delays resulted from legal proceedings; some were directly related to the nature of the lethal injection itself. The mixture of drugs had been chosen to simulate going to sleep, in order to bring about a "quick and painless" death, and from most accounts the fifty executions over the decade between 1982 and 1992 have gone without incident. However, some executions were smoother than others. In Stephen McCoy's case, on May 24, 1989, the reaction to the drugs induced a violent choking, gasping and writhing on the gurney—so much so that one witness fainted. In other cases, good veins (veins that would accommodate the needle) were hard to find. In the case of Stephen Peter Morin, executed on March 13, 1985, finding a good vein took approximately 45 minutes. In Raymond Landry's case, on December 13, 1988, two minutes after the solution was flowing, the syringe popped out, spraying the mixture of drugs across the room toward the witness window. The needle was reinserted and the execution proceeded fifteen minutes later. At Billy White's execution on April 23, 1992, the director of the Texas prison system at the time recalled, "He was a habitual drug user, and we had an extremely difficult time finding a vein suitable for the procedure." The inmate, however, was "very compliant, very courteous, very cooperative."[38]

Chronological Listing of Inmates Executed

Beginning with the execution of Charlie Brooks in December 1982 and ending with the execution of Robert Black on May 22, 1992, fifty men were put to death in Texas by lethal injection. The following is a chronological listing of these men and the crimes that led to their execution.

1. Charlie Brooks, Jr. (#592), executed December 7, 1982. On December 14, 1976, Brooks abducted from a used car lot a mechanic who had gone with Brooks for a test drive in one of the cars. The victim was bound and gagged with adhesive tape and a clothes hanger wire. He was taken to a motel, where he was shot once in the head. Brooks had been on death row at the time of his execution for just over four years.

2. James Autry (#670), executed March 14, 1984. On April 4, 1980, Autry and a codefendant, high on drugs, robbed a Sac and Pac store, killing the female clerk and a male customer and wounding two other men. His codefendant plea-bargained to a seven year sentence. Autry refused a thirty-five year plea bargain and was sentenced to death. Autry had been on death row at the time of his execution for three years and five months.

3. Ronald O'Bryan (#529), executed October 31, 1984. On October 31, 1974, O'Bryan returned from a neighbor's house with some Pixy Stix candy for his son and some friends who were trick-or-treating. After ingesting the candy, which had been poisoned, his son died a slow, painful death. The motive for the killing was insurance money. O'Bryan had recently increased his son's insurance premium. He made the poisoned Pixy Stix candies and handed them out to the boys after pretending to get them from a neighbor's house. This crime earned him the nickname "the Candyman." O'Bryan had been on death row at the time of his execution for eight years and seven months.

4. Thomas Barefoot (#621), executed October 30, 1984. On August 7, 1978, Barefoot, a fugitive from justice in New Mexico for allegedly kidnapping, raping, and otherwise sexually abusing a three-year-old girl, shot a police officer in the head just above the eye. Barefoot had been on death row at the time of his execution for five years and nine months.

5. Doyle Skillern (#518), executed January 16, 1985. On the night of October 23, 1974, Skillern and a codefendant attempted to sell drugs to a forty-year-old white male. Upon finding out that the buyer was an undercover Texas Department of Public Safety narcotics agent, they shot the victim six times in the chest with a pistol. Skillern's codefendant was also sentenced to death but later had his sentence commuted to life. Skillern had been on death row at the time of his execution for nine years and ten months.

6. Stephen Peter Morin (#712), executed March 13, 1985. On December 11, 1981, Morin killed a young woman at random and wounded another. After arrest, it was determined that he had raped, kidnapped, tortured, and

eventually killed at least nine women in a drifting crime spree. Morin had been on death row at the time of his execution for two years and nine months.

7. Jesse Sandoval De la Rosa (#713), executed May 15, 1985. On the morning of August 26, 1979, De la Rosa robbed a convenience store in San Antonio. He shot the clerk two times in the head with a .38 caliber pistol for six cans of beer. De la Rosa had been on death row at the time of his execution for two years and nine months.

8. Charles Milton (#628), executed June 25, 1985. On June 24, 1977, Milton robbed a female clerk at a liquor store in Fort Worth. Under the influence of drugs, he shot her one time. Although he had no prior record of violent crime convictions, he was later found guilty of committing three additional robberies three days prior to the shooting of the store clerk. Milton had been on death row at the time of his execution for six years and five months.

9. Henry Martinez Porter (#551), executed July 9, 1985. On November 29, 1975, Porter killed a Fort Worth police officer during a traffic stop. He was arrested three days later for aggravated robbery in San Antonio. Throughout his trial, he claimed he had killed the police officer in self-defense. He maintained this rationale throughout his appeals and finally even after being strapped to the gurney. Porter had been on death row at the time of his execution for nine years.

10. Charles Francis Rumbaugh (#555), executed September 11, 1985. On April 4, 1975, Rumbaugh robbed a jewelry store in Amarillo. Believing that the victim was reaching for a gun, Rumbaugh shot and killed him. Rumbaugh was seventeen at the time of the murder-robbery. Rumbaugh had been on death row at the time of his execution for nine years and one month.

11. Charles William Bass (#662), executed March 12, 1986. On August 16, 1979, Bass robbed a Houston lounge at gunpoint and fled. He was stopped by Houston city marshals and shot one of them in the stomach. He shot and missed the other marshal. He again shot the wounded officer who lay on the pavement dying. Bass had been on death row at the time of his execution for five years and seven months.

12. Jeffery Allen Barney (#714), executed April 16, 1986. On May 21, 1982, Barney raped, strangled to death, and sodomized the corpse of a female Pasadena resident in her home. He then took the victim's car, credit cards,

and cash and drove to Ohio, where he was arrested in the stolen car. When questioned about his motive for entering the home, Barney stated, "It's none of their fucking business." His rationalization for this offense was "The bitch deserved to die." Barney had been on death row at the time of his execution for three years and eight months.

13. Jay Kelly Pinkerton (#686), executed May 15, 1986. On October 26, 1979, Pinkerton robbed and knifed to death a thirty-year-old male. However, Pinkerton was also convicted of other capital murders involving rape-killings. One was the stabbing at a closed furniture store of a twenty-five-year old female who was waiting for a ride home. He was charged with this murder after a doctor was able to match Pinkerton's teeth to the marks found on the woman's body. Pinkerton had been on death row at the time of his execution for four years and eight months.

14. Rudy Ramos Esquivel (#606), executed June 9, 1986. Early in the morning on June 8, 1978, Esquivel, in order to avoid being searched for heroin, shot two police officers twice. One survived, the other died. He was shot once by one of the police officers during the shoot-out and was arrested at the scene. Esquivel had been on death row at the time of his execution for seven years and eight months.

15. Kenneth Albert Brock (#522), executed June 19, 1986. On May 20, 1974, Brock robbed a convenience store in Houston, killing the store manager in the process. He was executed in spite of pleas from the victim's father and the original prosecutor that the sentence be commuted to life in prison. Brock had been on death row at the time of his execution for eleven years and three months.

16. Randy Lynn Woolls (#646), executed August 20, 1986. On June 16, 1979, Woolls, along with accomplices, went to a drive-in movie in Kerrville. He approached the ticket booth, cut the woman teller's throat and wrist, hit her on the head with a tire iron, piled objects on top of her, and set her on fire. He then got into the victim's car and drove in to watch the movie, where he was later arrested. Woolls had been on death row at the time of his execution for six years and eight months.

17. Larry Smith (#643), executed August 22, 1986. On the night of February 2, 1978, in Dallas, Smith, along with a codefendant, robbed and then shot a twenty-six-year-old white male one time in the back with a .22 caliber pistol. Smith's codefendant received a life sentence. Smith had been on death row at the time of his execution for six years and nine months.

18. Chester Lee Wicker (#678), executed August 26, 1986. On April 4, 1980, Wicker abducted a twenty-two-year-old female from a Beaumont shopping center. He took her to an isolated location near Galveston beach, choked her, and then buried her alive in the sand. Wicker had been on death row at the time of his execution for five years and five months.

19. Michael Wayne Evans (#608), executed December 4, 1986. On June 26, 1977, Evans, along with a codefendant, abducted a couple leaving church. After robbing them, the offenders shot the man and shot and stabbed the woman. The victims' bodies were then dumped in separate locations. The codefendant received a life sentence. Evans had been on death row at the time of his execution for eight years and three months.

20. Richard David Andrade (#774), executed December 18, 1986. On March 22, 1984, Andrade, under the influence of heroin, entered a restaurant-bar in Corpus Christi and stabbed a twenty-eight-year-old female fourteen times while sexually assaulting her. Andrade had been on death row at the time of his execution for two years and one month.

21. Ramon Pedro Hernandez (#667), executed January 30, 1987. On June 20, 1980, Hernandez broke into an El Paso gas station. He then robbed and killed a mechanic who was sleeping in the station at the time of the break-in. Hernandez had been on death row at the time of his execution for six years and four months.

22. Eliseo Hernandez Moreno (#759), executed March 4, 1987. On October 11, 1983, Moreno engaged in a 5 1/2-hour, 160-mile crime spree. He first killed two in-laws who were sheltering his wife from him in College Station. After killing his in-laws, he headed south but was stopped by a trooper in Hempstead. Moreno shot the officer five times at close range, for which he received the death penalty. In Hempstead, he also killed three uncooperative elderly persons. He then abducted a family with three preschool children and forced them to drive him to Pasadena, near Houston. He then forced a man to drive him south toward his home in the Rio Grande Valley, but was captured in a roadblock between Wharton and El Campo. Moreno had been on death row at the time of his execution for three years and one month.

23. Anthony Charles Williams (#619), executed May 28, 1987. On June 12, 1978, Williams abducted a thirteen-year-old girl from the parking lot of a Houston bowling center. After sexually assaulting and strangling the

girl, he beat her to death with a two-by-four. Williams had been on death row at the time of his execution for eight years and six months.

24. Elliot Rod Johnson (#739), executed June 24, 1987. On April 8, 1982, Johnson, along with three accomplices, robbed a Beaumont jewelry store. Both the owner and a store clerk were shot at close range, execution-style, after being ordered to lie on the floor. One codefendant received death, another life, and another thirty years imprisonment. Johnson had been on death row at the time of his execution for four years and one month.

25. John Russell Thompson (#610), executed July 8, 1987. On May 21, 1977, Thompson, along with three codefendants, robbed a miniwarehouse in San Antonio, fatally shooting the seventy-year-old female proprietor. Thompson had been on death row at the time of his execution for eight years and eight months.

26. Joseph Blaine Starvaggi (#586), executed September 10, 1987. On November 19, 1976, Starvaggi, along with two accomplices, burglarized a juvenile probation officer/reserve duty sheriff's house to steal his gun collection. After being shot once, the victim begged for mercy. Starvaggi then shot the victim two more times. When urged by accomplices to shoot the victim's wife and daughter, he replied that he only killed "dopers and pigs." One codefendant received life and the other death. Starvaggi had been on death row at the time of his execution for nine years and five months.

27. Robert Lyndon Streetman (#746), executed January 7, 1988. On December 17, 1982, Streetman, along with three accomplices, entered a home to commit burglary. Finding the home occupied, the offenders shot and killed the female resident with a .22 rifle. Streetman had been on death row at the time of his execution for four years and four months.

28. Donald Gene Franklin (#546), executed November 3, 1988. On July 25, 1975, just after midnight, Franklin abducted a nurse from a hospital parking lot in San Antonio. Five days later, the nurse was found, nude and barely alive, in a field not far from the hospital. Suffering from irreversible shock, she died the next morning. Franklin had been on death row at the time of his execution for twelve years and five months.

29. Raymond Landry (#738), executed December 13, 1988. Landry was convicted for the murder-robbery of a thirty-three-year-old male restaurant owner in Houston. Landry was arrested three days after the offense at his

house, where the police found a bag from the restaurant. Landry had been on death row just under 5 1/2 years at the time of his execution.

30. Leon King (#624), executed March 22, 1989. On April 10, 1978, King, along with a codefendant, bludgeoned a man to death with the butt of a shotgun in the course of a robbery in Houston in which $11.50 was taken. Enraged over the amount, the two offenders took the victim and his girlfriend to a remote area, where they killed the man and repeatedly raped the woman. The codefendant received a life sentence. King had been on death row at the time of his execution for ten years and three months.

31. Stephen McCoy (#769), executed May 24, 1989. McCoy was convicted in 1981 for the slaying of Cynthia Johnson. Johnson was abducted and raped by McCoy and two codefendants. The victim, a stranded motorist awaiting help, was killed as part of a blood pact between McCoy and his two codefendants. McCoy had been on death row at the time of his execution for four years and eight months.

32. James Paster (#752), executed September 20, 1989. Paster was convicted of killing a thirty-eight-year-old man in Houston. With the victim's former wife and the former wife's husband as accomplices, Paster shot the victim in the head for $1,000. Paster had been on death row at the time of his execution for five years and eight months.

33. Carlos DeLuna (#744), executed December 7, 1989. DeLuna was convicted in the robbery-slaying of a female service station clerk in Corpus Christi. He stole an undetermined amount of money and fled on foot after stabbing the victim to death. DeLuna had been on death row at the time of his execution for six years and three months.

34. Jerome Butler (#852), executed April 21, 1990. Butler was convicted of the shooting death of a Houston taxi driver in 1986. The sixty-seven-year-old cab driver was robbed of just over $300 before being shot in the head with a pistol. Butler had been on death row at the time of his execution for three years and four months.

35. Johnny Anderson (#732), executed May 17, 1990. Anderson, a former mechanic with an IQ of 70, was convicted for the killing of his brother-in-law in Beaumont. He was allegedly offered $10,000 for the killing by his sister, the victim's wife. The victim was shot three times with a rifle and shotgun. Anderson had been on death row at the time of his execution for seven years and two months.

36. James Smith (#763), executed June 26, 1990. Smith was convicted of shooting a forty-four-year-old male manager of a Houston insurance office with a pistol during a store robbery. The victim was shot through the heart, allegedly as he begged for his life. Smith had been on death row at the time of his execution for six years and two months.

37. Mikel Derrick (#701), executed July 18, 1990. Derrick was convicted of killing a man with a handgun in the victim's apartment during the course of a robbery. The victim was stabbed nineteen times. Derrick had been on death row at the time of his execution for eight years and five months.

38. Lawrence Buxton (#743), executed February 26, 1991. Buxton was convicted of killing a supermarket customer in the course of a robbery. Apparently the shot was precipitated when the child the customer was carrying would not stop crying. Buxton had been on death row at the time of his execution for seven years and seven months.

39. Ignacio Cuevas (#526), executed May 23, 1991. Cuevas was executed for his part in an eleven-day prison siege in which he and other convicts attempted to escape. In the escape attempt four people were killed, including a prison librarian and a prison teacher who had been taken hostage. Two inmates working with Cuevas were also killed. Cuevas had been on death row at the time of his execution a few days short of sixteen years.

40. Jerry Joe Bird (#512), executed June 17, 1991. Bird was executed after being convicted of shooting an antique gun collector during a burglary of the man's home. Following the killing he set fire to the house, but the wife of the victim escaped through a window and was later able to testify. Bird had been on death row at the time of his execution for sixteen years and eight months.

41. James Russell (#579), executed September 19, 1991. Russell was executed after being convicted of killing a man who was going to testify against him at a robbery trial. The victim was kidnapped, locked in the trunk of a car, and driven to a remote location, where he was sexually abused before being shot. Russell had been on death row at the time of his execution for just under fifteen years.

42. G. W. Green (#576), executed November 12, 1991. Green was executed for his part in the robbery and murder of a probation officer, during which the wife and child were forced to listen as their husband and father begged for his life. Green did not fire the actual lethal shots, but evidence suggested that he would have if his gun had worked. One of his accomplices

in the crime had been executed in 1987. The second accomplice was given a life sentence. Green had been on death row at the time of his execution for just over fourteen years.

43. Joel Angel Cordova (#730), executed January 22, 1992. Cordova was allegedly high on beer and paint fumes when he, along with four juveniles, abducted and killed a man they spotted at a freeway pay phone, calling for aid after having locked himself out of his car. One of the juveniles was tried as an adult and given a fifteen-year sentence, while the others were sent to a juvenile detention home. Cordova had been on death row at the time of his execution for nine years and one month.

44. Johnny Garrett (#729), executed February 11, 1992. Garrett was executed after conviction for the rape and murder of an elderly nun. The case gained public attention when Governor Ann Richards granted a thirty-day reprieve after receiving a letter from the Vatican City ambassador to the United States requesting the stay in the name of Pope John Paul II, justified in part because of evidence of mental illness and a childhood of severe abuse. The Board of Pardons and Paroles voted 17–0 against commuting Garrett's sentence. Garrett had been on death row at the time of his execution for nine years and one month.

45. David Clark (#874), executed February 28, 1992. Clark, along with three accomplices, killed a man and woman he suspected of stealing chemicals used to manufacture illegal drugs. One accomplice, Clark's fiancée, was sentenced to a life prison term. The other two testified against Clark and his fiancée and pleaded guilty to lesser charges of burglary. Clark had been on death row at the time of his execution for four years and seven months.

46. Edward Ellis (#749), executed March 3, 1992. Ellis was sentenced to die for the robbery and strangling death of a seventy-four-year-old woman in Houston. Last-minute appeals by Ellis's attorneys claiming new evidence that another man had written a letter confessing to the crime failed. Ellis had been on death row at the time of his execution for nine years and five months.

47. Billy White (#585), executed April 23, 1992. White was executed for the 1976 robbery-slaying of a sixty-five-year-old woman who was a co-owner of a furniture store in Houston. White entered the store as the victim and her husband were closing for the evening. He was convicted of shooting the victim and taking $269 from the store's safe. White was shot in the groin in a struggle with the husband and then fled the scene. During his trial he was dubbed "Sleeping Billy" when he repeatedly went to sleep during his trial. White had

been on death row at the time of his execution for fourteen years and two months.

48. Justin Lee May (#783), executed May 7, 1992. May was sentenced to die for the 1978 killing of a woman in the course of a robbery. The woman's husband was also killed. May was not implicated in the robbery murder until 1984, when he was serving a fifteen-year sentence on another charge. A fellow inmate overheard May brag about the killing, reported it to prison authorities, and agreed to testify. May's accomplice also testified against him. May had been on death row at the time of his execution for seven years and two months.

49. Jesus Romero (#801), executed May 20, 1992. Romero was put to death for the kidnapping, rape, and murder of a teenage girl. The girl was abducted by Romero and three fellow members of a local gang. She was raped repeatedly, beaten with a pipe, and shot. One accomplice was also sentenced to death, while a second was convicted of capital murder and sentenced to life. The third was tried as a juvenile, convicted of sexual assault, and sentenced to twenty years. Romero had been on death row at the time of his execution for six years and eight months.

50. Robert Black (#819), executed May 22, 1992. Black was put to death after his conviction for hiring a man to kill his wife. Evidence also indicated that Black had paid the killer $10,000 in order to collect on his wife's recently purchased $175,000 life insurance policy. He had found the man through a classified ad in an issue of *Soldier of Fortune* magazine. The man hired to do the killing testified against Black and received a life sentence. At the time of his execution, Black had been on death row for six years and two months.

Four days after Robert Black became the fiftieth man to be executed in the post-*Furman* years, a Houston paper carried an in-depth story about the ten years that had elapsed since Charlie Brooks's execution.[39] With fifty executions Texas had become, by far, the nation's leader. The state next in line was Florida, with twenty-nine executions. The middle-of-the-night events at the Huntsville prison no longer drew the attention of the nation's news media. The circuslike atmosphere outside the walls with placard-carrying, slogan-chanting students and candle-burning protesters had become much more sedate, characterized by "the flicker of a lone candle raised by the remaining stalwart in local Amnesty International ranks." The removal of executions from the emotional tension and sometimes brutal conditions in local communities and the implementation of a "quick and painless death," sought by the reformers in the 1920s, had been realized. The ritualization of the latest death sentence proceedings had become institutionalized in finished form.

CHAPTER 7

STAGES OF SENTENCING AND FUTURE DANGEROUSNESS OF CONVICTS

■ ■ ■

Now, a person who will [commit that type of act] has got to be a threat to society. It has got to be a threat to all of us, to our wives, to our families, to everybody in this country. What would be more of a threat to society, is he going to stop, is he going to stop with these two? We don't know. How do we know? Are you going to go into the jury room and say two is okay, I don't think he will do it again?[1]

I tell you now that unless you do observe the evidence, and base your decision, and find beyond a reasonable doubt and find the answer [to the second, death-sentence issue] to be yes in this case, that upon your heads will lie the next man that's dead due to the defendant's hands.[2]

We are now in position to assess post-*Furman* death-sentencing patterns. Have statutory changes in Texas, with more restricted definitions of capital offenses and almost mandatory provisions for death once guilt is established, resulted in less arbitrary and capricious sentences and executions? Has the new death sentence scheme raised new problems associated with instructions to jury members that they predict how the recently convicted person is likely to act in the future?[3]

A Brief Review of Post-*Furman* Research

Researchers in the post-*Furman* years have taken their lead from the Court's concern with arbitrary and capricious sentences as defined by racial considerations. Whereas some justices in *Furman* emphasized the *defendant's* race as the determining influence, researchers in subsequent years have focused as well on the *victim's race* and the *victim-offender relationship*, as well as on whether noted racial discrepancies might be accounted for by factors other than racial bias.

For example, post-*Furman* researchers have consistently found that death sentences are most likely when the victim is Anglo and that this tendency is heightened when the offender is African-American. One explanation could be that prosecutors, judges, and juries are on the whole more protective of Anglo victims and more incensed by racially mixed crimes than crimes in which one African-American kills another from the same ethnic heritage.

On the other hand, the same punishment patterns may arise from the intermingling of other offense attributes. It might be that Anglos are more likely victims in lethal offenses involving robbery. Being proprietors of businesses vulnerable to robbery, Anglos may be confronted more frequently by robbers and be killed more frequently in the process. The presence of the aggravating second felony, rather than racial bias, may account for the overrepresentation of white-victim cases on death row. Similarly, rapes involving mixed-ethnicity characteristics may also be more likely to involve strangers.[4] Stranger-rape homicides may be treated by prosecutors, judges and juries, for any number of reasons, as more deserving of capital punishment. In brief, as post-*Furman* research has been careful to indicate, racial discrepancies in sentencing patterns do not automatically imply a racially arbitrary or capricious process.

Even when researchers, after investigating alternative explanations, conclude with "moral certainty" that racial bias is an important determining factor in capital sentencing patterns, the policy implications are not altogether obvious. Bias can be remedied with either more or fewer executions. For example, summarizing the implications of what is by all accounts the most comprehensive investigation of post-*Furman* death-sentencing patterns,[5] Richard Lempert noted that the haphazard patterns in earlier years had been reduced and that "the inconsistency that does exist . . . results more from the presence of eminently death-eligible defendants who escape the death sentence than it does from numbers of less culpable offenders being idiosyncratically sentenced to die."[6] Thus, the remedy for biased outcomes in the death-sentencing process may lie as obviously in executing more black offenders who kill black victims as in executing fewer blacks who kill whites; and as obviously in executing more whites convicted of murdering blacks as in fewer white offenders who kill white victims. Such a practice would greatly expand the number of offenders killed. The alternative, Lempert argues, is a more restrictive set of criteria or, recognizing the moral dilemmas involved, outright abolition:

> Where differences between offenders cannot be articulated or, as with the race of victim data, cannot withstand articulation, the more merciful disposition must control. If such a standard were faithfully applied we would soon find that capital punishment was confined to a small subset of the most heinous offenders. Other options are to turn a blind eye to the inequalities that permeate the system or to so increase the rate at which we sentence people to death that the state infliction of death will be, literally, an everyday occurrence. Or we may recognize that retribution by death inescapably conflicts with other deeply held and more civilized values, and for this reason we may cease to inflict it.[7]

With this quandary in capital punishment policy in mind, what more can be said of the research findings to date? The still-growing body of capital punishment sentencing research since 1974 can be divided by stage of criminal justice processing: presentencing, sentencing, and postsentencing. Presentencing research deals primarily with prosecutorial decisions to indict or charge offenders with capital murder. Indictment studies have reported racial sentencing discrepancies as defined by the race of the victim or offender-victim racial combinations in Florida and New Jersey, but another failed to find evidence of racial disparity in North Carolina. Studies of prosecutorial charging practices have reported victim or offender-victim discrimination in Florida, Kentucky, New Jersey, and South Carolina, while the North Carolina study found offender-based discrimination; a final study (from Florida) reported no evidence of race-based discrimination at this stage of the process.[8]

Sentencing research at both the conviction and punishment stages frequently compares characteristics of offenders sentenced to death with parallel characteristics of persons arrested for potential capital offenses. Comparisons of arrest and sentencing patterns provide a glimpse at differential treatment as cases move from the hands of the police to the prosecutors, judges, and jurors. Using this analytic method, researchers have reported evidence of victim-based or offender-victim-based racial discrimination in Arkansas, Florida, Georgia, Illinois, Louisiana, Mississippi, North Carolina, Ohio, Oklahoma, Texas, and Virginia. Two additional studies used summary measures of discrimination for nationwide data. The first such study completed after *Furman* found that racial composition of death row cases (in regard to both offenders and their victims) had not changed from 1971 to 1976 and concluded that discrimination still existed. Another study, which considered only race of offender, concluded that the race of offenders sentenced to death during 1967–1978 was not significantly different from patterns reflected in arrest data.[9]

Studies of conviction patterns have reported race-based discrimination (victim and victim-offender combinations) in Florida, Illinois, and North Carolina. One Florida study did not find evidence of discrimination, and another concluded that no discrimination existed even though findings were statistically significant. Studies of the actual punishment decision have found evidence of discrimination (victims or racial combinations) in Florida, Georgia, Illinois, and Kentucky. Other studies have reported no evidence of discrimination in Florida, Georgia, Kentucky, North Carolina, and South Carolina.[10]

Results from studies of postsentencing disparity likewise have been mixed. One study of appeals in Georgia and Florida reported no evidence of discrimination, while another concluded that there was on the basis of the offender's race. Studies of appellate review have found that state supreme courts have not rectified disparities occurring in the presentencing and sentencing stages in Georgia, Florida, and Texas.[11]

What can be said from this all too brief research review? Conclusions drawn by researchers at all stages of the sentencing process have been somewhat mixed. On balance, however, the data continue to reveal a race-linked bias. In the post-*Furman* years, race of the defendant has become less dominant than it apparently was in earlier years, though earlier studies do not provide the same statistical precision and thus comparisons are suspect. Discrepancies centered on the race of the victim and the racial composition of the offense remain. In view of these contradictory findings the post-*Furman* guided-discretion statutes cannot be said to have been totally successful in eliminating this source of the *Furman* Court's concern with arbitrary and capricious outcomes. The question now becomes whether we can shed further and more revealing light on the precise sources of the noted racial discrepancies in sentencing patterns.

Racial Bias and Post-*Furman* Supreme Court Decisions

The issue of racial bias in the post-*Furman* years came before the Supreme Court again in 1987 with a case involving Warren McCleskey,[12] an African-American who had been sentenced to death by a Fulton County, Georgia, superior court in 1978 following his participation, along with three accomplices, in a robbery of a furniture store in which a white police officer was shot and killed.

Appealing to the U.S. Supreme Court, McCleskey's lawyers rested their case on two arguments. In the first instance, the attorneys asked that the Georgia death penalty statute be found in violation of the equal protection clause of the Fourteenth Amendment in that racial bias continued to infect the administration of justice. Persons convicted of killing white victims were more likely to be sentenced to death than those convicted of killing black victims, and black murderers were more likely to be sentenced to death than white murderers. It followed, the lawyers argued, that McCleskey's death sentence also violated the Eighth Amendment's protection against cruel and unusual punishment in that the sentence was disproportionate to sentences imposed in other similar cases.

In support of these arguments, the lawyers offered a statistical study that went far beyond pre-*Furman* evidence the Court had drawn upon to support its finding that death sentences as then dispensed were arbitrary and capricious and therefore cruel and unusual.[13] In this study, researchers, employing a range of analytic strategies, separated Georgia capital punishment cases into different tiers, defined by aggravating or mitigating circumstances, and then adjusted for a wide range of contending explanations. This more elaborate examination of the data continued to reveal racial discrepancies in sentencing patterns.

For Justice Thurgood Marshall, writing in dissent from the *McCleskey* majority, these findings relentlessly documented the lasting legacy of racial bias. For the majority of the Court, however, the same data reflected discretionary judgments inherent in and indeed essential to the administration of justice.[14] Statistical models, the majority noted, reflected probability risks, not specific outcomes. The issue was the point at which the risk of racial discrimination becomes unconstitutional. McCleskey's lawyers asked the Court to hold that the constitutional threshold had been passed, noting among other findings that defendants charged with killing white victims in Georgia were 4.3 times as likely to be sentenced to death as defendants charged with killing blacks.

Justice Powell, writing for the majority, responded simply, "This we decline to do." Instead, the Court called for legislative action if sentencing schemes were found wanting. When appeals were filed, specific case-based evidence that police officers, prosecutors, judges or jurors had acted in an intentionally racially biased fashion was required.

Warren McCleskey's appeal thus set down a guidepost for the post-*Furman* era. When coupled with the number of persons then on death row across the nation, which was approaching two thousand, it brought forth predictions of an impending tidal wave of executions. There seemed little room for further appeals applicable to a broad base of convicted capital offenders following

McCleskey. What remained were tedious and expensive case-by-case appeals. The research director on capital punishment for the NAACP Legal Defense and Education Fund, Tanya Coke, commented: "Since *McCleskey,* there really are no issues that are germane to every inmate on the row, and what the capital defense lawyers now face is marshaling individual issues in individual cases, which takes long hours of expensive investigation."[15] Predictions notwithstanding, a rising tide of executions did not flood judicial shores, at least not in the next year. Nationwide, there had been twenty-one executions in 1984, eighteen in 1985 and in 1986, and twenty-five in 1987. In 1988, the year following *McCleskey,* the number dropped to eleven. Lawyers remained quite capable of finding ways to delay the ultimate outcome, though by 1990 the number of executions had climbed back to twenty-three.

Such delays increasingly became the focus of public concern. The familiar and increasingly bipartisan cry that justice delayed is justice denied was heard with increased frequency and volume. Among other accusations, lawyers were faulted for bringing issues before the courts in piecemeal fashion. Instead of raising all relevant grounds for appeal in a single petition, charges of error were partitioned into stages to stretch the appeals process out as long as possible. If appeals could be limited and consolidated, it was argued, both the certainty and swiftness of justice could be improved and thereby society might benefit from the much-discussed but little-evidenced deterrent influence of the execution process. There was little evidence of a collective memory that in the not so distant past executions had been carried out in a matter of months following conviction with little discernible influence on the rate of murder.

In early 1991 Warren McCleskey's attorneys once again secured the ear of the U.S. Supreme Court.[16] This time at issue was the claim that the most damaging evidence linking their client to the furniture store robbery and murder had been illegally gathered from a jailhouse informant planted by the Atlanta police. Without ruling directly on the legality of this evidence, on this occasion the Court denied the appeal, holding that the issue should have been raised earlier and that any legal problem with the evidence had not been responsible for McCleskey's conviction.

Five months later, on September 25, 1991, just shy of thirteen years following his conviction for the furniture store robbery and murder, and just after the denial of additional last-minute appeals, Warren McCleskey became the 155th person to be executed in the United States in the post-*Furman* years. At the time there were some 2,500 persons on death row. McCleskey's almost thirteen-year postsentence odyssey through the courts, along with similar cases in virtually every state with capital punishment statutes, energized a broad-based movement in the U.S. Congress to reform the death sentencing and appeals process.[17]

Post-*Furman* Patterns in Texas

Given this national context, what can we make of what was taking place in Texas? In *Furman*, the U.S. Supreme Court had asked states to provide sentencing guidance for jurors to reduce the level of capricious outcomes. Texas legislators responded with an almost mandatory statute. So limiting was the new Texas process that Justice Rehnquist, in a 1980 opinion, *Adams v. Texas*, found it hard to imagine any constitutionally acceptable statute allowing less discretion.[18] There were others, however, who remained skeptical. Five years after *Adams* Justices Brennan and Marshall, in *Degarmo v. Texas*, noted:

> When *Gregg* was decided several members of the Court expressed the belief that channeling juror discretion would minimize the risk that the death penalty "would be imposed on a capriciously selected group of offenders," thereby making it unnecessary to channel discretion at earlier stages in the criminal justice system. . . .
>
> But discrimination and arbitrariness at an earlier point in the selection process nullify the value of later controls on the jury. The selection process for the imposition of the death penalty does not begin at trial; it begins in the prosecutor's office. His decision whether or not to seek capital punishment is no less important than the jury's. Just like the jury, then, where death is the consequence, the prosecutor's discretion must be suitably directed and limited so as to minimize the risk of wholly arbitrary and capricious action.[19]

First Stage: Charge and Conviction

To obtain a picture of prosecutorial discretion, we need information on all death-eligible offenders: those arrested for crimes that could be charged as capital murder. We need to then compare the characteristics of these death-eligible arrestees with those eventually charged and tried for capital murder. Unfortunately, no list is available of cases tried as capital murder in Texas. The nearest approximation is a compilation of the cases that have resulted in a conviction for capital murder. Fortunately, for purposes of this research, comparing death-eligible arrestees with those convicted of capital murder is a rough measure of prosecutorial discretion in that very few capital cases result in acquittals. In Harris County (Houston), for example, that happened only once during 1983–1989.

We gathered data on death-eligible arrestees from Supplemental Homicide Reports (SHR) maintained by the Texas Department of Public Safety (DPS). SHR data include age, sex, and race/ethnicity of offenders and victims, the relationship between offenders and victims, the number of offenders and victims involved in a homicide incident, the weapon used, and the type of murder (e.g., lovers' quarrel, robbery-murder).

The SHRs have included information on ethnicity since 1980. Because race/ethnicity is a major consideration in this study, the years prior to 1980 were excluded from the following analysis. Also, homicide cases involving offender-victim racial combinations other than Anglo, African-American, or Hispanic were excluded from the analysis. Since these data are being compared with the pool of convicted capital offenders (both life- and death-sentenced) who were arrested and sentenced during 1980–1988, those arrested for capital murder during 1987 and 1988 were not included, so as to allow a two-year lag period for cases to be decided. A review of capital cases received on death row during 1989 confirmed that two years allowed an adequate period for case disposal. This resulted in a final pool of 1,149 death-eligible cases statewide.

The comparison group was further limited to only those murders that were categorized by police as involving rape, robbery, or burglary. These are the only categories explicitly defined in the SHR for which a person could be sentenced to death. Furthermore, since under current law only persons who are seventeen years or older at the time of their offense can be sentenced to death, all cases involving offenders under age seventeen were excluded from the analysis. Female offenders were also excluded from the analysis because of the rarity of cases in which a woman is involved in, and sentenced to death for, these types of murders. Since it was necessary to match the death and life sentences with the SHR data, cases missing information on any of the comparison variables (type of felony-murder, weapon, number of victims, relationship between victim and offender, victim's sex, and the race/ethnicity of offenders and victims) were excluded from the analysis.

In this more focused data set there were 213 offenders arrested for capital murder during 1980–1986 and subsequently convicted of capital murder in the course of a rape, robbery, or burglary.[20] The number of victims killed by these 213 offenders totaled 275. If an offender murdered, for example, an elderly white couple and was sentenced to death for killing the man but not the woman, the death of the woman should still be considered as resulting in a death sentence. It is impossible with these data to ascertain how much influence the killing of the woman had in the decision to try the case as a capital offense. In the following analysis, cases that involved multiple victims were weighted according to the number of victims killed. If two victims were killed by one offender, each offender-victim combination was assigned a weight of .50 (three victims killed by one offender were weighted .33, etc.) to prevent biased estimates that would overweight multiple-victim cases in subsequent statistical analysis.

There are many problems with SHR data.[21] First, the coding is, to some extent, not reliable. Incomplete information is coded as "unknown" in the SHR if it is so coded in initial police reports, even if the information comes to light later during an investigation. Police coding of incomplete information also varies by agency. While some departments may simply code incomplete information as missing, others may code what is typical of cases in similar circumstances. Nationwide, killings not classified, that is coded as "other," have been shown to constitute 14 percent of the total.[22] The "suspected felony" category is also large. This is particularly troubling in the present study because only rape, robbery, and burglary murders are selected for analysis. Many additional such murders are undoubtedly classified as "suspected felony," or "unknown," or are even erroneously coded as not involving felonious circumstances.

Maxfield found that murders in the unknown category are more likely to be felony-killings perpetrated by strangers, because leads usually exist in "conflict"-type murders, especially if among acquaintances or relatives.[23] Assuming that this is true, the death-eligible group of arrestees does not include all who could have been, or were, sentenced to death. However, this is not a problem if it can be assumed that the missing cases are randomly distributed on the relevant variables used in the analysis.

There is no reason to believe that this is not the case for variables other than type of homicide situation, offender-victim relationship, and sex of the victim. Rape-homicides are more likely to be coded as involving felony circumstances than robbery- and burglary-homicides because of the presence of obvious indicators. Hence, rape-homicides, and consequently homicides with female victims, are more likely to be included in the SHR data. Similarly, homicides that involve nonstrangers are more likely than those that involve strangers to have complete information on all relevant variables; and, therefore, nonstranger homicides are also more likely to be included in the study. If these limitations are kept in mind, the analytic strategy for matching cases and analyzing these data parallels the recent research of Gross and Mauro.[24]

In Table 7.1, the death-eligible arrestees eventually convicted of capital murder are compared with those who were not convicted, or presumably even charged, as capital murderers. By far, the single category of cases most likely to result in a conviction for capital murder involved the aggravating circumstance of rape. This is an even more striking finding in that, compared with other felony-homicides, rape-homicide cases are more likely to be included in the arrest comparison group than, say, burglary-homicides. Another significant variable is the number of victims involved in the homicide. Death-eligible cases involving multiple victims are nearly three times more likely to result in conviction for capital murder than cases involving a single victim. The type of weapon used and the relationship between the victim and offender are not significantly related to conviction in these bivariate comparisons.

A note of caution is warranted for the finding involving cases in which the

Table 7.1. *Proportion of Death-Eligible Offenders Convicted of Capital Murder, by Control Variables*

Control Variable	Proportion of Cases Convicted (213/1,149)		Attained Association[a] (Significance)*
Felony			.0721 (.0000)
Rape	55/97	= .566	
Robbery	138/891	= .155	
Burglary	20/111	= .124	
Weapon			.0006 (.4335)
Gun	126/709	= .178	
Other	86/439	= .197	
Number of Victims			.0389 (.0000)
Single	168/1,051	= .160	
Multiple	45/98	= .459	
Relation			.0031 (.0645)
Known	60/387	= .156	
Stranger	153/762	= .200	
Victim's gender			.0782 (.0000)
Male	115/907	= .126	
Female	98/242	= .406	
Victim's race			.0570 (.0000)
Anglo	168/651	= .258	
African-American	13/227	= .056	
Hispanic	32/271	= .119	
Offender's race			.0112 (.0021)
Anglo	91/379	= .240	
African-American	85/499	= .170	
Hispanic	37/271	= .137	

[a]Uncertainty coefficient.

* Likelihood ratio chi-square. Significance should be interpreted with caution given nonrandom nature of the sample.

victim and offender were strangers. Previous research has indicated that the victim-offender relationship is an important factor in the sentencing process.[25] In all likelihood, the reduced strength of this relationship in the present instance is due in part to the method of selecting cases for analysis. In our attempt to obtain records with complete information we have no doubt been more likely to eliminate cases involving strangers, which are precisely the cases for which less complete information is available when the police fill out the forms that are the basis of the Supplemental Homicide Reports. Checks of the data that were eliminated indicate this to be true.

Hence, in our attempt to gather information to facilitate the investigation of the most complete range of alternative explanations, we have in all likelihood produced an underestimation of the differential between cases involving strangers and those involving acquaintances. In the process we are also very likely underestimating the differential between inter- and intraracial offenses. While far from ideal, these are the blunt instruments accessible to us when we attempt to reconstruct the social complexity of the sentencing process. We would refer the reader to works cited for data shaped by compromises weighted toward uncovering the victim-offender relationship more precisely. Taken together with the current information, they reveal a more accurate picture.

Of further interest are the final three variables in Table 7.1. The victim's sex and race both are related to the probability of charge and conviction. Cases involving female and white victims are more likely to result in conviction, as are cases involving white defendants. Cases involving female victims are three times more likely to result in conviction than cases involving male victims. This relationship is due mainly to the offense of rape. In regard to the race/ethnicity of defendants, cases involving Anglo offenders are the most likely to result in conviction, followed by cases involving African-Americans. Hispanic offenders are the least likely to be convicted.

The latter findings refute simplistic suggestions that blatant defendant-based racial discrimination continues to drive the capital punishment charging and conviction process. To this extent there is some evidence that the post-*Furman* reforms in Texas may have worked. It is, of course, difficult to determine just how much of the apparent shift away from defendant-focused racism is due to the reformed statute itself, as opposed to a more general modification of beliefs and practices in the broader community. Whatever the source of the reduced defendant-race discrepancies, it appears that discrepancies that turn on the victim's race remain. As with findings in respect to the victim's sex, it is important to continue the analysis beyond the bivariate stage before reaching any final conclusions.

Table 7.2 reveals the remaining pattern of victim-based differences after controlling for the race of the defendant. Cases involving the racial combina-

Table 7.2. *Proportion of Death-Eligible Offenders Convicted of Capital Murder by Offender/Victim Racial Combination*

Racial Combination Offender × Victim	Proportion of Cases Convicted (213/1,149)
Anglo × Anglo	88/302 = .291
Anglo × African-American	0/30 = .000
Anglo × Hispanic	3/47 = .064
African-American × Anglo	63/257 = .245
African-American × African-American	11/183 = .060
African-American × Hispanic	11/59 = .186
Hispanic × Anglo	18/93 = .194
Hispanic × African-American	1/13 = .077
Hispanic × Hispanic	18/165 = .109

tion of Anglo defendants and Anglo victims are the most likely to result in a charge and conviction (29 percent); then come cases involving African-American defendants and Anglo victims (25 percent) and those with Hispanic defendants and Anglo victims (19 percent). The interracial homicides involving African-American offenders and Hispanic victims are the next most likely to result in conviction (19 percent). Intraracial cases involving Hispanics are next on the continuum, with an 11 percent charge and conviction rate.

These results, while instructive, are themselves incomplete in that in all likelihood interracial killings occur with greater frequency among strangers. As already noted, the statistical techniques selected for the present analysis underestimate this differential. To repeat: Other data, selected with an eye for including more cases with less information, reveal African-American-offender/white-victim cases are even more likely to result in a capital charge and conviction than our results show. This same pattern becomes evident as we institute more precise statistical controls while using the current data.

Using the techniques of logistic regression, with conviction as the dichotomized dependent variable (convicted/not convicted), and including measures for multiple victims, type of offense (rape- and robbery-homicides compared with other types), use of a gun, stranger/other relationship, and three combinations of ethnicity (African-American kills Anglo, Anglo kills Anglo, and African-American kills African-American compared with other), we were able to pursue more complex combinations of offense characteristics that might have influenced the charging and conviction process.

Three separate equations were calculated: One included three offense-related variables (victim, type of offense, and use of a weapon). The second was limited to victim-offender information (ethnicity, acquaintance/stranger, and sex of victim). The third included all variables, allowing for adjustments, such as the fact that the vast majority of homicide victims in rape cases are female and thus it is not possible to control for sex of the victim while simultaneously estimating the differential in conviction probabilities in rape cases.

These procedures revealed an overall probability of .185 that death-eligible offenders were charged and convicted of capital murder. The two variables that added the most to this mean probability of charge and conviction were rape and multiple-victim cases (.22 and .18, respectively). The other offense characteristics associated with statistically significant increases in charge and conviction probabilities, after simultaneous statistical adjustments, were African-American kills Anglo, Anglo kills Anglo, and stranger-relationship cases. In the last-named instances the increased probabilities ranged between .1 and .07, though for reasons cited the precision of these estimates should be viewed with substantial caution.

While these summary probabilities with simultaneous controls are useful, it is also instructive to take one last look at differences across categories of cases. To accomplish this, we divided cases into "aggravated" (multiple-victim, rape, or stranger) and "non-aggravated" (single-victim, offense other than rape, and acquaintance) offenses, according to findings in the above regression analysis, and examined differences in probabilities of charge and conviction across combination of racial and ethnic categories of victims and offenders. These results are presented in Table 7.3.

In Anglo- and Hispanic-victim cases, the presence of aggravating circumstances made a difference in outcome. Not so for cases involving African-American victims. In the records collected for this stage of the analysis, in no case (with or without aggravating circumstances) was an Anglo offender who killed an African-American victim charged with and convicted of capital murder. In only one instance did charge and conviction follow an Hispanic-defendant/African-American-victim case. When all cases are considered, the small number of offenders and victims in these categories becomes less dramatic, but the stark result remains that for both aggravated and non-aggravated offenses Anglo-victim cases are the most likely to result in a capital charge and conviction.

These, then, are the basic patterns during the initial stages of the sanctioning process, when prosecutorial influence is at its greatest. While there is little evidence of defendant-based discrimination, substantial differences remain in the probabilities of a capital charge and conviction across ethnic categories of victims and across mixtures of ethnicity when victims and offenders are considered together. It is possible, of course, that additional and more refined

Table 7.3. *Proportion of Death-Eligible Offenders Convicted of Capital Murder by Offender/Victim Racial Combination and Case Aggravation*

Racial Combination (Victim × Offender)	Proportion of Non-aggravated Cases Convicted (25/298)		Proportion of Aggravated Cases Convicted (188/851)	
Anglo	17/173	= .098	152/479	= .317
× Anglo	11/119		77/183	
× African-American	5/33		58/224	
× Hispanic	1/21		17/72	
African-American	4/69	= .058	8/157	= .051
× Anglo	0/7		0/23	
× African-American	4/59		7/124	
× Hispanic	0/3		1/10	
Hispanic	4/56	= .071	28/215	= .130
× Anglo	1/7		2/40	
× African-American	0/7		11/52	
× Hispanic	3/42		15/123	

information would narrow or expand the noted differences. However, at this point the evidence, consistent with a good deal of other post-*Furman* research findings, supports the idea that as the 1980s drew to a close, the capital punishment process had not been purged of all remaining racial bias.

Second Stage: Sentencing

We turn now to the next stage in the determination of who is to be sentenced to death. This analysis involves a comparison of the characteristics of the offenders, crimes, and victims of those sentenced to life imprisonment ($n = 126$) versus those sentenced to death ($n = 421$) following a conviction for a capital offense over the period 1974–1988 (Fig. 7.1). A list of those found guilty of capital murder and received at the Texas Department of Corrections was obtained through a computerized search of "new receives" admissions for each year from 1974 through 1988. These convicts were categorized according to the sentence received. Excluded from the list were eight offenders convicted of capital murder who were fifteen or sixteen years old at the time of their offense. Texas law stipulates that these offenders, if found guilty of capital murder, be automatically sentenced to life. No punishment hearing is held.

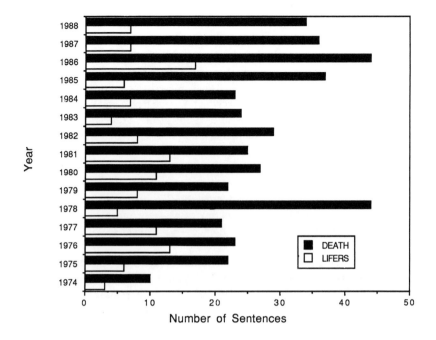

Figure 7.1. Total number of death and life sentences for capital offenses in Texas, 1974–1988.

Four categories of variables were gathered on these cases: offense information, criminal history, offender characteristics, and victim characteristics. Offense information includes the type of homicide according to statutory criteria, weapon used, presence of codefendants, whether multiple victims were killed, and the offender-victim relationship. Criminal history variables include prior prison incarcerations, Uniform Crime Report (UCR) violent crime convictions, UCR property crime convictions, arrests for violence, and arrests for any crimes except traffic violations. Offender characteristics include race, age, sex, occupation, and education. Victim characteristics include race, age, and sex.

The analytic techniques employed parallel those in the previous section. The first step involves a bivariate comparison of the proportions receiving death and life sentences across categories of offense, offender, and victim. Across the major types of offenses, there was little noticeable difference in the probability of receiving a death sentence, once convicted. The three major types of capital offenses (rape-, robbery-, and burglary-homicides) all had death sentence probabilities ranging between .76 and .80. The combined death sentence probability of the remaining offenses was .76. Similar minor differences were noted across type of weapon used, number of codefendants, number of victims, and whether the victim and offender knew each other. Thus, it would appear that whatever differences there are in the probability of a death sentence across these offense characteristics occur when the prosecutor makes the basic decision as to which charge to file and pursue. Over the decade and a half between 1974 and 1988, jurors, guided by post-*Furman* statutory restrictions, have not meted out statistically detectable differential treatment across basic categories of offenses.

There is some evidence of greater juror-produced variation when it comes to the characteristics of the offender and victim (Table 7.4). Males were more likely to be sentenced to death than females—77 percent (415/536) compared with 55 percent (6/11). Female-victim cases were more likely than male-victim cases to result in a death sentence—81 percent (195/242) compared with 75 percent (275/366).[26]

Contrary to the idea that only the poor are sentenced to die, "professionals" were more likely to receive the death sentence, once convicted, than were offenders whose occupation was categorized as "other"—82 percent (27/33) compared with 76 percent (389/509). It may be that the infrequency of capital murder charges among professionals produces a lowered tolerance among jurors for those who are so charged. The level of education made no statistically detectable difference. The age of the victim did. When cases involved young victims (twenty years or younger), 83 percent (83/100) of the offenders received the death penalty. The remaining combined victim age categories resulted in a 77 percent (316/412) death sentence rate. The age-based differential was reversed when it came to the age of the offender. Older offenders (25 years or older) were sentenced to death in 80 percent (230/286) of the cases, compared to 73 percent (191/261) in the younger category. The latter finding may also reflect the effect of a more lengthy criminal record, which was the strongest determinant of outcome at the sentencing stage.

The major source of discretion that jurors have under the post-*Furman* statute resides in their assessment of the offender's character and violent propensities once conviction is secured. A major indicator is past criminal behavior. The number of prior arrests by itself made little difference. Seventy-three percent (27/37) of the offenders with no record of prior arrests were sentenced to death, as opposed to 77 percent (394/509) of those with one or more arrests. By contrast, when there was some evidence of past *violent* activity, the probability of a death sentence went up, no doubt as a consequence of a yes to the question of whether the offender constituted a continuing violent threat. For example, if there was no prior record of a conviction of a violent offense, the probability of a death sentence, once conviction was decided, was .73 (260/354). With one or two prior convictions the probability was .82 (134/164), and with three or more it rose to .93 (27/29).

Table 7.4. *Proportion of Convicted Capital Murderers Sentenced to Death by Offender and Victim Characteristics*

Control Variables	Proportion of Defendants Receiving Death (421/547)	Attained Association[a] Signigicance[b]
Offender		
Age		.0068 (.0446)
17–24 years	191/261 = .732	
≥25 years	230/286 = .804	
Gender		.0046 (.0985)
Male	415/536 = .774	
Female	6/11 = .545	
Occupation		.0009 (.4655)
Professional	27/33 = .818	
Other	389/509 = .764	
Education		.0004 (.6238)
0–9 years	165/217 = .760	
≥10 years	253/325 = .778	
Victim		
Age		.0037 (.3687)
1–20 years	83/100 = .830	
21–51	234/304 = .770	
≥52 years	82/108 = .759	
Gender		.0045 (.1083)
Male	275/366 = .751	
Female	165/242 = .806	

[a]Uncertainty coefficient.
[b]Likelihood ratio chi-square.

Assuming that past behavior is the best predictor of future behavior, jurors seem to take their task seriously when asked to assess the chances that the offender will constitute a continuing violent threat to the community. While the large majority of offenders charged and convicted of a capital offense are eventually sentenced to death, what variation there is appears to be guided by an assessment of the defendant's propensities toward violence, as reflected in past criminal record.

Further evidence is available that juror estimates of violent propensities, rather than blatant racial biases, are driving the sentencing process. There are some differences across ethnically defined cases, but not as expected by traditional views of a race-conscious system. Eighty percent of the convicted Anglo defendants (205/257) and 79 percent of the convicted African-American defendants (157/199) were sentenced to die. Hispanic offenders were sentenced to death at lower rates: 63 percent (57/91). The death-sentence rates across ethnic categories of victims at this postconviction stage of juridical proceedings were almost identical; 77 percent (341/443) of Anglo-victim cases; 76 percent (31/41) of the African-American-victim cases; and 75 percent (47/63) of the Hispanic-victim cases resulted in death sentences once the jury had decided on guilt.

Characteristics of the offense situation, however, are not viewed in isolation by jurors as they pass judgment on the questions posed. In our quest to analyze the social variables involved in jury deliberations, the social complexity, as before, is reduced in statistical terms to a set of equations. The outcome is dichotomized and viewed as a joint probability: the likelihood that a death sentence will follow conviction for a capital offense when various combinations of offense, offender, and victim characteristics are present. The various characteristics were coded with a range of cutoff points and entered into the predictive equations in numerous combinations. With simultaneous controls, five variables emerged as statistically significant predictors of a death sentence, once guilt is established.

The overall probability of jurors' answering the three questions in the affirmative and thereby producing a death sentence following a conviction for capital murder was .77. The variable most likely to increase this probability was the offender's prior prison sentence ($Z = 4.08$). This factor, after being adjusted for a wide range of offense characteristics,[27] increased the likelihood of a death sentence by almost 8 percent. The second-largest increment came among cases involving multiple victims ($Z = 1.92$). Here the increase, again after adjustment for other offense attributes, was approximately 4.5 percent. Cases involving black offenders and white victims also were associated with the likelihood of a death sentence, but this initially statistically significant effect disappeared once type of offense, presence of codefendants, number of victims, and age and sex of the victim were controlled.

Summary of Conviction and Sentencing Patterns

Since the *Furman* decision in 1972, empirical studies have revealed continuing race-based differences in the death-sentencing process, especially surrounding the prosecutorial decision to charge and try a death-eligible case as capital murder. Less consistency is found at the sentencing stage.

The Texas statute, with its almost mandatory provisions at the final stage of the trial, provides occasion to pursue these issues further. During the guilt-determining stage of the process, when prosecutorial discretion is at the maximum (and when post-*Furman* guidelines are the least effective), evidence of race-based discrimination remains. In this sense the concerns noted by Justices Brennan and Marshall in *Degarmo v. Texas* are confirmed.

While we are confident of the results we have reviewed, we are also aware of many limitations in the present analysis. Available statistical tools and data leave us with several important notes of caution. First, evidentiary considerations determining the strength of the case, considerations that would influence the prosecutor's decision to pursue a capital charge, were not available. Had they been, the noted discrepancies across types of cases might have been reduced. In addition, the data used from the Supplemental Homicide Reports, while useful, are not ideal. Many cases were excluded because of missing data or because of coding practices applied to data derived from police reports during early stages of investigations that result in judgments of "possible felony" or "unknown" assailants. These incomplete or ambiguous reports are most likely to turn up in cases involving strangers and thus there is a persistent potential for biased results.

At the stage of sentencing, when the maximum discretion moves to the jury, little evidence of race-based discrepancies was found in the current study. Among the variables we were able to measure, prior criminal record and the presence of multiple victims—both legitimate considerations when assessing the continuing threat an offender poses to society—were the only factors that influenced the probability of a death sentence, once guilt was established, after simultaneous statistical controls were implemented. In this sense, the specific aim of the post-*Furman* statutory reforms in Texas appears to have been realized.

However, with these same reforms have come new questions. Given the vagaries of human behavior, how legitimate is it to impose a death sentence while relying on what often seems like little more than a gaze into a crystal ball? Can jurors, even with the sometimes substantial evidence offered at trial, predict with any degree of accuracy what offenders will do in the future? Is the level of this accuracy such as to justify a death sentence?

Gazing into the Crystal Ball: Predicting Future Dangerousness

Jurors' Predictions

Special Issue 2 in the sentencing stage of the Texas capital punishment statute asks jurors to sentence defendants not solely on the basis of the acts committed, but also on predictions about future behavior. Reviewing this provision of the statute, the U.S. Supreme Court upheld this predictive scheme, stating:

Prediction of future criminal conduct is an essential element in many of the decisions rendered throughout our criminal justice system. The task that a Texas jury must perform in answering the statutory question in issue is thus basically no different from the tasks performed countless times each day throughout the American system of criminal justice.[28]

In many capital trials the prediction of future dangerousness is a battle of the experts, given that both prosecutors and defense attorneys may hire psychiatrists, psychologists, criminologists, sociologists, and penologists to show that a defendant is or is not a "future threat" to society. In such situations there may be a tendency for the expert to become a "hired gun."

One particular psychiatrist, Dr. James Grigson, active in death-sentencing trials across Texas, has acquired a reputation for just such services, along with the title of "Dr. Death." With his long-standing involvement in forensic psychiatry (he has examined literally thousands of murderers for competency to stand trial), his often unequivocal testimony, and his reputed substantial folk charm, he has become a favorite witness for numerous prosecutors. To date he has testified for the prosecution in nearly one-third of the Texas cases involving death row inmates.

Examination of trial transcripts reveals a common testimony pattern. This expert witness begins by classifying the defendant as a "sociopath," a person who feels no remorse for acts committed, a person without conscience, a person highly skilled as an efficient manipulator. During a recent interview this expert witness reportedly stated, "Killing someone [for these persons] is less emotional than eating a plate of scrambled eggs . . . it's not much different from having a meal at a good restaurant. If you like it, you'll come back again."[29] There is no known cure within the field of psychiatry, he continued, and thus such acts will continue.

The following excerpts taken from capital trial transcripts are illustrative:

Prosecutor: In your opinion, will he kill again?
Grigson: Yes, he certainly will if there is any way at all he was given the opportunity to, he certainly will . . . Well, society can restrict him, confine him; yet even in areas of confinement, this behavior [killing people] will continue.[30]

Prosecutor: Can you tell us whether or not, in your opinion, having killed in the past, he is likely to kill in the future, given the opportunity?
Grigson: He absolutely will, regardless of whether he's inside an institution-type setting or whether he's outside. No matter where he is, he will kill again.
Prosecutor: Are you telling me, then, that even if he were institutionalized, put in a penitentiary for a life sentence—would he still be a danger to guards, prisoners and other people around him?

Grigson: Yes. He would be a danger in any type of setting, and especially to guards or to other inmates. No matter where he might be, he is a danger.[31]

Prosecutor: Doctor, based upon that hypothetical, those facts that I explained to you, do you have an opinion within reasonable medical probability as to whether the defendant, Aaron Lee Fuller, will commit criminal acts of violence that will constitute a continuing threat to society?

Grigson: Yes sir, I most certainly do have an opinion with regard to that.

Prosecutor: What is your opinion, please, sir?

Grigson: That absolutely there is no question, no doubt whatsoever, that the individual you described, that has been involved in repeated escalating behavior of violence, will commit acts of violence in the future, and represents a very serious threat to any society which he finds himself in.

Prosecutor: Do you mean that he will be a threat in any society, even the prison society?

Grigson: Absolutely, yes sir. He will do the same thing that he will do outside.[32]

As illustrated in the final excerpt, psychiatric experts often do not even talk to defendants. This practice was made much more likely in 1981, when the U.S. Supreme Court required *Miranda* warnings in psychiatric examinations used in the punishment phase of trials.[33] Following this ruling, prosecutors adjusted by often simply summarizing the facts and background of the defendant and then, using a hypothetical case as the vehicle, asking psychiatrists to testify as to the future dangerousness of the hypothetical offender. The jurors could draw their own conclusions.

In 1983, this strategy of assessing actual dangerousness on the basis of hypotheticals was upheld by the U.S. Supreme Court in *Barefoot v. Estelle*.[34] Thomas Barefoot had been convicted on November 14, 1978, of the capital murder of a police officer in Bell County, located about halfway between Waco and Austin. During the sentencing stage of the trial the prosecution had rested its case on two pillars of evidence. The first went to Barefoot's prior criminal record; he had two prior convictions for drug offenses and two prior convictions for unlawful possession of firearms. None of these convictions involved acts of violence. However, during the guilt-assessment stage of the trial the prosecution had also presented evidence that the defendant had escaped from jail in New Mexico, where he was being held on charges of statutory rape and unlawful restraint of a minor child with the intent to commit sexual penetration against the child's will. In addition, several character witnesses were called by the prosecution, who without mentioning particular examples testified that Thomas Barefoot's poor reputation as a "peaceable and law-abiding citizen" was well established.

The second body of evidence was offered in testimony by two psychiatrists, John Holbrook and James Grigson. Dr. Holbrook had experience that included a tenure as the chief of psychiatric services at the Texas Department of Corrections. Dr. Grigson established his expertise to testify as to the future dangerousness of individuals on the basis of experience that included examination of "between thirty and forty thousand individuals," including some eight thousand charged with felonies, approximately three hundred of whom had been charged with murder. Neither psychiatrist had examined Thomas Barefoot directly.

The attorneys for the prosecution presented both Grigson and Holbrook with an extended "hypothetical" that paralleled the facts in the case. If true of the defendant, the prosecutors wanted to know, what would be the diagnosis of Thomas Barefoot's potential for future dangerousness. Dr. Holbrook concluded "within a reasonable [psychiatric] certainty" that Barefoot was a criminal sociopath, that as a psychiatrist he knew of no treatment that would change this condition, that indeed the condition might accelerate in the next few years, and finally that the Thomas Barefoot in the hypothetical was likely to commit criminal acts in the future that would constitute a continuing violent threat to society, whether that society was in prison or on the streets.

On the basis of the same hypothetical Dr. Grigson was like-minded. He stated that he could diagnose Barefoot as a person with "a fairly classical, typical, sociopathic personality disorder." Thomas Barefoot, Dr. Grigson concluded, was in the "most severe category" of sociopaths—on a scale of one to ten Barefoot would be "above ten." There was, to Dr. Grigson's knowledge, no known cure for the condition. Finally, again on the basis of the hypothetical, Dr. Grigson was convinced that if placed in society, either in or out of prison, there was a "one hundred percent and absolute" chance that the hypothetical offender would commit future acts of criminal violence.

The American Psychiatric Association (APA) disagreed and filed *amicus* briefs on behalf of the offender. These briefs noted, among other things, that predictions such as "100% certainty that the defendant will kill again" are inappropriately prejudicial to the defendant and that such testimony "impermissibly distorts the fact-finding process in capital cases." The scholarly literature suggested ample reasons for the APA's findings.[35] In addition, the APA concluded, "[it] is unethical for a psychiatrist to offer a professional opinion unless he/she has conducted an examination."[36]

For its part, the majority of the Supreme Court in *Barefoot* held that while not infallible, such testimony could be admitted as part of the evidence for the jury to weigh in its deliberations. A year later Thomas Barefoot became the fourth person to be put to death by lethal injection. With this decision in hand, prosecutors have continued the practice of relying on hypotheticals to elicit psychiatric conclusions, and psychiatrists, even with the lack of professional backing, continue to travel the death-penalty circuit, drawing diagnostic and prognostic conclusions on the basis of hypotheticals, and in the process precipitating substantial continuing criticism among those who would change the process.[37]

The accuracy of such predictions can be tested, as indeed it has been.[38] The pattern is clear: Overprediction dominates. That is, there is a tendency to err on the side of predicting violent behavior when in the course of subsequent events none occurs. This tendency has been documented repeatedly, but perhaps most dramatically in two studies of persons diagnosed as criminally insane.[39] The motivation of this conservative tendency is to ensure that if errors are to be made, they should serve to further public protection so as to avoid even the possibility of future tragedies, such as that illustrated by the case of a former death row inmate, released on parole and subsequently charged with several murders.[40] While protective of the public, the high rate of false-positives raises substantial professional issues for psychiatrists who are willing to state with 100 percent certainty that persons will be violent in the future.

As noted in the last chapter, inmates spend long periods on death row awaiting their execution. Many of them have their sentences commuted. Some are eventually released into the community. Hence, it is possible to track behavior subsequent to a jury's prediction that a person constitutes a continuing threat of violence to society, and thereby at least partially assess the utility of the current Texas death penalty statute in this regard.

Postsentence Death Row Behavior

Even under the constraining conditions of death row, there is opportunity for inmates to do harm to each other and to prison guards. Over the fifteen-year period we have focused on between 1974 and 1988, with 421 persons passing through death row, sixty-three assaultive acts were reported to have been committed by 45 (10.7 percent) of the death row inmates. Thirty-seven of these assaults were attacks on other inmates with some kind of weapon. Twenty-four involved an attack on a guard with a weapon.

Two death row inmates killed again within the confines of death row. On August 28, 1979, at 8:30 A.M., the cell doors were opened so that the death row prisoners could enter the dayroom for recreation. Upon exiting from his cell, Anthony Pierce, a twenty-year-old recidivist, stabbed Edward King, a thirty-seven-year-old who had been sentenced to death for killing a Dallas police officer. Pierce had spent time in juvenile institutions for aggravated robbery and possession of marijuana, and had been arrested for burglary and several instances of arson. A year after being paroled from Gatesville, a state training school, the young Anthony Pierce was involved in another robbery in Houston, this one resulting in the death of the victim. According to inmates who witnessed the stabbing, King had threatened Pierce the night before, and Pierce, in fear of King, stabbed him for self-protection. Pierce claimed he did not intend to kill King. For the killing, he was sentenced to a three-year term for involuntary manslaughter.

The second killing involved the locally infamous James Demouchette. Demouchette's criminal history included five arrests for two burglaries, larceny, theft, shoplifting, and negligent homicide, for which he served three terms in juvenile institutions and one prior Texas Department of Corrections term. However, in his interview on admission to death row, he admitted to at least forty arrests. He also reported having been a heroin addict since age sixteen. Three months after his release from serving a five-year term for burglary and theft in TDC, Demouchette robbed a Pizza Hut in Houston with his brother. According to the Statement of Facts from the district attorney's office in Harris County:

At approximately 12:10 A.M., the three individuals, S.S., J.H., R.W., sat down to do the books when the two Demouchette brothers came up to sit down and talk to them. While the Demouchettes were sitting there talking to them, J.H. heard R.W. say "I wouldn't pull that trigger if I were you," and J.H. turned his head to look in the direction of R.W. and saw James Demouchette pull a gun and shoot R.W. once in the head and then turned again immediately to his left and shot J.H. in the head and then turned again and shot S.S. in the head. Having been shot, J.H. was able to retain consciousness and pretend that he was dead by slumping over the table, and heard the two Demouchette brothers run to the back office and rifle through the office. After about two or three minutes, he heard the two defendants come back up to where he and S.S. were slumped over the table. When James came over to the table, S.S. was making noises of choking in his own blood and upon hearing that, James proceeded to shoot S.S. one more time in the head then turned the gun on J.H. because he noticed that he was still alive and pulled the trigger, but the gun was empty. At that time, the defendants ran out of Pizza Hut.

Leaving J.H. alive would prove to be, according to this convicted capital murderer, "the onliest mistake I ever made." When trial time came, two other shootings were evidenced. It took the jury two hours to find James Demouchette guilty of capital murder, and another thirty-nine minutes to sentence the remorseless killer to death. Referred to as "the meanest man on death row," James Demouchette has been involved in numerous attacks with and without weapons on death row guards. He has also attacked two inmates, stabbing one. While awaiting retrial in Harris County, he raped and beat one inmate, stabbed another, destroyed a television and a commode, and set fire to his cell.[41]

On the night of August 2, 1983, Demouchette committed another murder, this time as a death row inmate. While on the way to shower, he went into the dayroom, where Johnny Swift, a forty-two-year-old inmate serving 101 years for murder with malice, was offering legal advice to death row inmates. After entering the dayroom, Demouchette approached Swift, and following a short verbal exchange, began stabbing him with a fourteen-inch "shank." He knocked Swift down and, sitting on top of him, continued stabbing even after an officer demanded that Demouchette give up the knife. Demouchette simply replied, "I ain't finished killing this nigger yet." After stabbing Swift sixteen times, he gave the knife to a sergeant stating, "The son of a bitch is dead now." For this murder, Demouchette received a life sentence on top of his existing death sentence. He was executed on September 22, 1992, just over fifteen years after his arrival on death row.

In addition to these two murders, much of the violent behavior on death row, as in the general prisoner population, stems from activities and disputes among prison gangs.[42] Warren Eugene Bridge, convicted of a robbery-murder at a Stop and Go convenience store in Galveston for the purpose of obtaining drug money, arrived on death row September 1, 1980. He had an extensive prior record, including four arrests for burglary and one for possession and sale of methamphetamines. On death row, he appeared to vie for Demouchette's "meanest inmate" title. A member of the Aryan Brotherhood (AB), a white supremacist gang, Bridge attempted to kill an inmate on the gang's "hit list" by fire-bombing his cell. The inmate saved his own life by throwing a mattress on top of the bomb. For this offense, Bridge was convicted of aggravated assault and received a ten-year sentence. He was also involved in the stabbing of another inmate and an attack on a correctional officer. His coconspirator and fellow AB member in the fire-bombing incident had a similar disciplinary record.

With these examples of severe death row violence in mind, it is important to remember that, while significant, they are the exceptions rather than the rule. The majority of inmates awaiting execution on death row have served their time without major incident. Many of them work in the garment factory with objects that might serve as weapons close at hand and yet do not commit any violent assaultive acts. The particularly constraining conditions on death row make any comparisons of the rates of assaultive behavior with events in the general prison population suspect. However, when former death row inmates are released into the regular cellblocks following a commutation of their sentence, comparisons become more appropriate.

Behavior of Post-1974 Commutees

Not all death row inmates are eventually executed. Neither are they kept on death row forever. In fact, nearly three times as many inmates have been released from death row by commutation or judicial reversals or dismissals as have been executed. To evaluate the institutional behavior of these inmates after their release from death row, we compared their records with those of three groups: (1) a control group of all 107 prisoners convicted of capital murder during 1974–1988 who were sentenced to life imprisonment because juries failed to answer yes to the "future dangerousness" question during the punishment stage of their trials; (2) the entire prison population in 1986; and (3) all inmates housed in a single high-security prison (the Darrington Unit) in TDC in 1986. If jurors, acting under the current death penalty statute, are accurate when predicting the future dangerousness of convicted capital murderers, we would expect that the ninety-two inmates under the sentence of death who were later released from death row would have a more violent record of institutional conduct than any of the comparison groups.

It is difficult to make direct comparisons between the groups because of the differences in time spent in prison, or the "at-risk" period. However, it is possible to make some general observations regarding prison behavior as well as the degree to which the commutees constituted a disproportionate threat to other inmates and the custodial staff. The data in Table 7.5 reveal that the yearly rate of weapon-related rule violations for those released from death row was somewhat lower than the rate for other groups.[43] One commuted capital murderer, however, was involved in a gang-related prison murder in July 1988. This inmate, a member of the Hispanic prison gang the Texas Syndicate (TS), and several fellow gang members murdered another TS member in a power struggle. He thus became the first inmate in Texas since the inception of state-imposed executions in 1924 to be released from death row and returned with a second death sentence for a new offense.

In total, eight inmates were identified as prison gang members. They are confined indefinitely in administrative segregation or high-security housing areas. By comparison, six control group members have been so identified and housed. With the noted important exceptions, murder and other forms of serious violence in prison was not as common as the testimony of psychiatrists such as "Dr. Death" would indicate. Nor were the death row releasees a dis-

Table 7.5. *Reported Serious Violent Rule Violations Committed by Commutees and Comparison Groups*[a]

Prison Rule Infraction	Released from Death Row (n = 90)[b]	Life Sentence (n = 107)	System-wide (1986) (n = 38,246)	Darrington (1986) (n = 1,712)
Murder of an inmate	1 (.18)	0	3 (.00)	1 (.05)
Aggravated assault on an inmate with a weapon	4 (.72)	7 (.90)	266 (.69)	23 (1.3)
Sexual attack on an inmate	0	1 (.13)	48 (.12)	1 (.05)
Murder of an officer	0	0	0	0
Asaulting an officer with a weapon	4 (.72)	12 (1.56)	4,144 (10.8)	308 (17.9)
Total violent infractions	9 (1.61)	20 (2.60)	4,461 (11.66)	333 (19.54)

[a]The first number represents the actual number of infractions; the number in parentheses is the average yearly rate per 100 inmates.
[b]Excludes two commutees who were discharged from death row to the community and did not serve any time in the general prisoner population.

proportionate threat to other inmates and staff once released to the general inmate population.

We examined the evidence of positive institutional behavior as well, including time-earning status, good time accumulated, and program enrollment. As of January 1, 1989, approximately 90 percent of both former death row inmates and the life-sentenced comparison cohort were in trusty status. Furthermore, four of the former death row prisoners had received a total of thirteen furloughs (a four-day stay with family members), while two of the life-sentenced inmates had a attained total of fourteen furloughs. Inmates from both groups completed these furloughs without incident. Two-thirds of both groups have never been in solitary confinement, a punishment for serious disciplinary infractions. One former death row inmate graduated cum laude with a bachelor's degree in psychology from Sam Houston State University in May 1988. One-fifth of offenders in both groups (27 percent of the commuted group and 22 percent of the control group) had no record of rule violations of any type, minor or major, during their prison stay.

Twelve of the commutees have been released from prison. One died shortly after his release in a construction accident. The average time in the free community for the releasees as of December 1988 was 4.5 years. The only inmate to be returned to prison from this group was convicted in 1985, five years after his release. Of the thirteen control group members released to society, one has been reincarcerated on several different occasions for possession of drugs, aggravated assault, and aggravated robbery. As this is being written, he is on parole.

Conclusion

In this chapter we have taken a final look at patterns of death sentences handed out under the post-*Furman* statute in Texas. The intended purpose of this revised statute was to reduce the level of arbitrary and capricious outcomes through more rigid guidelines aimed primarily at the decisions of juries. In this regard, the statute may be linked to some progress. While it is not possible to attribute all of the apparent reduction in racial bias in sentencing patterns to this reform statute, it is clear that blatant racism at the sentencing stage of the proceedings is no longer a major factor.

On the other hand, it appears that prosecutorial decisions remain tainted with the remnants of the racially biased system that was noted so dramatically in the early chapters of this book. In this sense, the results reported in this chapter are quite consistent with those summarized in a comprehensive study of death-sentencing practices in Georgia, in which it is noted that "the exercise of prosecutorial discretion [in seeking a death sentence] is the principal source of the race-of-victim disparities observed in the system."[44]

The post-*Furman* remnants of racism are most apparent in cases involving black defendants and white victims. While further statutory modifications designed to provide further restrictions on prosecutorial discretion might reduce these race-based discrepancies in sentencing patterns, the specific nature of the reforms to be instituted is not altogether clear. Should we fashion statutes to maximize executions of white and black offenders who kill black victims, or should we work toward a reduction in the number of black-on-white case executions. It is in choosing between these paths that we move away from questions to which findings such as those presented in this book are addressed and into a realm in which our beliefs regarding the value of life, the protection of society, and the importance of revenge or retribution take over.

CHAPTER 8

SOME CLOSING THOUGHTS

■ ■ ■ This brings me back to the question,
"What is a just punishment for crime?"
Who is wise enough, just and fair enough,
and impartial enough to say? There may
be humans who possess the qualities to
correctly determine this question. I
cannot.[1]

***Governor Richards Praised and
Blasted for Delaying Inmate's
Execution***
[Governor Ann Richards] granted a 30-
day stay of execution [of Johnny Garrett]
after receiving pleas from Pope John Paul
II, members of [the victim's] religious or-
der and 16 bishops.[2]—*Austin American-
Statesman*, 1/8/92

This much we know. Slavery, criminal justice, lynchings, and capital punishment are historically closely intertwined in the United States. Texas is no
exception.

In December of 1865, with the ratification of the antislavery amendment
and its loophole clause that slavery was henceforth illegal "except as punishment of crime," the United States joined more distant Aztec, Chinese, and
Egyptian civilizations in which the dominant image of the slave "was that of
an insider who had fallen, one who ceased to belong and had been expelled

from normal participation in the community because of a failure to meet certain minimal legal or socioeconomic norms of behavior."[3]

This slave-of-the-state legacy for duly convicted felons held center stage for the next hundred years. In the end, it energized the reform movements that were reshaping criminal proceedings and prison life during the middle decades of the twentieth century. The most onerous portion of this legacy was a thoroughgoing dishonoring exclusion: "Alienated from all 'rights' or claims of birth, [the slave] ceased to belong in his own right to any legitimate social order. All slaves experienced, at the very least, a secular excommunication."[4] From this exclusion much followed.

In particular, the image of prisoner as slave of the state placed convicted felons outside the protective boundaries of community life, thus loosening the normally binding imperative against the intentional infliction of suffering or death. Whippings and other forms of corporal punishment were routine. State-sanctioned executions eventually became concentrated most heavily in the former Confederacy. The frequency of illegal lynchings, phenomena that also were found disproportionately in the South, rose and fell, often in concert with the rhythms of local economic and political life, when the boundaries separating insiders from outsiders, "us" from "them," became most salient.

The threat to those boundaries, and the consequent impetus to lynchings, constituted by economic and political cycles has been noted by numerous researchers.[5] For example, Beck and Tolnay[6] have provided careful confirmation of Raper's[7] and Hovland and Sears's[8] earlier conclusions regarding the link between the incidence of lethal mob violence against black southerners and the shifting economic conditions of the cotton market. Using annual time-series data for the period 1882–1930 in six Deep South states (not including Texas), Beck and Tolnay reported "that advances in the constant dollar price of cotton are associated with *fewer* black lynchings, while inflationary shifts in the price of cotton are associated with *increased* mob violence against blacks" (p. 536). However, they found that when the data were disaggregated by means of moving time-series analysis[9] across successive fifteen-year intervals, the noted relationships were valid only for the period up until about 1905–1910. Thereafter, there was virtually no connection between the vagaries of the cotton market and illegal lynchings.

The question raised is, Why? What had changed by the first decade of the twentieth century to reduce the relationship between the cotton market and lethal mob violence in the Deep South? Just as important is the question, Why did lynchings eventually disappear altogether? One possible explanation is that by the early years of the twentieth century, through the enactment of Jim Crow and related disenfranchising legislation,[10] buttressed by the Supreme Court's *Plessey v. Ferguson*[11] decision in 1896, the descendants of slaves, along with other African-Americans whose relatives had enjoyed greater freedom, had been segregated from the mainstream of social, political, and economic life. With effective, ongoing exclusion, economic competition became less menacing. The issue of "place" was settled.

Thus, with more than a touch of irony, greater legal and social exclusion may have meant fewer local lynchings. With increasingly effective exclusionary laws, local mobs gave way to centralized state-sanctioned executions. At times there seemed to be almost a one-for-one trade-off. We have seen, for example, that during the first year after the 1923 Texas capital punishment statute took effect, twelve of the thirteen persons electrocuted were black; the thirteenth was Hispanic. However, this idea of a simple substitution of formal for informal control, perhaps intensified by economic competition, takes us only a short way toward understanding what was happening.[12]

We have argued that shifting currents of beliefs hold the key to a more complete picture of capital punishment practices over these decades. Our basic position is this: The pattern of post–Civil War lynchings can be traced directly to struggles over social, political, and economic "place" in the community and thus to the exclusionary legacy of slavery. Illegal lynchings decreased over time not only with the introduction of exclusionary Jim Crow laws, but eventually in proportion to the success of efforts, such as those of the Association of Southern Women for the Prevention of Lynching (noted in Chapter 1), to redefine the boundaries of "place" in a more inclusive fashion. As cultural beliefs became more inclusive, illegal lynchings gave way to legal executions. Further legal reforms gave rise to three trends over the decades covered in the preceding chapters: The differential sentencing patterns, comparing blacks and whites, narrowed; the locus of discretionary bias became more focused; and the reluctance to execute rose.

Each of these trends suggests that more than transformation of sanctions and decreased social and economic competition is involved in the patterns explored in this volume, though clearly these forces also played a role. This "more" has been a shifting set of cultural beliefs. This cultural shift has come in large measure from what is perhaps the most important purposive social movement of the twentieth century—a movement to expand access to civil rights to include economic opportunities and legal protections. Our closing comments will be directed at a set of ideas germane to investigating this possibility. First, a brief review of the three major trends.

Three Trends

The data presented in Chapter 2 indicate that the majority (some 66 percent) of persons sentenced to die over the total time period were those who would today be categorized as members of minority groups. This was not stable over time. In the 1920s and 1930s the figure fluctuated around 70 percent to

80 percent. By the 1960s it had fallen to around 50 percent. In the post-*Furman* decades Anglos constitute the majority of persons arriving on death row. This trend has been generated largely by decreasing differentials between black offenders' and white offenders' chances of being sentenced to death once convicted.

While this trend has been evident for all types of capital offenses, it has been less marked among offenses involving rape. This finding, along with the dramatic upswing in the 1930s in the ratio of black rapists' odds of receiving death sentences to those of white rapists noted in Chapter 3, suggests a continuing link between economic strains and the death-sentencing process as well as a lingering presence of an exclusionary and "peculiarly construed" chivalry. Thus, while there is evidence of a systematic change in capital sentencing over the years that reflects, we would argue, a continuing reduction in exclusionary racial beliefs, there is also evidence that the shift toward a more inclusive perspective came slower in some social areas (in particular, sexual relations) than in others. It should also be remembered that not a single Anglo capital offender was executed between 1924 and 1990 for the killing or rape of an African-American victim.

As these patterns unfolded, the locus of bias became more focused. Data presented in Chapters 6 and 7 suggest that for the post-*Furman* years the almost mandatory provisions for guiding jury decisions in the newly crafted Texas statute had an effect. The continuing race-based discrepancies appear to arise not from jury deliberations, but largely from the stage of proceedings at which prosecutorial decisions are most important. Once there was a conviction, the jurors' role in determining the sentences added little if anything to the noted gaps across types of victims or offenders.

In this sense, the locus of discrimination has been narrowed by a Supreme Court decision grounded in the due process clause of the Fourteenth Amendment, which was originally designed to limit lingering injustices visited on former slaves. Thus, capital punishment reform in the twentieth century, embodied in *Furman*, was deeply embedded in a broader and long-standing movement to erase exclusionary scars left by the days of slavery.

The same can be said for what is perhaps the most dramatic shift in capital sentencing patterns across the seven decades we have investigated in this volume: the increased time between conviction and execution. During the 1920s and 1930s executions most often came within the second month following conviction. By the 1990s this had increased to many years. For example, the three offenders executed in May, June, and July of 1990 had been on death row for 7, 6, and 8 1/2 years, respectively.

This dramatic trend was clearly grounded in an increased reluctance to lethally cast persons outside the human community without first ensuring that all due process steps had been followed. For many, this reluctance has become tiresome. There is now a well-established counter movement to push the time-to-execution trend in the opposite direction, in part to reassert victims' over defendants' rights and in part to reestablish a more direct link between a crime and its punishment and thereby strengthen whatever deterrent effect there might be in the capital punishment process. It is in such crosscurrents of debate that cultural practices are forged.

Legal Reform and Social Movements

In this regard, the works of Gamson, Fireman, and Rytina,[13] Snow et al.,[14] and Collins[15] are particularly noteworthy. In their investigations of how shifts in cultural practices and beliefs are grounded in social movement efforts, Gamson, Fireman, and Rytina have singled out three long-term reform mobilization processes; of these, "the process of replacing a dominant belief system that legitimizes the status quo with an alternative, mobilizing belief system that supports collective action for change" (p. 14) is the most relevant.

Much of the practice of illegal lynchings in the Reconstruction South was rooted in the struggle for legitimate authority between local and federal officials. Without consensus, legitimacy remained an unsettled issue, an issue often resolved in local fact by the situational dispute-settling mechanism of lynching. The local beliefs and mythology that patterned such incidents were embedded in a broader cultural readiness to engage in what we have called a logic of exclusion.

The struggle to replace this dominant practice became above all else a struggle to redefine the boundaries of rightful "place" in the social, economic, and political life of the community. The core problem for reformers was to define the framework for interaction in such a way as to convince others that "the unimpeded operation of the authority system would result in an injustice."[16] The more general process of "framing" an issue, as discussed by Snow et al.,[17] deserves a central place in the study of capital punishment reform.

The history of the NAACP and related social movement organizations is as much as anything the chronicle of a struggle to reframe our conceptions of justice.[18] Lynchings were the most dramatic example of the injustices inherent in that period's definitions of social, economic, and political status; thus they provided a solid motivational basis for early recruitment to reform efforts. In a development of the deepest irony, the tragic inequities of lynchings became the reframing lever for mobilizing resources[19] and were thus instrumental in getting the NAACP-led social movement off the ground.

By publishing such documents as *Thirty Years of Lynchings*, by joining forces with other organizations in support of federal antilynching legislation, and by publicizing "critical incidents" such as the "Waco Horror" in 1916 and the Longview and Chicago riots in the summer of 1919 in their journal, *The Crisis*,

NAACP leaders hoped to further generate a sudden discontinuity in the collective belief framework and thereby increase their capacity for collective action.[20]

It is just such a framework-changing incident (the burning of three persons accused of a crime) in 1922 that spurred a local Texas legislator to push for and secure passage of capital punishment legislation designed to reduce the probability of lynchings in local communities. Such catalytic incidents would repeatedly occur over the ensuing decades.[21] Given the often precipitous effect of such events, Collins's suggestion[22] that broad trends can be understood only with a solid understanding of specific events becomes all the more persuasive.

While lynchings continued to occur well into the 1950s,[23] eventually they virtually ceased. This trend toward greater equity and formality in the sanctioning process was buttressed by awakened sensitivities to civil and human rights occasioned by World War II and the Nuremberg Trials.[24] This broader attention to the protection of rights, along with the associated hesitancy to exclude individuals from the life-protecting boundaries of the community, are specifically evidenced in the three trends we have noted in the post-*Furman* years: decreased sentencing disparities, narrowed locus of discrimination, and lengthened time from conviction to execution.

We would not, of course, argue that an end point has been reached. Indeed, there is evidence that the more cautious and hesitant approach to capital punishment has been accompanied by a well-documented trend in the opposite direction—the execution on April 21, 1992, of Robert Alton Harris, the first person to be executed in California in twenty-five years, being a recent concrete example. In the week prior to that execution, the president of the Criminal Justice Legal Foundation, a group self-described as supporting law enforcement, noted his satisfaction that the fourteen-year battle in this case was drawing to a close: "I'm not shouting with glee, but I think the gas chamber is going to be busy. . . . This case has cleaned out the pipeline in the toughest legal battle zone in the country: California."[25] Thus, our willingness to visit death on those who violate our central norms is still very much alive and evolving.

The Continuing Debate

The evolution proceeds along two fronts—public opinion and legal precedent. In the early to middle 1960s approval of capital punishment for murder hovered in the 40 percent range.[26] Over the past twenty years support has increased. For example, the General Social Surveys (GSS), administered yearly since 1972[27] by the National Opinion Research Center, reflect a national climate of opinion that has moved from a 60 percent approval of capital punish-

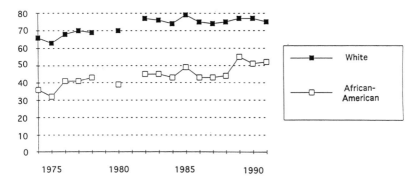

Figure 8.1. Approval of capital punishment, 1974–1991. (Respondents were asked, "Do you favor or oppose the death penalty for persons convicted of murder?")

ment in the case of murder in the 1970s to a level equal to about three-quarters of the population as the final decade of twentieth century begins to unfold. These same surveys suggest that this trend is intimately tied to a more general concern with crime and the idea that courts do not deal harshly enough with criminals.

Equally interesting, in light of the historical roots and patterns of capital punishment that we have noted throughout this book, are the differences between white and black respondents. The two approval-of-capital-punishment trends are summarized in Figure 8.1. In the early 1970s approximately one-third of the black respondents approved of capital punishment for the crime of murder, thirty percentage points lower than the level of their white counterparts. Throughout the ensuing years this thirty-point spread was maintained, until the late 1980s, when the difference began to narrow as, for the first time nationwide, a majority of black respondents reported approval of the death penalty for persons convicted of murder. Specifically, in 1991 52 percent of those classified as black respondents, compared with 75 percent of those classified as white, favored the death penalty for persons convicted of murder. When these figures are broken down by region of the country in which the interview was conducted, the lowest approval rating for capital punishment is found among black respondents residing in the southern region of the country (44 percent), the only combination of race and region that has yet to reach majority approval.[28]

There are, of course, a number of factors, both historical and more contemporary, that might account for these trends and differences. Looking to more immediate circumstances, the most obvious opinion-related shift has been a growing public frustration with the perceived inability of a badly flawed criminal justice system to deal with what appears to be an ever-threatening rate of crime. Influenced, however indirectly, by these currents of public concerns, the majority on the Supreme Court has shifted back and forth in the conflicting currents of a dilemma-ridden sanctioning system.

Whereas *Furman* and its immediate progeny signaled a system of justice too little concerned with the rights of defendants and too much dominated by the wanton and freakish imposition of the death penalty, more recent decisions have aimed at identifying procedural abuses that seem to drag the appellate process out to intolerable lengths. Lamenting the latter, Justice Powell pointed to the prolonged and permissive nature of the appellate process (which he helped fashion in *Gregg, Woodson,* and *Lockett*), which "irrationally permits the now familiar abuse of process . . . that both Congress and the Courts tolerate." Justice Powell concluded that the remedy resided in either a speedier process for death penalty appeals or the total abolition of capital punishment.[29]

Currently the Supreme Court, Congress, and state legislatures are leaning toward expedited proceedings. Early indications of heightened Supreme Court concern with the expeditious handling of death penalty appeals appeared about ten years after *Furman* with a case from Texas, *Barefoot v. Estelle.* In an unusually quick turnaround—a single day, despite little chance to review a 258-page transcript of a federal hearing and a 1,400-page state court trial transcript—the Fifth Circuit Court of Appeals, in a departure from then recent practices, refused to stay the execution. The Supreme Court agreed. Thus, through its emphasis on the states' interest in expeditious executions "the Court not only permitted but encouraged the federal courts to adopt procedures that would expedite appeals in capital cases and thereby hasten the journey toward execution."[30] As we have seen in the preceding chapter, this line of reasoning continues.[31]

Advocates of more expeditious appellate proceedings frequently justify their case on the basis of an increased deterrent effect or on a sense of injustice substantially heightened by years of postponed punishment. Relying on these or other rationales, advocates of a speedier process must confront two knotty problems—equity and accuracy—if we are to construct a system of capital punishment worthy of support. Without equity and accuracy, the case for outright abolition becomes strong indeed, whatever the rationale for continued use.

Evidence of the deterrent impact of capital punishment depends on what we mean. In the case of the convicted offender, the incapacitating effect is as obvious as it is absolute. While the impact is obvious, speed of punishment in this context matters little. However, when deterrence is couched in terms of the impact capital punishment has on the general rate of murder or other forms of violence, the case is more complex. It is possible that more certain and expeditious proceedings could have behavior-reducing potential for future offenders. Although that is a logical possibility, the available evidence is fuzzy at best, and perhaps inaccessible at worst.

A thorough review of general deterrence research is not called for here. We have not dealt with this topic in the preceding chapters and there are numerous other sources.[32] However, it can be said that there is little reason to revise, some two decades later, Gibbs's pessimistic introduction to his comprehensive review and reformulation of the deterrence question, in which he states that his work reveals "a continuous denial of immediate prospects for satisfactory answers to questions about crime, punishment, and deterrence."[33] The evidentiary situation for present purposes is complicated further in that most studies aimed at investigating the deterrent effect of capital punishment have not even bothered with the speed-of-punishment variable.

Nevertheless, two sets of studies are of interest. The first deals with evidence regarding variation in the connection between capital punishment and the murder rate over time; the second with short-term effects of well-publicized executions. In the first instance, we have seen that the time-to-execution has increased over the seven decades between the 1920s and 1990s. If more expeditious handling of cases meant a stronger deterrent effect, we would expect to find that during the earlier decades, when punishments were more frequent and swifter in coming, the deterrence effect would be more noticeable. In fact, although time-series comparisons face the daunting difficulty of shifts in data collection strategies, researchers have reported quite the opposite. Ehrlich's widely cited evidence for a deterrent effect was immediately criticized on the basis that when the period after 1964 is excluded, the deterrent effect disappears, and even reverses. Relying on more recent evidence through the middle 1980s, Layson, who generally supports the idea of a deterrent effect, has concluded that "the case for the effectiveness of capital punishment as a deterrent hinges in *including* the post-1963 data in the sample."[34] This, of course, is precisely the opposite of what one would expect on the basis of time-to-execution alone. However, this is not the most important critique of deterrence research.

As Gibbs and others have noted, the inconclusiveness of evidence on the deterrence question is not likely to go away.[35] In the statistician's cliché, "Correlation does not mean causation." Whenever we find correlational evidence either supporting or contradicting the deterrence hypothesis, we are left with contending explanations. Denied experimental designs, clearly out of the question, and confronted with weak and contradictory correlational findings, cautious researchers from both camps will continue to disagree. In the foreseeable future the debate will hinge more firmly on moral arguments. It is here that equity and accuracy move center stage.

The issue of equity comes in at least two general forms. In the first, we simply ask whether capital punishment is an equitable response to any activity, however heinous. Is there some threshold that when crossed negates the normal protections we ascribe to life? Hitler-like events are offered up most frequently to establish the moral acceptability and even necessity of such thresholds. Surely, the argument goes, at some point we have an affirmative duty to put an end to atrocities, by whatever means. "Just war" theories have been developed to morally clarify our threshold thinking in this regard. The same rationale can be applied to capital punishment. Given such moral thresholds, which we would agree are clearly present, the task becomes one of determining where to draw the line: Currently, murder with heinous and brutal circumstances—Yes. Rape—No. Shoplifting—Certainly not.

Once it is established that capital punishment equitably fits some infractions of our core beliefs, a second issue of equity becomes whether punishment is being distributed in an even-handed fashion. Here, final agreement on equity-related evidence has proved elusive.

The Supreme Court in *McCleskey v. Kemp* has set the high standard of "exceptionally clear proof" before discrimination in capital punishment cases is established. Statistical patterns, even those revealing a heightened "significant risk" among identified groups of cases, are not enough. Thus, the data presented in this volume, or the more exhaustive information compiled in preparation for *McCleskey*, fall short. Instead, it must be shown that decision makers in individual cases must act with "discriminatory purpose." Some disparities in punishment patterns, the Court stated, are inevitable. With such a stand, the majority in *McCleskey* seemed to back away from the decisions reached by the majority of justices in *Furman*.

In this debate over sentence disparity, we seem to vacillate on the horns of the dilemma that pits strict disparity-reducing guidelines, with the accompanying injustice of rigid mandatory sentences, against the necessary discretion for individualized justice, with the accompanying intrusion of personal biases and the potential for "arbitrary and capricious" outcomes. It is a dilemma that goes beyond capital punishment, being demonstrated amply by the heated debate over mandatory sentencing guidelines advanced by the Sentencing Reform Act of 1984.[36] It is a debate made more intense by the finality of the sanctions imposed.

While proof of unconstitutional levels of discrimination has become more difficult to reach, presumably no one would argue that innocent persons should be put to death for crimes they did not commit. Even here, unfortunately, it has been argued that, given human frailty, some such injustice is inevitable and even justifiable in light of a perceived greater good. It is a justification the present authors readily reject. Indeed, this potential for executing the innocent, a potential adequately demonstrated in fact,[37] a potential that can only be heightened with the recent move toward more expeditious proceedings, is the strongest single argument for the complete abolition of capital punishment.

While proving innocence, like proving discriminatory bias, is an elusive enterprise, three recent cases in Texas are illustrative. The first involves Randall Adams. The prosecution's case was based largely on the account of a man who had offered Adams a ride, supplemented by what later turned out to be questionable corroborating testimony. In addition, the psychiatrist highlighted in the preceding chapter for his notoriously unwavering assessment of future dangerousness once again offered his opinion that this defendant constituted a continuing violent threat to society.

Adams was convicted of the November 28, 1976, shooting of a Dallas police officer and sentenced to die. Had it not been for a subsequent film documentary, *The Thin Blue Line*, in which the principal witness admitted to his false testimony, the case against Randall Adams in all likelihood would not have unraveled. As it happened, it did. Upon further investigation, additional "irregularities" in the prosecution's case came to light. On the basis of this new information, a writ of habeas corpus was granted. The Texas Court of Criminal Appeals affirmed. The prosecutor declined to retry. Twelve years after he arrived on death row, Randall Adams was released, cleared of the charges brought against him. Had the system worked more expeditiously and the sentence carried out without further investigation before the documentary was released, the state, in all likelihood, would have been guilty of executing an innocent man.

The second case involves Clarence Brandley. After an initial mistrial, Brandley was convicted of the August 23, 1980, rape and murder of a teenage girl and sentenced to die. His conviction was affirmed on appeal and a date for his execution was twice set and twice postponed. In 1987, six days prior to execution, a stay was obtained when a witness came forward to identify the real killers. Eventually, two of Brandley's coworkers, who had testified against him, admitted to perjured testimony and a third coworker changed his story. After nine years on death row, amid charges of professional misconduct on the part of prosecuting officials reminiscent of racist East Texas stories in the 1930s and 1940s, Brandley was released in 1990. Had his case been "expeditiously" handled, there is a high probability that the state would have been guilty in this case also of killing an innocent man.[38]

The third case involves the conviction of Leonel Herrera for the murder of a police officer and state trooper in 1981. Some eleven years later Herrera's lawyers had compiled evidence that included, they claimed, eyewitness testimony that Leonel Herrera was not guilty. In what reads like rather bizarre logic, the appeals court ruled that Herrera's "actual innocence" presented no substantial claim for relief under federal law. Innocence or guilt is a matter determined at trial.

Faced with this decision, Herrera's attorneys took their case to the Supreme Court. On February 19, 1992, five justices refused to block Herrera's execution. However, whereas it takes five justices to grant a stay of execution, it takes only four to grant a full hearing of the case before the Court. On the same day the Court refused to grant a stay of execution, four justices agreed to hear arguments in this case as related to the Eighth Amendment's prohibition of cruel and unusual punishment, applied to a convicted capital murderer who may be innocent on the basis of newly obtained evidence.

While the hearing was granted, it would not occur until after the scheduled execution, which the five justices continued to resist. This left the rather uncomfortable possibility of executing a man prior to the final review of his case. Two days before Herrera's scheduled execution, the Texas Court of Criminal Appeals, in a 5–3 vote, halted the execution until the U.S. Supreme Court had time to decide whether newly found evidence, once a conviction is final, must be considered before an execution is carried out. The Supreme Court ruled that such new evidence need not be considered. On May 12, 1993, Leonel Herrera was executed by lethal injection.

APPENDIX A

STATUTE PROVIDING FOR THE ELECTROCUTION OF CONVICTS CONDEMNED TO DEATH

■ ■ ■   [S.B. No. 63]   Chapter 51

An Act providing for the execution of convicts, condemned to death, by electrocution; prescribing the procedure in such cases; providing the means for accomplishing the purposes of this Act and making an appropriation therefor; prescribing fees to be paid; repealing certain statutes with saving clauses, and all laws or parts of laws in conflict herewith, and declaring an emergency.

Be it enacted by the Legislature of the State of Texas:

Sec. 1. From and after the taking effect of this Act whenever the sentence of death is pronounced against a convict, the sentence shall be executed at any time before the hour of sunrise on the day set for the execution, not less than thirty days from the date of sentence, as the court may adjudge, by causing to pass through the body of the convict a current of electricity of sufficient intensity to cause death, and the application and continuance of such current through the body of such convict until such convict is dead.

Sec. 2. The warden of the State Penitentiary at Huntsville, or in case of his death, disability or absence, his deputy, shall be the executioner. In the event of the death or disability or absence of both the warden and his deputy, the executioner shall be that person appointed by the Board of Prison Commissioners for that purpose.

Sec. 3. Whenever any person is sentenced to death, the clerk of the court in which the sentence is pronounced, shall, within ten days after sentence has been pronounced, issue a warrant under the seal of the court for the execution of the sentence of death, which shall recite the fact of conviction, setting forth specifically the offense, the judgment of the court, the time fixed for his execution, and directed to the warden of the State Penitentiary at Huntsville, commanding him to proceed, at the time and place named in the sentence, to carry the same into execution, as provided in Section 1 of this Act, and shall deliver such warrant to the sheriff of the county in which such judgment of conviction was had, to be by him delivered to the said warden, together with the condemned person, as provided in the following section.

Sec. 4. Immediately upon the receipt of such warrant, the sheriff shall transport such condemned person to the State Penitentiary at Huntsville, and shall there deliver him and the warrant aforesaid into the hands of the warden and shall take from the warden his receipt for such person and such warrant, which receipt the sheriff shall return to the office of the clerk of the court where the judgment of death was rendered. For his services, the sheriff shall be entitled to the same compensation as is now allowed by law to sheriffs for removing or conveying prisoners under the provisions of Section 5 of Articles 1122 or 1130 of the Code of Criminal Procedure, as the case may be.

Sec. 5. Upon the receipt of such condemned person by the warden of the State Penitentiary, he shall be confined therein until the time for his execution arrives, and, while so confined, all persons outside the said prison shall be denied access to him, except his physician and lawyer, who shall be admitted to see him when necessary to his health or for the transaction of business, and the relatives, friends and spiritual advisors of the condemned person, who shall be admitted to see and converse with him at all proper times, under such reasonable rules and regulations as may be made by the Board of Prison Commissioners.

Sec. 6. The execution shall take place at the State Penitentiary at Huntsville, in a room arranged for that purpose. It shall be the duty of the Board of Prison Commissioners of this State to provide the necessary room and appliances to carry out the electrocution as provided in this Act and the sum of five thousand ($5,000.00) dollars is hereby appropriated out of the General Revenue of the State to be expended by the Board of Prison Commissioners for said purposes.

Sec. 7. The following persons may be present at the execution, and none other; the executioner and such persons as may be necessary to assist him in conducting the execution; the Board of Prison Commissioners, two physicians, including the prison physician, the spiritual advisor of the condemned;

the chaplain of the penitentiary, the county judge and sheriff of the county in which the penitentiary is situated, and any of the relatives or friends of the condemned person that he may request, not exceeding five in number, shall be admitted, provided no convict shall be permitted by the prison authorities to witness the execution.

Sec. 8. If the person condemned escapes after sentence and before his delivery to the warden, and be not rearrested until after the time fixed for execution, any person may arrest and commit him to the jail of the county in which he was sentenced; and thereupon the court by whom the condemned was sentenced, either in term time or vacation, on notice of such arrest being given by the sheriff, shall again appoint a time for the execution, not less than thirty days from such appointment, which appointment shall be by the clerk of said court immediately certified to the warden of the State Penitentiary and such clerk shall place such certificate in the hands of the sheriff, who shall deliver the same, together with the warrant aforesaid and the condemned person to the warden, who shall receipt the sheriff for the same and proceed at the appointed time to carry the sentence of death into execution as herein above provided.

Sec. 9. If the condemned person escapes after his delivery to the warden, and be not retaken before the time appointed for his execution, any person may arrest and commit him to the State Penitentiary whereupon the warden shall certify the fact of his escape and recapture to the court in which sentence was passed; and the court, either in term time or vacation, shall again appoint a time for the execution, which shall not be less than thirty days from the date of such appointment; and thereupon the clerk of such court shall certify such appointment to the warden, who shall proceed at the time so appointed to execute the condemned, as herein above provided. The sheriff or other officer or other person performing any service under this and the preceding Article shall receive the same compensation as is provided for similar services under the provisions of Articles 1122 or 1130 of the Code of Criminal Procedure.

Sec. 10. When execution of sentence is suspended or respited to another date, the same shall be noted on the warrant and on the arrival of such date, the warden shall proceed with such execution; and in case of the death of any condemned person before the time for his execution arrives, or if he should be pardoned, or his sentence commuted by the Governor, no execution shall be had, but in such case, as well as when the sentence is executed, the warden shall return the warrant and certificate, with a statement of any such act and with his proceedings endorsed thereon, together with the statement that the body of the convict was decently buried or delivered to his relatives or friends, naming them, or to some other person, by consent of the convict, naming such person, and naming two or more witnesses to the fact that the convict consented that his body might be delivered to such person to the clerk of the court in which the sentence was passed, who shall record said warrant and return in the minutes of the court, provided that the body of the person electrocuted may be returned to the county in which conviction was had at the expense of the county, when so requested by the convict's relatives.

Sec. 11. The warden, or other person, conducting the execution, shall be allowed therefor the sum of twenty-five ($25.00) dollars to be paid out of the treasury of the county in which judgment of execution was rendered; and it shall be the duty of the commissioners' court of such county to approve such account and order it paid, out of the general funds of the county, upon the certificate of the district clerk of such county, showing the return by the warden of the death warrant, with execution of sentence endorsed thereon.

Sec. 12. The sheriff may, when he supposes there will be a necessity, order such number of citizens of his county, or any military or militia company, to aid in preventing the rescue of a prisoner.

Sec. 13. That Articles 863, 864, 865, 883, 884, 885, 886, 887, 889, 890 and 892 of the Code of Criminal Procedure of 1911, be, and the same are hereby specifically repealed and all other laws and parts of laws in conflict herewith are herewith repealed. Provided that where the sentence of death has been or may hereafter be imposed upon a convict, under existing laws, previous to the time when this Act takes effect, and where the day of execution has been or may be set at a date either prior to or subsequent to the time this Act becomes effective, the same shall not be affected by the repeal herein of any such existing laws but the execution shall take place as if the laws repealed had still remained in force.

Sec. 14. The fact that our present method of putting to death condemned convicts by hanging the condemned in the counties where the judgment of death is obtained, frequently creates great disturbance in the county, and the further fact that the system is antiquated and has been supplanted in many states by the more modern and humane system of electrocution create an emergency and an imperative public necessity demanding the suspension of the constitutional rule requiring bills to be read on three several days in each House and that this Act shall take effect and be in force from and after its passage and said rule is hereby suspended, and it is so enacted.

[Note. Senate Bill No. 63 passed the Senate, yeas 16, nays 11; and passed the House of Representatives with amendments, no vote given; and the Senate concurred with the House amendments, no vote given.]

Approved June 4, 1923.
Effective 90 days after adjournment.

APPENDIX B: DEATH ROW PRISONERS, 1923–1988

Execution No.	Name	Race[a]	County	Offense[b]	Date of Birth	Executed	Commuted	Status
1	Mack Matthews	B	Tyler	Murder	1885	02/08/24		
2	George Washington	B	Newton	Murder	1885	02/08/24		
3	Melvin Johnson	B	Liberty	Murder	1904	02/08/24		
4	Ewell Morris	B	Liberty	Murder	1901	02/08/24		
5	Charles Reynolds	B	Red River	Murder	1897	02/08/24		
6	Blaine Dyer	B	Dallas	Murder	1888	03/28/24		
7	Earnest Lawson	B	Dallas	Murder	1885	03/28/24		
8	Booker Williams	B	Angelina	Murder	1905	04/04/24		
9	Tommie Curry	B	Smith	Murder	1899	04/17/24		
10	Harle Humphreys	B	Falls	Murder	1905	05/22/24		
11	Frank Cadena	H	Bexar	Murder	1889	05/23/24		
12	Ed Henderson	B	Polk	Rape	1879	06/09/24		
13	Ed Kirby	B	Colorado	Murder	1867	10/10/24		
14	Roy Mitchell	B	Lamar	Murder	12/1894		04/29/25	
15	Newt DeSilva	W	Jefferson	Murder	01/1892		03/20/25	
16	Sidney Welk	W	Dallas	Murder	01/1894	04/03/25		
17	Lavannie Twitty	B	Dallas	Murder	03/1901	06/05/25		
18	Salvador Jacques	H	El Paso	Murder	1902		07/22/25	
19	Frank Noel	B	Dallas	Rape	04/1902	07/03/25		
20	Lorenzo Noel	B	Dallas	Rape	04/1900	07/03/25		

Note: "Executed," "Commuted," and "Status" columns updated through May 1992.

[a] B = Black; H = Hispanic; N = Native American; S = Samoan; V = Vietnamese; W = White.

[b] Jailbreak = murder in the course of jailbreak; Policeman or Prison guard = murder of a policeman or prison guard; Remuneration = murder for remuneration; Robbery = robbery by firearms for pre-*Furman* convictions, murder in the course of robbery for post-*Furman* convictions; Arson, Burglary, Kidnapping, or Rape = the stipulated offense in connection with another felony for post-*Furman* convictions.

APPENDIX B: DEATH ROW PRISONERS, 1923–1988 (continued)

Execution No.	Name	Race[a]	County	Offense[b]	Date of Birth	Executed	Commuted	Status
21	Joe Brown	B	Harris	Murder	05/1890		07/19/25	
22	G. C. Gray	W	Titus	Murder	12/1884	08/07/25		
23	Edwin Rushing	B	Anderson	Murder	01/1900	07/17/25		
24	Arnuflo Valles	H	El Paso	Murder	1904		07/30/25	
25	Melton Carr	B	Walker	Rape	05/1902	01/02/26		
26	Agapito Rueda	H	El Paso	Murder	11/1896	01/09/26		
27	W. T. Aven	W	McLennan	Murder	1886		03/27/26	
28	Willie Vaughn	B	Bexar	Rape	03/1903	03/12/26		
29	S. A. Robinson	B	Dallas	Murder	03/1898	04/06/26		
30	Forest Robinson	B	Dallas	Murder	04/1900	04/06/26		
31	John Smith	B	Brown	Murder	02/1902	04/16/26		
32	T. Harris	B	Harris	Murder	12/1893	05/03/26		
33	Sam Phillips	B	Fort Bend	Murder	1895	05/14/26		
34	Fred Tilford	B	Navarro	Murder	02/1902	07/09/26		
35	Alex Maxey	B	Shelby	Murder	05/1882		08/24/26	
36	F. D. Baines	B	Bexar	Murder	1898	02/18/27		
37	George Hassell	W	Parmer	Murder	07/1888	02/10/28		
38	Bryant Satchell	B	McLennan	Murder	1905	03/17/27		
39	Matthew Briscoe	B	Bexar	Rape	12/1889	05/10/27		
40	Pete McKinney	B	Fort Bend	Murder	1902		09/08/27	
41	E. M. Snow	W	Erath	Murder	1878	08/12/27		
42	Ed Joshlin	B	Victoria	Rape	1869	08/22/27		
43	Tillman Simmons	B	Bexar	Murder	1877	09/26/27		
44	A. V. Millikin	W	Caldwell	Murder	1887	11/05/27		
45	Willie Robinson	B	Denton	Murder	1904	09/23/27		
46	Anastacio Vargas	H	Bexar	Murder	02/1892		03/09/28	

#	Name	Race	Offense	County	Born	Date	Date
47	Pete Banks	B	Murder	Fayette	1887		04/14/28
48	Robert Lee Benton	B	Murder	Crosby	06/1904	02/10/28	07/29/29
49	Juan Flores	H	Murder	Bexar	1906		
50	Willie Fisher	B	Murder	Harris	1897	04/12/28	
51	Bill Smith	W	Murder	Jones	1903	10/17/30	
52	Lawrence Davenport	B	Murder	Harris	1906	06/01/28	
53	Garrett Thomas	B	Murder	Live Oak	1896	08/03/28	
54	Esequiel Servina	H	Rape	Bexar	03/1905	09/07/28	
55	Clemento Rodriguez	H	Rape	Bexar	03/1906	09/07/28	
56	Tom Ross	B	Murder	Nacogdoches	1893	09/28/28	
57	J. R. Silver	W	Robbery	Tarrant	Unknown		10/25/28
58	O. T. Alexander	B	Murder	Harris	1888	09/28/28	
59	Floyd Byrnes	W	Murder	Tom Green	1903	01/11/29	
60	Robert Blake	W	Murder	Swisher	1904	04/19/29	
61	John McKenzie	W	Murder	Bexar	1904		09/28/29
62	H. J. Leahy	W	Murder	Williamson	1888	09/02/29	
63	Wade Wilborn	B	Murder	Titus	1882	04/12/29	
64	P. W. Howard	W	Murder	El Paso	1887		05/08/30
65	Mathis Sanders	B	Rape	Brazos	1903	04/27/29	
66	O. C. Wells	W	Murder	Coleman	1897	06/20/29	
67	Silas Jarman	B	Robbery	Grayson	1911	05/24/29	
68	Willie Grady	B	Rape	Hunt	10/1909	07/25/29	
69	Jessie Charles	B	Murder	Liberty	1905		09/13/29
70	Henry Helms	W	Robbery	Eastland	1896	09/05/29	
71	Lee Roy Merriman	W	Rape	Dallas	1902	11/29/29	
72	E. V. Allen	W	Robbery	Eastland	1899		05/13/30
73	Ben Aldridge	W	Rape	Dallas	11/1903	12/19/29	
74	Bishop Adams	B	Murder	Travis	1889	03/13/30	
75	William Pruitt	W	Murder	Dallas	1905	06/06/30	
76	Jordan Scott	B	Murder	McLennan	1900	05/22/30	
77	Raney Williams	B	Rape	Jefferson	07/1892	08/08/30	
78	Lee Davis	B	Murder	Brazoria	1909	08/22/30	

APPENDIX B: DEATH ROW PRISONERS, 1923–1988 (continued)

Execution No.	Name	Race[a]	County	Offense[b]	Date of Birth	Executed	Commuted	Status
79	Jesse Lee Washington	B	Roberts	Murder	1909	09/12/30		
80	Lus Arcos	H	Medina	Murder	1900	11/07/30		
81	Monty Jackson	B	Fort Bend	Murder	1876		10/23/30	
82	J. J. Maple	W	Harris	Murder	1895	11/28/30		
83	Clyde Thompson	W	Eastland	Murder	1911		08/06/31	
84	Moncus Twitty	W	Gray	Rape	1900	04/24/31		
85	Ofilio Herrera	H	Mason	Murder	1894	06/19/31		
86	Nicando Munoz	H	Hidalgo	Murder	1905	10/30/31		
87	Victor Rodriguez	H	Hidalgo	Murder	1911	10/30/31		
88	Joshua Riles	B	Galveston	Rape	09/1902	07/24/31		
89	Dave Goodwin	W	Bowie	Murder	1889		08/06/31	
90	Will Jenkins	B	Harris	Rape	06/1886	07/28/31		
91	Joe Shield	W	Brown	Murder	1895	08/14/31		
92	Red Wing	N	Comal	Murder	1892	11/30/31		
93	Alfred Jackson	B	Bexar	Murder	1881	01/08/32		
94	Will Fritts	W	Kent	Murder	1890	12/18/31		
95	Bonnie Lee Ross	B	Morris	Rape	11/1909	12/18/31		
96	Ira McKee	W	Dawson	Murder	1899	01/08/32		
97	Jake White	B	Dallas	Murder	1887	04/01/32		
98	James Williams	B	Hunt	Murder	1904	05/20/32		
99	Earnest Johnson	B	Caldwell	Murder	1911	06/05/32		
100	Estamistado Lopez	H	Willacy	Murder	1902	06/10/32		
101	Richard Johnson	B	Wichita	Murder	1901	08/10/32		
102	Charlie Grogans	B	Jefferson	Rape	07/1907	07/28/32		
103	John Green	B	Medina	Murder	1913	08/05/32		
104	Richard Brown	B	Young	Murder	1912	08/10/32		

	Name	Race	County	Crime	Birth		
105	Guadalupe Garza	L	Refugio	Murder	1882		01/09/33
106	Carter Rolling	B	Tarrant	Murder	1913		01/06/33
107	Hilton Bybee	W	Cottle	Robbery	1910		01/28/33
108	Aaron Johnson	B	Walker	Murder	1912		02/23/33
109	Castleton Whitfield	B	Austin	Murder	1905		03/13/33
110	Walter Haskins	B	Ellis	Murder	1901	04/07/33	
111	Robert Cubit	B	Caldwell	Murder	1907		07/21/33
112	Louis Rogers	B	Caldwell	Murder	1903		07/21/33
113	Walter Frienney	B	Falls	Murder	1867		06/06/33
114	R. T. Bennett	B	Dallas	Murder	1909	08/18/33	
115	Pantaleon Ortiz	H	Refugio	Murder	1898	12/12/33	
116	Marshall Williams	B	Walker	Murder	1909	11/20/33	
117	Ira Kelley	W	Harris	Rape	03/1895	01/18/34	
118	Tom Cook	B	Harris	Murder	08/1899	12/19/33	
119	Leon Aubry	B	Harris	Murder	1892		01/17/34
120	Clarence Booker	B	Travis	Murder	1908	12/29/33	
121	Carl Stewart	B	Travis	Murder	1909	12/29/33	
122	Paul Mitchell	W	Lubbock	Robbery	1909		02/03/34
123	Dewey R. Hunt	W	Dallas	Murder	1906	12/29/33	
124	Clarence Thomas	B	Hunt	Murder	1914	12/15/33	
125	Frank Flours	B	McLennan	Murder	1894	02/02/34	
126	Thurman Burkley	B	Dallas	Murder	1915	02/09/34	
127	Bluit Burkley	B	Dallas	Murder	1914	02/09/34	
128	Jesse Mott	B	Dallas	Murder	1900	02/09/34	
129	Sack Jackson	B	Rusk	Rape	1907	04/06/34	
130	Nathan Brooks	B	Harris	Murder	1905	06/01/34	
131	Charlie Outlaw	W	Angelina	Murder	1874	04/27/34	
132	Johnnie Williams	B	Harris	Murder	1904	05/01/34	
133	Ed Stanton	W	Swisher	Murder	1889	09/28/34	
134	Jack Jackson	B	Liberty	Murder	1898	11/19/34	
135	June Woolfolk	B	Bexar	Murder	1897	11/23/34	
136	J. E. Hogan	W	Hidalgo	Murder	1882		12/20/34

APPENDIX B: **DEATH ROW PRISONERS, 1923–1988** (continued)

Execu-tion No.	Name	Race[a]	County	Offense[b]	Date of Birth	Executed	Commuted	Status
137	Leroy Lane	W	Dallas	Murder	1910	01/25/35		
138	C. B. Dobbins	W	Harris	Murder	1899	02/01/35		
139	Leonard Burns	W	Bowie	Murder	1898	02/15/35		
140	Cecil Short	W	Dallas	Murder	1903		02/02/35	
141	Jose Sanchez	H	Comal	Murder	1915		03/01/35	
142	Gabe Smith	B	Harris	Murder	1910	03/19/35		
143	Ira Rector	B	Grimes	Murder	03/1914	04/02/35		
144	Doye Arnold	W	Callahan	Murder	02/1907	04/19/35		
145	Albert Carr	B	Harris	Rape	11/1908	06/07/35		
146	Joe Palmer	W	Grimes	Murder	09/1902	05/10/35		
147	Raymond Hamilton	W	Walker	Murder	05/1913	05/10/35		
148	Lewis Cernock	W	Williamson	Murder	11/1894	07/12/35		
149	Jon B. Willis	W	Smith	Rape	03/1893	06/12/35		
150	Eligha Stewart	W	Harris	Murder	04/1907	06/12/35		
151	Ben Boyd	B	Wharton	Murder	06/1904	08/30/35		
152	Bernard Lacume	W	Angelina	Murder	01/1911	08/23/35		
153	Hugh McCann	W	Bell	Murder	11/1899		08/05/35	
154	Johnnie Dade	B	Brazoria	Murder	09/1912	08/16/35		
155	John Trapper	B	Uvalde	Murder	12/1884	08/14/35		
156	W. D. May	W	Tarrant	Murder	10/1895	09/06/35		
157	W. R. Hildreth	W	Howard	Murder	04/1886	11/25/35		
158	Pierson Cantrell	W	Wood	Murder	05/1996	12/06/35		
159	Ramiro Galvin	H	El Paso	Murder	08/1903		02/13/36	
160	G. B. James	W	Tyler	Murder	12/1903	12/31/35		
161	Henry Carr	B	Tyler	Murder	01/1992	01/03/36		
162	Fred Hill	B	Travis	Murder	05/1912	01/10/36		

No.	Name	Race	County	Crime			
163	John Rivera	H	Bastrop	Rape	02/1912	06/23/36	
164	Willie Green	B	Liberty	Murder	12/1882		06/12/36
165	Virgil Stalcup	W	Lubbock	Murder	12/1907	05/04/36	
166	Theo Mitchell	B	Harris	Murder	12/1905		05/19/36
167	Willie Dickerson	B	Cass	Rape	06/1916	05/29/36	
168	Aria Tance	B	Harris	Murder	03/1907	05/30/36	
169	William Davis	B	Travis	Murder	08/1915	06/05/36	
170	James McCallister	W	Hidalgo	Murder	06/1898	06/05/36	
171	Glenn Warren	W	Angelina	Murder	06/1902	07/20/36	
172	Grady Warren	W	Upshur	Murder	09/1910	07/10/36	
173	Oscar Brown	B	Refugio	Murder	11/1909	07/10/36	
174	Mack Brown	B	Refugio	Murder	05/1901	07/10/36	
175	Antonio Carrasco	H	Hudspeth	Murder	01/1901	10/23/36	
176	Elmo Banks	B	Lynn	Murder	Unknown	10/23/36	
177	Lonnie Joiner	W	Newton	Murder	04/1899	05/28/37	
178	Elmer Pruitt	B	Henderson	Murder	12/1913	05/30/37	
179	Dwight Beard	W	Dallas	Murder	04/1910	06/04/37	
180	Wisie Ellison	B	Caldwell	Murder	11/1900	06/04/37	
181	Earnest McCarty	W	Tarrant	Rape	09/1917	07/09/37	
182	Clemens Matura	B	Stonewall	Murder	02/1871	07/02/37	
183	Harry Alex	B	Wharton	Murder	07/1912		08/16/37
184	Peo Quezada	H	Willacy	Murder	04/1889		09/30/37
185	George Patton	W	Ellis	Murder	06/1882	07/30/37	
186	Humphrey Henderson	B	Galveston	Murder	04/1905		08/16/37
187	Luke Trammell	W	Brazoria	Murder	10/1908	08/20/37	
188	Albert Lee Hemphill	B	Dallas	Murder	11/1914	01/14/38	
189	Virgil Terrill	W	Gregg	Rape	05/1912	04/01/38	
190	Leroy Kelly	B	Lamb	Murder	04/1898	03/15/38	
191	Johnnie Banks	B	Brazoria	Murder	09/1912	04/29/38	
192	Salenes Canedo	H	Bexar	Murder	12/1911	10/28/38	
193	John W. Vaughn	W	Bexar	Murder	05/1905	04/30/38	
194	Paul Layes	W	Hays	Murder	02/1904	05/10/38	

APPENDIX B: **DEATH ROW PRISONERS, 1923–1988** (continued)

Execu-tion No.	Name	Race^a	County	Offense^b	Date of Birth	Executed	Commuted	Status
195	Roscoe Young	B	Harrison	Robbery	04/1920	05/06/38		
196	Henderson Young	B	Harrison	Rape	05/1921	05/06/38		
197	Tommie Moore	B	Limestone	Murder	09/1911	06/03/38		
198	Charlie Brooks	B	Cass	Murder	05/1897	05/31/38		
199	Mark Henry Calhoun	B	Dallas	Rape	09/1919	06/17/38		
200	Tommie Wells	B	Bowie	Rape	06/1915	06/17/38		
201	Fobie Grays	B	Wharton	Murder	10/1915	07/20/38		
202	Sam Cash	B	Wharton	Murder	11/1917		11/16/38	
203	Vince Boss	W	Caldwell	Murder	09/1916	08/02/38		
204	Willie Caesar	B	Harris	Murder	05/1897		07/07/38	
205	Collin Morgan	W	El Paso	Murder	04/1901	08/19/38		
206	Carlos Fernandez	W	Bexar	Murder	09/1917		09/16/38	
207	Jesse Palanco	H	Bexar	Murder	06/1916	08/19/38		
208	Morris Norman	B	Donley	Rape	11/1918	12/16/38		
209	Dan Sims	W	Harris	Robbery	02/1891		01/16/39	
210	Winzell Williams	B	Dallas	Murder	04/1920	03/06/39		
211	Harvey Nealy	B	Dallas	Murder	12/1919	04/10/39		
212	Jesus Herrera	H	Wilson	Murder	01/1891	04/15/39		
213	Genaro Lugo	H	San Patricio	Murder	09/1910	04/23/39		
214	James Miles	B	Dallas	Rape	01/1917	04/23/39		
215	Bennie Randall	B	Colorado	Rape	08/1912	05/07/39		
216	Johnnie Caesar	B	Dallas	Murder	01/1909	05/21/39		
217	James Ervin	B	Tarrant	Rape	10/1900	05/19/39		
218	Ladell Rhodes	B	Harrison	Murder	01/1912	06/26/39		
219	Lee Walker	B	Freestone	Rape	11/1906	06/30/39		
220	Bob White	B	Montgomery	Rape	03/1910			Killed at retrial

	Name	Race	County	Crime			
221	Francis Marion	W	Brewster	Murder	01/1910		08/15/39
222	Harry Lacy	B	Montgomery	Murder	01/1897	12/19/39	
223	Frank Salazar	H	Nolan	Murder	01/1915	12/16/39	
224	J. W. Richman	W	Collin	Murder	02/1918	03/18/40	
225	Bluitt Hampton	B	Dallas	Murder	06/1911	03/31/40	
226	Robert Walker	W	Dallas	Murder	05/1914	04/19/40	
227	Webster Lyons	B	Bexar	Murder	01/1911	04/28/40	
228	Robert Manning	B	Bexar	Murder	06/1919	04/28/40	
229	Burton Franks	W	Ellis	Murder	09/1917	06/07/40	
230	Placido Handy	H	Hidalgo	Murder	01/1904	06/09/40	
231	Florence Murphy	B	Kaufman	Rape	03/1909	08/30/40	
232	Ascension Martinez	H	Hidalgo	Murder	08/1903	02/21/41	
233	Theodia Muldrow	B	Dallas	Rape	02/1922	02/21/41	
234	George Griffin	B	Nueces	Rape	12/1914	04/20/41	
235	Tommie Harris	B	Tarrant	Murder	01/1921	06/06/41	
236	Arlin Reese	W	Limestone	Murder	01/1895	08/24/41	
237	Nehemiah Glover	B	Harris	Murder	08/1913	01/28/42	
238	Albert Wesley, Jr.	B	Dallas	Rape	03/1922	12/28/41	
239	Richard Robinson	B	Harris	Rape	12/1903	02/15/42	
240	Charlie Goldsby	B	Jefferson	Rape	07/1904	01/22/42	
241	James Alford	W	Bexar	Murder	09/1915	05/08/42	
242	Rogers Lee King	B	Johnson	Murder	04/1922	03/22/42	
243	McKinley Morris	B	Wilson	Murder	12/1908	05/16/42	
244	Emeliano Benavidez	H	Schleicher	Murder	01/1911	08/08/42	
245	Orrin J. Brown	W	Hansford	Murder	08/1886	06/15/42	
246	Luther Hill	B	Panola	Murder	07/1913	07/05/42	
247	Edward Hart, Jr.	B	Dallas	Rape	05/1917	07/29/42	
248	Ben Walker	B	Harrison	Rape	05/1907	08/01/42	
249	C. L. Turner	B	Dallas	Murder	06/1906	09/02/42	
250	Fidel Contreras	H	El Paso	Murder	01/1911		01/12/43
251	Leo Lera	W	Fort Bend	Murder	03/1909	02/19/43	
252	Arthur Wilson	B	Dallas	Murder	11/1918	07/21/43	

APPENDIX B: DEATH ROW PRISONERS, 1923–1988 (continued)

Execu-tion No.	Name	Race[a]	County	Offense[b]	Date of Birth	Executed	Commuted	Status
253	Rex Beard	W	Fisher	Murder	10/1922	09/03/43		
254	Dolores Quiroz	W	Jeff Davis	Murder	09/1912	10/29/43		
255	Juan Gutierrez	H	Hidalgo	Murder	06/1901	05/02/44		
256	Bruce Jordan	W	Colorado	Murder	09/1918	04/16/44		
257	Willie Worlds	B	Travis	Murder	05/1908		05/26/44	
258	Harold Minor	W	El Paso	Murder	03/1896		05/30/44	
259	David Williams	B	Travis	Rape	01/1925	07/09/44		
260	Bennie Johnson	B	Chambers	Murder	06/1903	07/09/44		
261	Ramon Munoz	H	Bexar	Murder	11/1921		06/27/44	
262	Clay Whittle	W	Houston	Murder	08/1906	07/30/44		
263	Willie Johnson	B	Fayette	Murder	07/1908	08/27/44		
264	George Johnson	B	Bowie	Murder	10/1913	08/27/44		
265	Allen Murray	B	Denton	Rape	12/1912	12/31/44		
266	J. B. Stephens	W	Ellis	Murder	12/1907	12/19/44		
267	George Luke	W	Tarrant	Murder	04/1904		01/03/45	
268	Henry Williams	B	Gonzales	Murder	01/1887	03/04/45		
269	Robert Holloway	B	McLennan	Murder	11/1921	03/25/45		
270	Louis Klander	W	Harris	Rape	12/1920		07/07/45	
271	Julius Harper	B	Harris	Murder	06/1927	07/07/45		
272	Jose Rocha	H	Caldwell	Rape	03/1905		07/30/45	
273	Joseph Oglesby	B	Reeves	Rape	10/1923	09/02/45		
274	C. L. Akins	B	Dallas	Murder	08/1914		10/02/45	
275	Jarvin Elliott	B	Bowie	Murder	09/1922	01/18/46		
276	Joseph Van Hodge	B	Harris	Murder	02/1914		03/06/46	
277	L. C. Newman	B	Polk	Murder	01/1920	07/19/46		
278	Clyde Moore	B	Henderson	Rape	11/1924	05/08/46		

No.	Name	Race	County	Crime	Date 1	Date 2	Date 3
279	Roberto Campos	B	Hudspeth	Murder	08/1912		05/25/46
280	Richard Gamble	B	Tarrant	Murder	09/1913	06/28/46	
281	Edgar Dotson	W	Dallas	Murder	06/1912		08/06/46
282	Harold Palm	B	Bexar	Rape	09/1911	09/01/46	
283	Joe Leza	H	Bexar	Murder	09/1915	09/01/46	
284	Louis Jones	B	Gonzales	Murder	04/1917	06/02/47	
285	P. H. Zachary	B	Williamson	Murder	12/1919	04/01/47	
286	L. D. Henderson	B	Grimes	Murder	01/1926	03/21/47	
287	Gaither Lovelady	B	Lee	Murder	07/1903		04/20/47
288	Huey Wilson	B	Harris	Murder	06/1910	05/02/47	
289	Oscar Allen	B	Dallas	Murder	03/1902	05/29/47	
290	William A. Norris	B	Hudspeth	Murder	02/1924	06/07/47	
291	Charlie Allen	B	Dallas	Murder	06/1910	06/26/47	
292	Walter Young	W	Dallas	Rape	01/1918		06/20/47
293	Arthur Adams	B	Tarrant	Murder	09/1909	09/05/47	
294	Elijah Pearson	B	Harris	Murder	12/1900	09/12/47	
295	Raymond Davis	B	Newton	Murder	12/1929	10/05/47	
296	Lonnie Cline	W	Dallas	Murder	12/1919	01/02/48	
297	Nolan West	W	Harris	Murder	07/1922	02/04/48	
298	Bennie Johnson	B	Fort Bend	Rape	06/1922	03/28/48	
299	Clayton Rushing	W	Jasper	Murder	12/1921	03/28/48	
300	Willie Sims	B	Harris	Rape	03/1912	04/25/48	
301	Joseph Saulter	W	Galveston	Murder	12/1914	07/09/48	
302	Miguel Flores	H	Goliad	Murder	05/1917		06/25/48
303	George Gardner	W	Harris	Murder	01/1915		06/11/48
304	John Coleman	B	Gregg	Rape	03/1891	07/18/48	
305	Ernest Williams	B	Caldwell	Murder	10/1900		07/23/48
306	Riley McCane	W	Jefferson	Murder	01/1905	08/20/48	
307	Henry Brown	B	Harrison	Murder	01/1925	08/01/48	
308	Cleo Smith	B	Bowie	Rape	12/1918	08/24/48	
309	Andrew Hill	B	Bowie	Murder	11/1924	10/03/48	
310	Wilson Moore	B	Harris	Rape	04/1919	02/01/49	

APPENDIX B: DEATH ROW PRISONERS, 1923–1988 (continued)

Execution No.	Name	Race[a]	County	Offense[b]	Date of Birth	Executed	Commuted	Status
311	Thurman Williams	B	Harris	Murder	06/1925	02/13/49		
312	Thomas Larkin	B	Harrison	Murder	12/1925	02/21/49		
313	Buster Northern	W	Dallas	Murder	06/1928	04/16/49		
314	Amberto Valtiero	H	Dallas	Murder	09/1926		09/29/49	
315	James Blackmon	B	Harris	Murder	06/1925	04/05/50		
316	W. Fred Jones	W	Crosby	Murder	01/1909	08/10/49		
317	William Wilson, Jr.	B	Harris	Rape	12/1918	02/05/50		
318	General Kerzee	B	Dallas	Murder	11/1895	08/10/49		
319	F. M. McClendon	B	Lee	Murder	06/1926	08/14/49		
320	Cleveland Stovall	B	Tarrant	Rape	02/1927	09/11/49		
321	J. W. Morrow	W	Harris	Murder	11/1920	02/09/50		
322	Cerillo Zamora	H	El Paso	Rape	07/1912		02/03/50	
323	Samuel Gibson	B	Howard	Murder	11/1925	01/29/50		
324	William Smith, Jr.	B	Harris	Murder	02/1928	04/05/50		
325	Lee Bunn	B	McLennan	Murder	06/1922	05/03/50		
326	Nathaniel Edwards	B	Harris	Rape	11/1922	05/17/50		
327	William Ray	W	Navarro	Rape	08/1914	06/09/50		
328	Felix Lewis	W	Live Oak	Rape	04/1903	06/21/50		
329	Porter Henderson	B	Harris	Murder	03/1903	06/14/50		
330	Ben Pickett	B	Harris	Rape	08/1915	01/13/51		
331	Dan White	W	Palo Pinto	Murder	05/1901	06/02/50		
332	Eugene McFarland	B	Harris	Rape	05/1924	06/30/50		
333	Edward Johnson	B	Harris	Rape	03/1919	12/29/50		
334	Herman Ross	B	Galveston	Murder	08/1919	06/04/52		
335	Thomas Price	W	Dallas	Murder	04/1920	02/01/51		
336	J. B. Patterson	W	Harris	Murder	08/1906	03/14/51		

#	Name	Race	County	Crime	Birth	Date	Date
337	Allen Williams	W	Harris	Rape	11/1910	03/21/51	
338	Fred Adair, Jr.	W	Dallas	Rape	02/1924	09/05/51	
339	Abbie Mouton	B	Jefferson	Murder	05/1919	12/08/51	
340	Emma Oliver (Fe)	B	Bexar	Murder	09/1910		06/29/51
341	Morris Bessard	B	Harris	Rape	08/1928	06/27/51	
342	Sam Williams	B	Harris	Murder	09/1897	07/03/51	
343	Y. B. Robinson	B	Wichita	Murder	03/1918	07/16/51	
344	Richard McGee	W	Lubbock	Murder	06/1924		10/26/59
345	Steve Mitchell	W	Harris	Murder	01/1902	09/25/51	
346	Albert Edwards	W	Harris	Murder	04/1912	10/09/51	
347	Allen Matthews	B	Harris	Murder	03/1927	09/05/51	
348	Richard McMurrin	B	Galveston	Rape	11/1930	01/08/52	
349	L. C. Sims	B	Collin	Rape	04/1925	09/05/51	
350	Bob Wall	W	McLennan	Murder	09/1920		03/25/52
351	Billy McCune	W	Tarrant	Rape	05/1928		03/06/52
352	T. C. Saucier	W	Wichita	Murder	11/1915		01/08/52
353	Harrell King	W	Travis	Murder	09/1924		03/18/52
354	Robert Johnson	W	Dallas	Murder	Unknown	03/12/52	
355	William Jones	W	Jones	Murder	06/1893	04/26/52	
356	James Craft	W	McLennan	Murder	04/1917		03/25/52
357	Booker Reed	B	Dallas	Murder	04/1906	10/28/52	
358	Marvin Johnson	W	Brown	Murder	05/1930	04/09/52	
359	Henry Savage	B	Grimes	Rape	04/1926	04/30/52	
360	Darious Goleman	W	Liberty	Murder	08/1921	02/04/53	
361	Thomas Haley	W	Tarrant	Rape	01/1925	07/10/52	
362	Major Preston	B	Trinity	Rape	09/1917	08/08/52	
363	Foley Gephart	W	Travis	Rape	08/1912		09/18/52
364	Alton Paris	B	Anderson	Murder	01/1892	12/02/52	
365	Lester Stevens	W	Bailey	Murder	06/1901		12/02/52
366	Robert Miers	W	Bexar	Murder	06/1931		01/09/53
367	R. J. Hulen	W	Potter	Murder	06/1909	02/06/53	
368	Samuel Gasway	W	Potter	Rape	11/1917	03/21/53	

APPENDIX B: DEATH ROW PRISONERS, 1923–1988 (continued)

Execu-tion No.	Name	Race[a]	County	Offense[b]	Date of Birth	Executed	Commuted	Status
369	Jack Farmer	W	Floyd	Murder	08/1899	06/10/53		
370	Lewis Allison	B	Harris	Rape	09/1930	10/17/53		
371	Charles Clark	W	Tom Green	Murder	09/1910	03/25/54		
372	Walter Green	W	Culberson	Murder	01/1929	02/19/54		
373	Willie Gage	B	Tarrant	Rape	03/1912	04/23/54		
374	Charles Klinedinst	W	Dallas	Rape	12/1924	06/19/54		
375	Jimmy Richardson	B	Freestone	Rape	04/1922	06/24/54		
376	Charles Barnes	B	Harris	Murder	05/1930	07/14/54		
377	Marvin Rayson	B	Palo Pinto	Murder	09/1925	07/17/54		
378	Donald Brown	W	Dallas	Murder	09/1928	01/22/55		
379	Walter Whitaker, Jr.	W	Wilbarger	Murder	04/1932	09/01/54		
380	Maurice Sampson	B	Harris	Murder	08/1933	09/29/54		
381	Morris Addison	B	Travis	Murder	01/1926		02/08/55	
382	Gordon Morris	W	Harris	Murder	08/1923		02/24/55	
383	Harry Butcher	W	Midland	Rape	12/1925	05/20/55		
384	Henry Meyer	W	Harris	Murder	12/1889	06/08/55		
385	Lonnie Brinkley	W	Harris	Murder	09/1891		01/08/57	
386	Floyd Jackson	B	Dallas	Rape	04/1934	08/18/55		
387	Johnnie Gordon	B	Harris	Rape	08/1930	01/24/56		
388	Carrol Farrar	W	Harris	Murder	12/1919	01/04/56		
389	Merle Ellisor	W	Harris	Murder	08/1922	04/04/57		
390	Tommie Walker	B	Dallas	Murder	12/1934	05/12/56		
391	Marion Washington	B	McLennan	Murder	01/1927	06/08/56		
392	Billy Houston	W	Dallas	Rape	09/1928		01/25/60	
393	Flandell Fite	B	Dallas	Rape	10/1928	08/23/56		
394	Yancy McGowen	W	Harris	Murder	03/1893	04/24/57		

#	Name	Race	County	Crime			
				Rape	06/1955	06/30/56	
396	Leonard Bingham	W	Pecos	Murder	09/1930	10/30/56	
397	Leslie Webb	B	Wood	Murder	03/1924	01/04/57	
398	John McHenry	B	Harris	Rape	08/1930	01/03/57	
399	Alvaro Alcarta	H	Bexar	Murder	10/1919		01/01/59
400	Junior Williams	B	Wharton	Rape	01/1930	03/05/60	
401	Wilburn Hall	W	Harris	Murder	09/1927	08/21/57	
402	Marshall Lamkin	B	Caldwell	Murder	08/1905	09/19/58	
403	John Wright	B	Bell	Rape	12/1918	09/14/57	
404	Jimmy Shaver	W	Bell	Murder	07/1925	07/25/58	
405	Charlie White	W	Travis	Murder	02/1912	02/06/58	
406	John Mack	B	Dallas	Rape	07/1932	03/06/58	
407	Theodore Thompson	B	Dallas	Rape	10/1934	06/20/58	
408	Alvin Blankenship	B	Harris	Robbery	09/1930	06/11/58	
409	Norman Kizzee	B	Robertson	Murder	02/1939		08/26/58
410	James Bell	B	Dallas	Murder	10/1920		09/25/58
411	Phillip Slater	B	Montgomery	Murder	07/1922	02/04/59	
412	Milton Williams	B	Lee	Rape	02/1931	05/28/59	
413	Jessie Smith	B	Harris	Murder	04/1917	08/04/59	
414	George Moses	B	Harris	Murder	02/1930	08/12/60	
415	Albert Davis, Jr.	B	Brazoria	Rape	03/1940		02/12/60
416	Nearvel Moon	W	Harris	Murder	05/1940	04/28/60	
417	Howard Draper, Jr.	B	Dallas	Rape	03/1932	05/26/60	
418	Samuel Holmes	B	Travis	Rape	02/1938	11/30/60	
419	George William	B	Williamson	Murder	06/1930	07/08/60	
420	Willie Philpot	B	Gregg	Murder	05/1933	07/15/60	
421	Eusebio Martinez	H	Midland	Murder	12/1933	08/27/60	
422	Charles Williams	B	Houston	Rape	08/1940	06/03/61	
423	Howard Stickney	W	Harris	Murder	03/1938	05/23/62	
424	Adrian Johnson	B	Harris	Murder	05/1942	04/19/62	
425	Ernesto Lopez	H	Dallas	Murder	03/1937		04/07/61
426	James Edwards	B	Dallas	Rape	10/1930	06/23/61	

APPENDIX B: DEATH ROW PRISONERS, 1923–1988 (continued)

Execu-tion No.	Name	Race[a]	County	Offense[b]	Date of Birth	Executed	Commuted	Status
427	Maggie Morgan (Fe)	B	Harris	Murder	09/1912		07/25/61	
428	Joe Singleton	B	Jefferson	Rape	11/1936		08/11/72	
429	Fred Leath	W	Tarrant	Murder	02/1921	11/09/61		
430	Roosevelt Wiley	B	Johnson	Murder	06/1932	01/11/62		
431	Charles Forgey	W	Dallas	Rape	Unknown	01/10/62		
432	Leo Luton	W	Dallas	Murder	07/1928	02/20/63		
433	Joe Smith	B	Harris	Murder	03/1942		10/30/72	
434	Donald Wilson	W	Johnson	Murder	01/1940	03/20/62		
435	Herbert Bradley	B	Dallas	Robbery	06/1941	05/15/62		
436	Cecil Brown	B	Harris	Rape	01/1943		06/28/62	
437	Walter Mosley	W	Harris	Murder	12/1935	07/18/62		
438	Bobby Stein	B	Harris	Murder	05/1933	09/05/62		
439	Joe Sneed	B	Dallas	Rape	09/1933	01/03/63		
440	Roscoe Gibson	B	Harris	Rape	07/1923	10/06/62		
441	Bennie McIntyre	B	Lynn	Rape	07/1942	01/20/63		
442	Leslie Ashley	W	Harris	Murder	01/1928		01/14/66	
443	Carolyn Lima (Fe)	W	Harris	Murder	02/1942		04/03/65	
444	John Lavan	B	Harris	Murder	11/1928	03/31/63		
445	Curtis Roberts	B	Ward	Robbery	05/1941		06/17/63	
446	Oscar O'Brien	B	Harris	Murder	11/1931		07/19/63	
447	Jesse Parker	B	Dallas	Rape	08/1940	02/12/64		
448	James Echols	B	Harris	Rape	Unknown	05/07/64		
449	Bobby Bradford	B	Ellis	Murder	02/1932	03/11/64		
450	Edward Hagans	W	Nacogdoches	Murder	07/1933		11/05/73	
451	Eugene Welch	B	Grayson	Murder	03/1935		12/08/72	
452	Lawrence O'Connor	B	Harris	Rape	03/1938	04/26/64		

No.	Name	Race	County	Crime	Date	Date	Note
454	Edwin Bertsch	W	Fayette	Murder	08/1912	08/15/72	Died 10/04/1967
455	James Graves	W	Harris	Murder	09/1942	11/08/72	
456	Benny Longoria	H	Ellis	Murder	09/1932	05/17/71	
457	James Marion	B	Lubbock	Murder	04/1942	08/18/72	
458	John Burns	W	Harris	Murder	10/1927	12/01/69	
459	Leon Spencer	B	Jefferson	Murder	12/1927	10/20/65	
460	Robert Freeman	W	Harris	Murder	09/1939	04/15/69	
461	Harold Hintz	W	Tarrant	Murder	04/1920	05/06/69	
462	Clifford Carroll	W	Tarrant	Murder	08/1942	11/21/72	
463	Ralph Powers	W	Bexar	Murder	11/1942	12/04/68	
464	Leon Johnston	W	Palo Pinto	Rape	09/1938	08/18/72	
465	Melvin Dixon	B	Harris	Murder	01/1943	09/18/72	
466	Melvin Payton	B	Harris	Murder	06/1942	09/21/72	
467	Johnny Clemons	B	Gregg	Rape	01/1938	10/30/72	
468	John Young	W	Harris	Robbery	11/1938	10/30/72	
469	Walter Siros	W	Harris	Rape	10/1940	06/15/66	
470	Oscar Cook	W	Falls	Murder	07/1938	10/30/72	
471	Jimmie Guilbry	W	Montgomery	Murder	07/1939	10/30/72	
472	Calvin Sellars	W	Harris	Robbery	08/1941	08/18/72	
473	Kenneth Martin	W	Dallas	Murder	03/1935	11/03/73	
474	Robert Jackson	B	Newton	Murder	01/1942	10/30/72	
475	Nelson Chevallier	B	Harris	Murder	11/1920	10/30/72	
476	Paul Crain	W	Harris	Murder	08/1934	12/28/71	
477	William Bryan	W	Fort Bend	Murder	03/1939	06/09/71	
478	Jimmy Chavez	H	Potter	Rape	04/1940	07/31/72	
479	Jesse Ellison	B	Falls	Robbery	06/1934	09/11/69	
480	Reginald Wright	W	Tarrant	Murder	02/1916	09/20/72	
481	Claude Edwards	W	Young	Murder	10/1942	07/10/69	
482	Earlando Williams	B	Dallas	Rape	12/1947	09/20/72	
483	Juan Enriquez	H	Karnes	Murder	03/1947	08/18/72	
484	Jerry Ward	W	Harris	Murder	04/1944	09/20/72	

APPENDIX B: DEATH ROW PRISONERS, 1923–1988 (continued)

Execu-tion No.	Name	Race[a]	County	Offense[b]	Date of Birth	Executed	Commuted	Status
485	Kenneth McDuff	W	Tarrant	Murder	03/1946		09/18/72	
486	William Scott	B	Brazoria	Rape	10/1948		12/13/72	
487	Melvin Pittman	W	Tarrant	Murder	01/1948		09/18/72	
488	William Marshall	W	Dallas	Murder	09/1935		09/05/72	
489	Tracey Whan	W	Harris	Murder	12/1935		12/28/71	
490	Daniel Quintana	H	Dallas	Rape	09/1949		11/18/71	
491	Hershel Joseph	W	Harris	Murder	02/1934		08/18/72	
492	Elmer Branch	B	Wilbarger	Rape	11/1946		10/20/72	
493	Arlice Huffman	W	Harris	Murder	02/1919		08/18/72	
494	F. L. McKenzie	B	Tarrant	Murder	05/1941		09/18/72	
495	Eddie Grant	B	Harris	Murder	02/1941		08/18/72	
496	Theo Thames	W	Tarrant	Murder	12/1947		09/20/72	
497	Guadalupe Sanchez	H	Nueces	Murder	07/1947		11/22/72	
498	Cornelius Tea	B	Harris	Murder	03/1941		09/20/72	
499	Roy David	B	Harris	Murder	04/1941		08/25/72	
500	Carl Harris	W	Galveston	Murder	06/1946		08/18/72	
501	Leopoldo Morales	H	El Paso	Murder	01/1940		10/30/72	
502	Robert Curry	B	McLennan	Murder	07/1948		10/30/72	
503	Billy Stanley	W	Collin	Murder	05/1938		11/08/72	
504	Samuel Matthews	B	Refugio	Murder	12/1949		11/10/72	
505	Larry Lane	B	Harris	Murder	08/1938		08/18/72	
506	Arthur Broussard	B	Harris	Murder	11/1941		08/11/72	
507	John DeVries	W	Jefferson	Burglary	11/1920			Suicide 07/1/1974
508	Jerry Jurek	W	DeWitt	Robbery	02/1951		01/29/82	
509	Leonard Freeman	W	Armstrong	Kidnapping	07/1945		04/11/83	
510	James Burn	W	Ector	Robbery	06/1953		02/23/81	

No.	Name	Race	County	Crime	Birth			Notes
511	Excell White	W	Collin	Robbery	03/1938			On death row
512	Jerry Joe Bird	W	Nueces	Robbery	04/1937	06/17/91		
513	Mark Moore	B	Dallas	Rape	07/1952		09/04/82	
514	Howie Robinson	B	Dallas	Robbery	11/1951		06/24/81	
515	Earnest Smith	B	Dallas	Robbery	12/1947		06/24/81	
516	Doyle Boulware	W	Dallas	Policeman	03/1929		11/01/82	
517	Anderson Hughes	B	Dallas	Burglary	12/1955		06/17/82	
518	Doyle Skillern	W	Live Oak	Policeman	04/1936			
519	Wilbur Collins	B	McLennan	Robbery	08/1950	01/16/85	11/29/82	
520	Selwyn Gholson	B	Bell	Robbery	08/1954		07/13/82	
521	Larry Ross	B	Bell	Robbery	11/1953		07/13/82	
522	Kenneth Brock	W	Harris	Robbery	08/1948		03/11/87	
523	Calvin Woodkins	B	Harrison	Robbery	03/1955	06/19/86		
524	Walter Bell, Jr.	B	Jefferson	Rape	12/1953		04/06/83	On death row
525	James Livingston	W	Dallas	Robbery	04/1947		11/23/77	
526	Ignacio Cuevas	H	Harris	Murder	07/1931	05/23/91		
527	Robert Kleason	W	Travis	Robbery	09/1932		07/14/82	
528	Fred Durrough	W	Bexar	Robbery	03/1941			
529	Ronald O'Bryan	W	Harris	Remuneration	10/1944	03/31/84		
530	Albert Castro	H	Bexar	Robbery	10/1954		08/02/79	
531	Jessie Jones	B	Dallas	Robbery	10/1946		03/27/86	
532	Moses Garcia	H	Harris	Robbery	02/1953		04/06/83	
533	Kenneth Granveil	B	Tarrant	Rape	08/1950			On death row
534	Jesse Villareal	H	Harris	Robbery	07/1941		01/18/85	
535	Richard Vargas	H	Harris	Robbery	05/1951			Died 5/31/81
536	Don Warren	W	Lubbock	Burglary	03/1950			
537	William Hovila	W	Dallas	Burglary	12/1947		03/29/79	
538	Edwin Corley	W	McLennan	Rape	09/1947		01/08/82	
539	Ronald Chamber	B	Dallas	Robbery	01/1955			On death row
540	John Shippy	W	Bell	Burglary	02/1952		12/06/83	On death row
541	Raymond Riles	B	Harris	Robbery	06/1950			
542	Kenneth Palafox	W	Nacogdoches	Burglary	01/1947		12/12/80	On death row

APPENDIX B: DEATH ROW PRISONERS, 1923–1988 (continued)

Execu-tion No.	Name	Race[a]	County	Offense[b]	Date of Birth	Executed	Commuted	Status
543	Gerald Bodde	W	Harris	Rape	04/1947			Died 8/10/87
544	James Whitmore	W	Tarrant	Remuneration	07/1941		08/07/79	
545	Kenneth Stogsdill	W	Wichita	Robbery	07/1940		07/29/77	
546	Donald Franklin	B	Nueces	Rape	09/1951	11/03/88		
547	Eddie Robinson	B	Bexar	Robbery	11/1952		07/28/78	
548	Billy Battie	B	Tarrant	Robbery	08/1957			On death row
549	Herbert Washington	B	Harris	Robbery	11/1949		02/08/78	
550	Sammie Felder	B	Harris	Burglary	09/1945			On death row
551	Henry Porter	H	Tarrant	Murder	12/1941	07/09/85		
552	Billie Woods	W	Harris	Rape	12/1946			On death row
553	William Cortez	H	Nueces	Robbery	04/1938		11/26/80	
554	Richard Smith	W	Coryell	Robbery	10/1950		11/27/78	
555	Charles Rumbaugh	W	Potter	Robbery	06/1957	09/11/85		
556	Billie Hughes	W	Matagorda	Policeman	01/1952			On death row
557	Felix Ochoa	H	DeWitt	Policeman	03/1943		08/24/79	
558	Alton Byrd	W	San Augustine	Rape	02/1953		01/03/84	
559	Richard Denny	W	Cameron	Robbery	10/1929		08/04/82	
560	Jimmie Vanderbilt	W	Potter	Kidnapping	11/1952			On death row
561	Thelette Brandon	B	McLennan	Policeman	05/1953		07/08/82	
562	John Wilder	B	Bowie	Robbery	05/1954		10/23/81	
563	Artis Armour	B	Bowie	Robbery	10/1954		10/23/81	
564	Bobby McCormick	W	Panola	Remuneration	02/1948		09/20/83	
565	Billie McMahon	W	Panola	Remuneration	07/1946		09/22/83	
566	Mark Fields	W	Wichita	Burglary	03/1952		02/16/84	
567	Margarito Bravo	H	Karnes	Policeman	02/1921		10/31/86	
568	Vernon McManus	W	Harris	Robbery	02/1943		01/21/87	

	Name		County	Crime				
569	Murrel Crawford	W	Potter	Robbery	04/1957		10/27/87	
570	Bernard Ferguson	W	Bell	Robbery	08/1959		12/13/82	
571	Jerry Hartfield	B	Wharton	Rape	03/1956		04/08/83	
572	James Demouchette	B	Harris	Robbery	05/1955			On death row
573	Edward King	B	Dallas	Policeman	11/1942			Murdered 8/28/1979
574	Larry Fortenberry	W	Hale	Robbery	01/1948		05/24/79	
575	Pedro Muniz	H	Williamson	Rape	09/1956			On death row
576	G. W. Green	W	Montgomery	Burglary	11/1936	11/12/91		
577	Harvey Earvin	B	Angelina	Robbery	04/1958			On death row
578	William Hammett	W	Brazoria	Robbery	06/1947		10/23/81	
579	James Russell	B	Fort Bend	Kidnapping	03/1949	09/19/91		
580	Joseph Foulder	W	Gregg	Burglary	10/1937			On death row
581	Randy Green	W	Harris	Robbery	09/1955			On death row
582	John Zimmerman	W	Harris	Rape	11/1946			On death row
583	Sammie English	B	Harris	Robbery	01/1956		12/07/82	
584	Harvey Duffy	W	Bexar	Burglary	06/1951		05/15/81	
585	Billy White	B	Harris	Robbery	10/1957	04/23/92		
586	Joseph Starvaggi	W	Montgomery	Robbery	11/1952	09/10/87		
587	Anthony Pierce	B	Harris	Robbery	07/1959			On death row
588	Magdolino Rodriguez	H	Bexar	Robbery	05/1959		10/19/81	
589	James Williams	B	Harris	Robbery	03/1954		10/17/88	
590	Samuel Hawkins	B	Lubbock	Rape	09/1943			On death row
591	Clarence Lackey	W	Tom Green	Rape	08/1954			On death row
592	Charlie Brooks, Jr.	B	Dallas	Robbery	09/1942	12/07/82		
593	Robert May	W	Harris	Multiple murder	08/1925		05/18/82	
594	James Richardson	W	Brazoria	Burglary	02/1958		10/22/80	
595	Woodie Loudres	B	Tarrant	Kidnapping	12/1943		12/31/82	
596	Phillip Brasfield	W	Lubbock	Kidnapping	08/1949		02/17/80	
597	Charles Sanne	W	Live Oak	Policeman	02/1933		11/19/80	
598	Charles O'Brient	B	McLennan	Rape	06/1957		03/21/80	
599	Stanley Burks	B	Dallas	Burglary	07/1958		09/21/83	
600	Kerry Cook	W	Smith	Rape	04/1956			On death row

Execution No.	Name	Race^a	County	Offense^b	Date of Birth	Executed	Commuted	Status
601	Kenneth Davis	B	Dallas	Robbery	02/1957		11/31/81	
602	Randall Adams	W	Dallas	Policeman	12/1948		07/16/80	
603	Paul Rougeau	B	Harris	Robbery	12/1947			On death row
604	Jeremiah O'Pry	W	Freestone	Burglary	08/1947		06/03/81	
605	William Horne	W	Harris	Robbery	08/1954		03/17/81	
606	Rudy Esquivel	H	Harris	Policeman	08/1935	06/09/86		
607	Mary Anderson (Fe)	W	Wharton	Remuneration	09/1943		10/31/78	
608	Michael Evans	B	Dallas	Robbery	11/1956			On death row
609	Clarence Jordan	B	Harris	Robbery	05/1956	12/04/86		
610	John Thompson	W	Bexar	Robbery	01/1955		10/29/81	
611	James Pierson	W	Dallas	Robbery	01/1948	07/08/87		
612	David Powell	W	Travis	Policeman	01/1951			On death row
613	John Quinones	H	Harris	Rape	12/1958		05/21/81	
614	William Davis	B	Harris	Robbery	04/1957			On death row
615	Jack Smith	W	Harris	Robbery	12/1937			On death row
616	Ernest Holloway	W	Gregg	Robbery	12/1953			On death row
617	Feryl Granger	W	Fort Bend	Remuneration	11/1948		06/19/81	
618	Jackie Osteen	W	Galveston	Robbery	11/1958		06/24/81	
619	Anthony Williams	B	Harris	Rape	11/1959	05/28/87		
620	Charles Evans	B	Harris	Robbery	06/1952		02/17/81	
621	Thomas Barefoot	W	Bell	Policeman	02/1945	10/30/84		
622	David Roder	W	Harris	Robbery	07/1957		11/24/87	
623	George Clark	W	Travis	Rape	04/1956		11/13/81	
624	Leon King	B	Harris	Rape	05/1944		05/03/81	
625	Silguero Reyes	H	Hidalgo	Rape	02/1926	03/22/89		
626	John Fearance	B	Dallas	Rape	10/1954			On death row

	Name		County	Crime				Status
627	Mark Cass	W	Harris	Robbery	07/1955			On death row
628	Charles Milton	B	Tarrant	Robbery	03/1951	06/25/85		
629	David Grijalva	H	Tarrant	Robbery	01/1952		05/20/82	
630	Jamers Buffington	W	Bexar	Remuneration	04/1944		01/03/89	
631	John McCrory	W	Wichita	Rape	09/1950		10/11/83	
632	Linda Burnett (Fe)	W	Jefferson	Kidnapping	02/1948		08/31/83	
633	Carl Johnson	B	Harris	Robbery	03/1955			On death row
634	Joseph Cannon	W	Bexar	Burglary	01/1960			On death row
635	James Simmons	B	Hill	Robbery	06/1958		08/21/81	
636	Arturo Anderson	H	Wharton	Policeman	05/1948			On death row
637	Curtis Harris	B	Brazos	Robbery	08/1961			On death row
638	Donald Vigneault	W	Wharton	Rape	02/1950			On death row
639	Edward Payne	B	Harris	Kidnapping	04/1951			On death row
640	Larry White	W	Harris	Robbery	03/1950			On death row
641	Charles County	B	Cameron	Robbery	03/1949			On death row
642	Jonathan Reed	W	Dallas	Rape	06/1954			On death row
643	Larry Smith	B	Dallas	Robbery	08/1955	08/22/86		
644	David Wallace	B	El Paso	Robbery	01/1959		07/24/81	
645	Ovide Dugas	W	Nueces	Kidnapping	04/1946			Killed in escape attempt 6/20/83
646	Randy Woolls	W	Tom Green	Robbery	11/1949	08/20/86		
647	Jeffery Griffin	B	Harris	Robbery	01/1945			On death row
648	Claude Wilkerson	W	Harris	Robbery	04/1954		09/01/83	
649	Danny Harris	B	Brazos	Robbery	07/1960			On death row
650	Cesar Fierro	H	El Paso	Robbery	10/1956			On death row
651	John Satterwhite	B	Bexar	Robbery	05/1946			On death row
652	John Selvage	B	Harris	Robbery	08/1950			On death row
653	Roger Degarmo	W	Fort Bend	Kidnapping	11/1954			On death row
654	John Penry	W	Polk	Rape	05/1956			On death row
655	James Roney	W	Harris	Robbery	04/1962		04/08/83	
656	Richard King	W	Wichita	Burglary	05/1952		01/17/84	
657	Kent Graham	W	Hunt	Robbery	02/1950		01/08/82	

■ ■ ■ 223

APPENDIX B: DEATH ROW PRISONERS, 1923–1988 (continued)

Execution No.	Name	Race[a]	County	Offense[b]	Date of Birth	Executed	Commuted	Status
658	Charles Russell	W	Taylor	Robbery	08/1961			On death row
659	Jimmie Mead	W	Tarrant	Policeman	03/1943		07/01/85	
660	Jerry Hogue	W	Tarrant	Robbery	09/1950			On death row
661	Ernesto Garcia	H	Cameron	Robbery	09/1948		12/30/81	
662	Charles Bass	W	Harris	Robbery	01/1957	03/12/86		
663	Bobbie Moore	B	Harris	Robbery	10/1959			On death row
664	Darryl Stewart	B	Harris	Burglary	04/1955			On death row
665	Pamela Perillo (Fe)	W	Harris	Robbery	12/1955			On death row
666	Calvin William	B	Harris	Rape	07/1960			Murdered 8/26/90
667	Ramon Hernandez	H	El Paso	Burglary	03/1942	01/30/87		
668	Warren Bridge	W	Galveston	Robbery	07/1960			On death row
669	James Session	B	Smith	Robbery	06/1957			On death row
670	James Autry	W	Jefferson	Robbery	09/1954	03/14/84		
671	Delma Banks	B	Bowie	Robbery	11/1958			On death row
672	Paul Bush	W	Wichita	Burglary	01/1953			Died 6/17/86
673	Danny Barber	B	Dallas	Rape	05/1955			On death row
674	Noble Mays	W	Denton	Robbery	08/1953			On death row
675	Kenneth Dunn	B	Harris	Robbery	10/1959			On death row
676	Andrew Mitchell	B	Smith	Robbery	02/1961			On death row
677	Willie Williams	B	Harris	Robbery	02/1956			On death row
678	Chester Wicker	W	Galveston	Kidnapping	08/1948	08/26/86		
679	Dave Gardner	W	Parker	Kidnapping	09/1959			On death row
680	Clarence Brandley	B	Montgomery	Rape	09/1951			Charges Dropped[c]
681	Efren Ibanez	H	El Paso	Robbery	10/1962			On death row
682	Joseph Turner	W	El Paso	Robbery	08/1959			Suicide 7/5/86
683	Harold Barnard	W	Galveston	Robbery	11/1942			On death row

No.	Name	Race	County	Crime			Birth	Status
684	Allen Janecka	W	Harris	Remuneration			11/1949	On death row
685	Max Soffar	W	Harris	Robbery			12/1956	On death row
686	Jay Pinkerton	W	Randall	Rape	05/15/86		12/1962	On death row
687	Phillip Tompkins	B	Harris	Rape			02/1954	On death row
688	Carl Kelly	B	McLennan	Robbery			03/1959	On death row
689	James Meanes	B	Harris	Robbery			06/1955	On death row
690	Noe Beltran	H	Willacy	Robbery		09/09/87	08/1955	On death row
691	Miguel Richardson	B	Bexar	Robbery			07/1954	On death row
692	William Burns	B	Bowie	Robbery			07/1958	On death row
693	Victor Burns	B	Bowie	Robbery		12/04/86	09/1963	On death row
694	Markum Duff-Smith	W	Harris	Remuneration			01/1947	On death row
695	Carlos Santana	H	Harris	Robbery			10/1952	On death row
696	Garry Graham	W	Harris	Robbery			09/1963	On death row
697	Raymond Beasley	W	Hidalgo	Burglary		12/04/87	02/1951	On death row
698	Stephen Nethery	W	Dallas	Policeman			06/1960	On death row
699	Joseph Jernigan	W	Navarro	Burglary			01/1954	On death row
700	Antonio Bonham	B	Harris	Rape			02/1960	On death row
701	Mikel Derrick	W	Harris	Robbery			02/1957	On death row
702	Leonel Herrera	H	Cameron	Policeman	07/18/90		09/1947	On death row
703	Micheal Goodman	B	Harris	Robbery			12/1955	On death row
704	Caruthers Alexander	B	Bexar	Rape			09/1948	On death row
705	Fletcher Mann	W	Dallas	Rape			04/1961	On death row
706	George Cordova	H	Bexar	Rape			03/1959	On death row
707	Kerry Armstrong	B	Johnson	Robbery		12/23/87	10/1961	On death row
708	Robert Carter	B	Harris	Robbery			02/1964	On death row
709	Joseph Nichols	B	Harris	Robbery			09/1961	On death row
710	Danny Thomas	W	Harris	Rape			08/1955	On death row
711	James Briddle	W	Harris	Robbery			04/1955	On death row
712	Stephen Morin	W	Nueces	Kidnapping	03/13/85		02/1951	On death row
713	Jesse De La Rosa	H	Bexar	Robbery	05/15/85		09/1960	On death row

*Conviction overturned by Texas Court of Criminal Appeals; prisoner released January 23, 1990.

APPENDIX B: DEATH ROW PRISONERS, 1923–1988 (continued)

Execution No.	Name	Race[a]	County	Offense[b]	Date of Birth	Executed	Commuted	Status
714	Jeffery Barney	W	Harris	Rape	03/1958	04/16/86		
715	Heran Clark	B	Harris	Rape	07/1946			On death row
716	Stephen Mattox	W	Harris	Robbery	01/1954			Suicide 6/26/83
717	Bruce Cullins	B	Tarrant	Robbery	02/1960			On death row
718	Lee Roy Barrow	W	Travis	Robbery	08/1962		02/26/86	
719	David McKay	W	Dallas	Robbery	07/1958			On death row
720	Wayne East	B	Taylor	Robbery	10/1955			On death row
721	Charles Rector	B	Travis	Robbery	04/1954			On death row
722	Walter Williams	B	Bexar	Robbery	01/1962			On death row
723	Clifford Phillips	B	Harris	Robbery	12/1934			On death row
724	John Pyles	W	Dallas	Burglary	12/1957			On death row
725	Maurice Andrews	B	Jefferson	Robbery	12/1955			On death row
726	Paul Bush	W	Hemphill	Policeman	01/1953			Died 6/17/86
727	Ricardo Guerra	H	Harris	Policeman	04/1962			On death row
728	Donald Miller	W	Harris	Robbery	06/1962			On death row
729	Johnny Garrett	W	Potter	Rape	12/1963	02/11/92		
730	Joe Cordova	H	Harris	Robbery	03/1952	01/22/92		
731	Robert West	W	Harris	Rape	12/1961			On death row
732	Johnny Anderson	W	Jefferson	Remuneration	12/1959	05/17/90		
733	Larry Anderson	W	Harris	Robbery	08/1952			On death row
734	John Lamb	W	Hunt	Robbery	07/1957			On death row
735	Manuel Perez	H	El Paso	Robbery	03/1945			On death row
736	Arthur Williams	B	Harris	Policeman	10/1959			On death row
737	Ramon Montoya	H	Dallas	Policeman	08/1954			On death row
738	Raymond Landry	B	Harris	Robbery	05/1949	12/13/88		
739	Elliot Johnson	B	Jefferson	Robbery	08/1958	06/24/87		

No.	Name	Race	County	Crime	Birth	Date 1	Date 2	Status
740	Michael Sharp	W	Crockett	Kidnapping	04/1954			On death row
741	James Morland	W	Henderson	Robbery	05/1960			On death row
742	John Sawyers	W	Harris	Robbery	07/1955			On death row
743	Lawrence Buxton	B	Harris	Robbery	09/1952	02/26/91		On death row
744	Carlos DeLuna	H	Smith	Robbery	03/1962	12/07/89		
745	Harold Lane	W	Dallas	Robbery	08/1945			On death row
746	Robert Streetman	W	Hardin	Burglary	03/1960	01/07/88		On death row
747	James Ross	B	Harris	Robbery	09/1959			On death row
748	Larry Robinson	W	Tarrant	Robbery	08/1957			On death row
749	Edward Ellis	W	Harris	Burglary	06/1953	03/03/92		On death row
750	John Skelton	W	Ector	Arson	05/1929			Acquitted 10/10/90
751	Billy Gardner	W	Dallas	Robbery	07/1943			On death row
752	James Paster	W	Harris	Rape	01/1945	09/20/89		On death row
753	Ricky Morrow	W	Dallas	Robbery	04/1951			On death row
754	Marlyn Marrs	W	Harris	Robbery	03/1943		02/08/88	
755	Robert Drew	W	Harris	Robbery	04/1959			On death row
756	Richard Wilkerson	B	Harris	Robbery	04/1964			On death row
757	James Wyle	B	Culberson	Robbery	04/1960		12/07/90	
758	Calvin Burdine	W	Harris	Burglary	03/1953			On death row
759	Eliseo Moreno	H	Fort Bend	Robbery	09/1959			On death row
760	Kenneth Gentry	W	Denton	Robbery	01/1961	03/04/87		On death row
761	Curtis Johnson	B	Harris	Robbery	04/1954			On death row
762	Jewel McGee	B	Hardin	Robbery	09/1964			On death row
763	James Smith	B	Harris	Robbery	10/1952	06/26/90		On death row
764	Lester Bower	W	Grayson	Robbery	11/1947			On death row
765	Justin Cruz	H	Navarro	Robbery	04/1951			Acquitted 06/15/85
766	Jose Guzman	H	Navarro	Robbery	01/1963		05/15/87	
767	Joe Trevino	H	Tarrant	Rape	07/1962			On death row
768	Raymond Murtinez	H	Harris	Robbery	07/1946			On death row
769	Stephen McCoy	W	Harris	Rape	12/1948	05/24/89		
770	David Castillo	H	Hidalgo	Robbery	08/1964			On death row
771	Federico Macias	H	El Paso	Robbery	10/1952			On death row

APPENDIX B: DEATH ROW PRISONERS, 1923–1988 (continued)

Execu- tion No.	Name	Race[a]	County	Offense[b]	Date of Birth	Executed	Commuted	Status
772	Kenneth Ransom	B	Harris	Robbery	04/1963			On death row
773	David Spence	W	Brazos	Kidnapping	07/1956			On death row
774	Richard Andrade	H	Nueces	Rape	04/1961	12/18/86		
775	Jim Huffman	W	Lubbock	Rape	04/1961		04/04/88	
776	Mario Marquez	H	Bexar	Rape	08/1958			On death row
777	Karla Tucker (Fe)	W	Harris	Robbery	11/1959			On death row
778	Pedro Sosa	H	Atascosa	Robbery	12/1951			On death row
779	Daniel Garrett	W	Harris	Robbery	04/1946			On death row
780	Willie Modden	B	Angelina	Robbery	04/1948			On death row
781	Randy Mayo	W	Tom Green	Rape	04/1960			On death row
782	Thomas Dunn	B	Smith	Rape	08/1951		04/15/87	
783	Justin May	W	Brazoria	Robbery	04/1946	05/07/92		
784	Troy Kunkle	W	Nueces	Robbery	05/1966			On death row
785	James Beathard	W	Trinity	Robbery	02/1957			On death row
786	James Davis	B	Travis	Rape	02/1963			On death row
787	Bonnie Erwin	B	Harris	Kidnapping	03/1942			On death row
788	William Little	W	Liberty	Rape	01/1961			On death row
789	Jeffery Motley	B	Harris	Robbery	09/1965			On death row
790	Robert Purtell	W	Palo Pinto	Robbery	05/1959			On death row
791	Samuel Smith	W	Lubbock	Rape	06/1951		11/20/89	
792	Maneer Deeb	W	McLennan	Remuneration	04/1959			On death row
793	Antonio Barrientes	H	Cameron	Robbery	04/1955			On death row
794	Terry Sterling	B	Lamb	Rape	05/1959			On death row
795	Bobby Wills	B	Orange	Robbery	01/1967			On death row
796	Emile Duhamel	W	Cameron	Rape	03/1948			On death row
797	Anthony Westley	B	Harris	Robbery	07/1960			On death row

	Name	Race	County	Offense	Born			Status
798	David Lozada	H	Cameron	Rape	04/1965			On death row
799	Henry Lucas	W	Tom Green	Rape	08/1936			On death row
800	Gene Hathorn	W	Trinity	Burglary	09/1960			On death row
801	Jesus Romero	H	Cameron	Rape	02/1965	05/20/92		On death row
802	Charlie Livingston	B	Harris	Robbery	02/1962			On death row
803	Denton Crank	W	Harris	Robbery	10/1955			On death row
804	Ruben Cantu	H	Bexar	Robbery	12/1956			On death row
805	Norman Green	B	Bexar	Robbery	11/1960			On death row
806	Toby Williams	B	Panola	Kidnapping	08/1964			On death row
807	Rodolpho Hernandez	H	Comal	Robbery	11/1949			On death row
808	Raymond Kinnamon	W	Harris	Robbery	11/1941			On death row
809	Patrick Harvard	W	Walker	Policeman	10/1961			On death row
810	Betty Lou Beets (Fe)	W	Henderson	Remuneration	03/1937			On death row
811	David De Blanc	B	Liberty	Robbery	01/1956			On death row
812	Baby Ray Bennett	B	Newton	Burglary	05/1961			On death row
813	William Robinson	B	Harris	Rape	02/1958			On death row
814	Muriano Rosales	H	Harris	Multiple murder	07/1939			On death row
815	Richard Foster	W	Parker	Robbery	08/1952			On death row
816	Patrick Rogers	B	Collin	Robbery	01/1964			On death row
817	Ramone Mata	H	Madison	Prison guard	04/1949			On death row
818	Ronald Allridge	B	Tarrant	Robbery	09/1960			On death row
819	Robert Black	W	Brazos	Remuneration	01/1947	05/22/92		On death row
820	David Holland	W	Jefferson	Robbery	07/1935			On death row
821	Tommy Jackson	B	Williamson	Rape	11/1956			On death row
822	Robert Madden	W	Leon	Robbery	09/1963			On death row
823	James Knox	W	Galveston	Robbery	07/1951			On death row
824	Sam Cumbo	B	Brazos	Robbery	10/1960		12/18/89	On death row
825	David Gibbs	W	Montgomery	Burglary	03/1961			On death row
826	Randall Hafdahl	W	Randall	Policeman	06/1953			On death row
827	David Harris	W	Jefferson	Kidnapping	10/1960			On death row
828	Rogelio Hernandez	H	Zapata	Jailbreak	03/1950			On death row
829	Perry Keeton	B	Navarro	Robbery	12/1960		04/08/87	On death row

APPENDIX B: DEATH ROW PRISONERS, 1923–1988 (continued)

Execu- tion No.	Name	Race[a]	County	Offense[b]	Date of Birth	Executed	Commuted	Status
830	Jeff Emery	W	Brazos	Rape	06/1959			On death row
831	Troy Farris	W	Tarrant	Policeman	02/1962			On death row
832	Kavin Lincecum	B	Brazoria	Rape	06/1963			On death row
833	Jackie Upton	W	Lamar	Robbery	06/1949			On death row
834	Thomas Miller-El	B	Dallas	Robbery	04/1951			On death row
835	John Carter	B	Harris	Robbery	01/1967			On death row
836	John Matson	B	Harris	Rape	11/1967			On death row
837	Juan Soria	H	Tarrant	Robbery	05/1967			On death row
838	Gerald Mitchell	B	Harris	Robbery	07/1967			On death row
839	Johnny James	W	Chambers	Rape	01/1954			On death row
840	William Kitchens	W	Taylor	Rape	04/1963			On death row
841	Clifton Belyeu	W	McLennan	Robbery	06/1958			On death row
842	Lesley Gosch	W	Victoria	Kidnapping	07/1955			On death row
843	Ava Lauti	S	Harris	Robbery	06/1954			On death row
844	John Barefield	B	Harris	Rape	03/1964			On death row
845	Angel Rivera	H	El Paso	Arson	10/1957			On death row
846	Richard Drinkard	W	Harris	Burglary	07/1957			On death row
847	Irineo Montoya	H	Cameron	Robbery	06/1967			On death row
848	Freddie Webb	B	Nueces	Robbery	08/1960			On death row
849	Delbert Teague	W	Tarrant	Rape	11/1962			On death row
850	Dorsie Johnson	B	Scurry	Robbery	03/1967			On death row
851	Michael Riley	B	Wood	Robbery	05/1958			On death row
852	Jerome Butler	B	Harris	Robbery	04/1936	04/21/90		On death row
853	Benjamin Boyle	W	Potter	Rape	07/1943			On death row
854	John Cockrum	W	Bowie	Robbery	12/1958			On death row
855	Ernest Baldree	W	Navarro	Robbery	03/1942			On death row

856	Willie Washington	B	Harris	Robbery	01/1959		On death row
857	Vernon Satterwhite	B	Bexar	Kidnapping	09/1955		On death row
858	Carlos Ramirez	H	Harris	Rape	01/1963		On death row
859	Jose Moreno	H	Bexar	Kidnapping	12/1967		On death row
860	Robert Tennard	B	Harris	Robbery	11/1962		On death row
861	John Elliot	H	Travis	Rape	03/1960		On death row
862	David Long	W	Dallas	Robbery	07/1953		On death row
863	Banda Esquel	H	Hamilton	Rape	12/1963		On death row
864	James Gunter	W	Harris	Rape	02/1965		On death row
865	Karl Hammond	B	Bexar	Rape	07/1964		On death row
866	David Lewis	W	Angelina	Burglary	05/1965		On death row
867	James Richardson	B	Navarro	Robbery	09/1967		On death row
868	Nelson Mooney	W	Liberty	Robbery	08/1955		On death row
869	Thomas Kenneth	B	Dallas	Burglary	02/1961		On death row
870	James Allridge	B	Tarrant	Robbery	11/1962		On death row
871	Kenneth First	W	Lubbock	Multiple murder	01/1960		On death row
872	Jesse Jacobs	W	Walker	Remuneration	02/1950		On death row
873	Michael Norris	B	Harris	Multiple murder	Unknown	02/28/92	On death row
874	David Clark	W	Brazos	Multiple murder	03/1959		On death row
875	Jerry McFadden	W	Bell	Rape	03/1948		On death row
876	Bruce Jacobs	W	Dallas	Robbery	10/1946		On death row
877	Andre Lewis	B	Dallas	Robbery	09/1966		On death row
878	Martin Draughon	W	Harris	Robbery	08/1963		On death row
879	Alvin Goodwin	W	Montgomery	Robbery	12/1963		On death row
880	Carl Napier	W	Harris	Robbery	10/1945		On death row
881	Ernest Willis	W	Pecos	Arson	09/1945		On death row
882	Richard Jones	W	Tarrant	Kidnapping	04/1960		On death row
883	Tony Rice	W	Houston	Remuneration	01/1958		Acquitted 04/12/91
884	Terry Washington	B	Brazos	Robbery	09/1963		On death row
885	Jonathan Nobles	W	Travis	Burglary	08/1961		On death row
886	Brian Roberson	B	Dallas	Burglary	10/1963		On death row
887	Clifford Boggess	W	Clay	Robbery	06/1965		On death row

APPENDIX B: DEATH ROW PRISONERS, 1923–1988 (continued)

Execution No.	Name	Race^a	County^c	Offense^b	Date of Birth	Executed	Commuted	Status
888	Alvin Crane	W	Denton	Murder	05/1958			On death row
889	Roger McGowen	B	Harris	Robbery	12/1963			On death row
890	Michael Richards	B	Harris	Rape	08/1959			On death row
891	Charles Boyd	B	Dallas	Burglary	08/1959			On death row
892	David Stroker	W	Hale	Robbery	01/1959			On death row
893	Ricky Blackmon	W	Shelby	Burglary	11/1957			On death row
894	Thomas Eliason	W	Tarrant	Burglary	07/1967			On death row
895	Jesse Turner	B	Harris	Robbery	06/1960			On death row
896	Mark Fronkiewicz	W	Limestone	Remuneration	07/1958			On death row
897	James Wilkens	W	Smith	Burglary	07/1961			On death row
898	Eddie Johnson	B	Aransas	Kidnapping	07/1952			On death row
899	Richard Brimage	W	Kleberg	Kidnapping	12/1955			On death row
900	Monty Delk	W	Anderson	Robbery	02/1967			On death row
901	Kenneth Harris	B	Harris	Rape	08/1962			On death row
902	Orien Joiner	W	Lubbock	Rape	10/1949			On death row
903	Michael McBride	W	Lubbock	Multiple murder	01/1962			On death row
904	Hai Hai Vuong	V	Jefferson	Multiple murder	09/1955			On death row
905	James Earhart	W	Lee	Kidnapping	04/1943			On death row
906	Ted Cole	W	Tom Green	Robbery	07/1956			On death row
907	Alberto Valdez	H	Nueces	Policeman	08/1955			On death row
908	Jose Delacruz	H	Nueces	Robbery	04/1968			On death row
909	Emanual Kemp	B	Tarrant	Rape	09/1965			On death row
910	Syed Rabbani	W	Harris	Robbery	06/1965			On death row

911	Gary Johnson	W	Walker	Robbery	10/1950	On death row
912	Cornelius Goss	B	Dallas	Burglary	05/1961	On death row
913	Marlin Nelson	W	Harris	Robbery	07/1968	On death row
914	Earl Behringer	W	Tarrant	Robbery	01/1964	On death row
915	Damon Richardson	B	Taylor	Multiple murder	12/1963	On death row
916	Richard Beavers	W	Harris	Rape	12/1955	On death row
917	Michael Lockhart	W	Bexar	Policeman	09/1960	On death row
918	Anthony Cook	W	Milam	Robbery	01/1959	On death row
919	Michael Jones	B	Jefferson	Burglary	08/1949	On death row
920	Peter Miniel	H	Harris	Robbery	06/1962	On death row
921	James Clayton	B	Taylor	Robbery	11/1966	On death row
922	Frances Newton (Fe)	B	Harris	Multiple murder	04/1965	On death row
923	Leopoldo Narvaiz	H	Bexar	Multiple murder	03/1968	On death row
924	Domingo Cantu	H	Dallas	Rape	06/1968	On death row
925	Steven Butler	B	Harris	Rape	04/1962	On death row
926	Bernard Amos	B	Dallas	Burglary	12/1961	On death row
927	Vincent Cooks	B	Dallas	Robbery	07/1964	On death row
928	Warren Rivers	B	Harris	Rape	03/1967	On death row

On death row at Furman but not given a death row number

995	Larry Twine	B	McLennan	Murder	03/1950	01/16/73
996	James Farris	W	Grayson	Murder	01/1958	08/21/73
997	Michael Jewell	W	Hansford	Murder	06/1947	05/14/73
998	Michael Paprskar	W	Tarrant	Murder	07/1941	08/18/72

APPENDIX C

POST-1974 DEPARTMENT OF CORRECTIONS PROCEDURES FOR THE EXECUTION OF DEATH-SENTENCED INMATES
■ ■ ■

The following procedures shall be followed when an inmate sentenced to death is to be executed:

I. Two weeks prior to date of execution:
    Huntsville Unit Warden shall request the Ellis I Unit Warden to gather the following information from the inmate:

    A. Witnesses to Execution: Condemned inmate shall be informed that five (5) witnesses will be authorized to witness the execution. These witnesses must be on their approved computerized data processing visitors list.
        This list may be changed at the inmate's request. This request must be submitted at least seven (7) days prior to date of execution in order to get the changes processed.

    B. Disposition of Personal Property: Receive instructions from condemned inmate as to disposition of property. If no authorization is given, the elected next of kin will have to file through small claims court to obtain the property.

    C. Inmate Trust Fund: Request that the inmate make out a withdrawal slip if the condemned inmate has any money in the Inmate Trust Fund. This withdrawal slip will be made payable to the elected next of kin. If no authorization is given, the elected next of kin will have to file a claim through the small claims court to obtain the money.

II.   One week prior to the execution:
        The Huntsville Unit Warden shall complete the following items:
        A. Department of Public Safety—Notify the DPS Sergeant at the
            Huntsville station to have the DPS riot team in Huntsville the
            night of the execution. Team will be picked up by bus at 5:00
            p.m. from the DPS station in Huntsville.
        B. Walker County Sheriff—Notify the Walker County Sheriff of
            pending execution and to have officers on standby.
        C. Huntsville Police Department—A request from the Huntsville Po-
            lice Chief for five (5) mobile units to block designated streets dur-
            ing the execution shall be made.
        D. Texas Rangers—Company A Captain shall be contacted and asked
            to bring (5) to seven (7) of his men for the execution.
        E. Internal Affairs—shall be contacted to provide (3) or four (4) men
            to assist during the execution.
        F. Training Department—Notify the Assistant Director for Security
            and Training to provide training staff and officer trainees for se-
            curity during the execution.
        G. Warden, Goree Unit—To provide three (3) to four (4) officers in
            the rank of Sergeant and above to assist for the execution.
        H. Warden, Diagnostic Unit—To provide three (3) to four (4) offi-
            cers in the ranks of Sergeant and above to assist for the execution
            and have two (2) buses with drivers available.
        I. Justice of the Peace, Precinct III—Notified and advised to be pre-
            pared to hold an inquest. A history of the condemned inmate will
            be given to the Justice of Peace so that necessary paperwork can
            be completed.
        J. Huntsville Unit Warden and Ellis I Unit Warden shall establish
            the transfer procedures of the condemned inmate. The actual time
            that the condemned inmate will be transferred shall be restricted
            to the knowledge of the two (2) Wardens.
        K. There will be two (2) practice sessions on the Huntsville Unit with
            the total execution team.

III.   Three days prior to the execution:
        A. Preliminary contact shall be made with the Attorney General's of-
            fice and the Governor's office in Austin to establish telephone con-
            tact times, telephone numbers, and verification of the Personnel
            that the Warden's office will be in contact with the night of the
            execution.
        B. At the time the funeral home is contacted, if the Huntsville Unit
            has knowledge of the disposition of the body (who will claim the

body) this information will be related to the funeral home. If the family has requested that TDC bury the inmate in the Joe Byrd Cemetery or if they plan to claim the body at the funeral home, this information is given to the funeral home by the Huntsville Unit Warden. If the family claims the body the only financial obligation that TDC has is the transporting of the body to the Harris County Morgue and to pay for the autopsy; all other expenses incurred will be responsibility of the family.

C. A TDC physician will be advised to be on stand-by for immediate call upon completion of the lethal injections to evaluate and pronounce the condemned inmate's death time and verify that the inmate is dead. The physician will enter his remarks in the inmate's medical file. This will be the only input into the execution that a physical [sic] will have.

IV. Two days prior to the execution:

A. The injection team will assume the responsibility of preparing the necessary paperwork for procuring the lethal injection dosage on the day before the execution. This team will also assume the responsibility of getting the proper forms together for the Director's signature to obtain the lethal injection substance in accordance with the FDA regulations. The injection team commander will also be responsible for seeing that all necessary equipment is accounted for in the injection chamber.

B. The Huntsville Funeral Home will be contacted the afternoon prior to the execution and will be instructed to be at the Huntsville Unit east gate at ten minutes until twelve to be escorted to the rear of the death chamber to await the end of the execution and remove the body and transport it to the Harris County Morgue.

V. Day prior to execution:

A. Upon the arrival of the inmate at the Huntsville Unit, an execution log book will be energized and documented. Times and remarks will be entered on all the inmate's activities throughout his stay in the death chamber of the Huntsville Unit.

B. The inmate will enter the death house; he will be placed in the holding cell; his restraints will be removed and he will be strip searched and his property inventoried by the two officers that have been assigned to stay with him in the death house. When this shift changes, these two officers will be relieved by two officers from the next shift.

C. His clothing size will be obtained from him. The clothes that he will be executed in will be procured.

D. After his property has been inventoried, he will be advised that he may have in his cell any of his property that he desires as long as it is not considered contraband.

E. The Huntsville Unit Chaplain will visit the inmate shortly after his arrival to advise him that he will be visiting him thoughout his stay at the Huntsville Unit and making the inmate aware that he will be available to help him with his needs throughout his stay in the Huntsville Unit.

F. At approximately 10:00 a.m. the Food Service Manager shall visit with the condemned inmate and advise him of the menu for the noon meal. He will also ask him for his last meal request which will consist of the preparation of anything within reason that is stocked in the Food Service Department.

G. At approximately 10:30 a.m. the inmate will be fingerprinted to re-verify his identity.

H. There will be no media visits allowed for the condemned inmate throughout his stay at the Huntsville Unit.

I. The inmate may receive visits from his family or friends who are on his approved visitors computer list. In the event the inmate has a visitor, he will be removed from his holding cell and placed in the visitors cell in the death chamber. The visitor(s) will be placed in front of the cell with the mesh screen. No physical contact will be allowed.

J. He may be visited by TDC Chaplains, ministers, family members and friends who are on his approved list. All visitors will be approved by the Warden with the exception of the chaplain who visits. All visits will be terminated by 6:00 p.m. on the day immediately prior to the execution.

K. The Warden's office will be responsible for continuously advising the Assistant Director of Public Relations of any and all activities of the inmate that have any merit so that he may evaluate the information and release it to the media.

L. The last meal will be served between 6:30 and 7:30 p.m. Prior to midnight the inmate will shower and dress in his execution clothes.

M. The following security measures will be established at approximately 5:00 p.m.:

  1. A police barricade ribbon will be stretched from the south door of the Administration Building to the Huntsville Unit to allow

a walkway for TDC Personnel. The media will not be allowed in this area. They will be contained in an area from the east side of the ribboned crossway walk to the rodeo ticket office Public Relations area. Upon completion of the execution and when five media personnel witnesses exit and arrive at the landing above the steps in the Administration Building, the rest of the step area as the ribbon is removed [sic].

2. The five Huntsville Police Department Mobile Units block designated streets in the immediate Huntsville Unit perimeter. One TDC officer with a walkie-talkie radio will be stationed with each unit.

3. The DPS Riot Team will be picked up at the Huntsville DPS station and transported by bus to the Diagnostic Unit for their evening meal and then to the TDC Administration Building. This team will remain in the Conference Room until the execution is completed.

4. Security Officers and Training Academy Staff will be placed around the areas of the police ribbon barricades which encircle the Administration Building and walkway from the south door of the Administration Building to the Huntsville Unit.

5. Internal Affairs Personnel will assist in checking credentials of those requesting to park around the Administration Building and to observe the crowd.

VI. Execution:

A. The inmate will be removed from his cell at 12:01 a.m. after the Director has given the warden permission to proceed with the execution. The inmate will be strapped to the gurney and catheters placed in each arm. The saline solution will begin flowing in each arm. When the saline solution has begun it's flow, the media representatives (Attachment A) who will witness the execution as well as the five family or friends he has selected as witnesses and those outlined in the statute who are allowed to witness the execution, will be summoned and escorted to the death chamber viewing room. Prior to the visitors (those other than TDC Personnel) entering the death chamber viewing room, they will be I.D.'d and shook down. When the last visitor has entered the death chamber viewing room and the door has been closed, the Huntsville Unit Warden will proceed after being given a verbal order by the Director. The Warden will then ask the condemned inmate for his last statement. If the inmate has a statement, he is allowed to make it. The Warden then states, "We are ready."

B. At this time, the designee(s) of the Directors, shall begin the flow of substance(s) necessary to cause death. This individual(s) shall be visually separated from the execution chamber by a wall and locked door, and shall not be identified.

C. A TDC physician shall be summoned and ascertain that the inmate is dead, and then pronounce his death, but shall have no further function in the execution. This information will be recorded in the inmate's medical file.

D. After the inmate is pronounced dead, he shall be immediately removed from the death chamber, taken to an awaiting ambulance, and delivered to the Harris County Morgue

E. When the inmate has been pronounced dead, the Warden then orders the witnesses to be escorted from the death chamber to the outside of the compound.

F. The inmate's property is immediately taken to the Warden's office and his family or the person he has designated to pick up his property is allowed to pick up his property after signing a release for it. If the family or designee wishes to pick up the property at a later date, those arrangements are made with Warden's office at that time.

G. During the execution procedures, one Assistant Warden mans the telephone to the Attorney General's office in Austin and another Assistant Warden mans the telephone to the Governor's office in Austin. Constant voice-communication is established and continued throughout and after the execution.

H. An accounting of timed activities starting with the time the inmate is removed from the holding cell is maintained and a copy is given to the Assistant Director of Public Relations at the end of the execution so that he may release this information to the news media. This same information is related to the Governor's office and the Attorney General's office by the two Assistant Wardens.

VII. Any request for Security Personnel shall be submitted to the Assistant Director for Security and Training at least seven days prior to an execution by the Huntsville Warden.

EXECUTION PROCEDURES AND THE MEDIA

Media witnesses are persons provided for in Vernon's Ann. C.C.P., Article 43.20.

Media—One Texas bureau representative designated by the Associated Press, one Texas bureau representative designated by the United Press

International, one representative of the Huntsville Item newspaper, and one representative each from established separate rosters of Texas print and broadcast media will be admitted to the execution chamber as witnesses, provided those designated agree to act as pool reporters for the remainder of the media present and to meet with all media representatives present immediately subsequent to the execution. No recording or transmitting devices, either audio or video, shall be permitted either in the unit or the execution chamber.

NOTES

■ ■ ■

1. From Lynchings to Electrocutions

1. Justice Brennan concurring in *Furman v. Georgia*, p. 290.

2. Statement of prosecutor reported in "Condemned Negro Fails to Save Life on a Technicality," *Austin American-Statesman*, February 8, 1924, p. 1.

3. See, for example, Steve J. Martin and Sheldon Ekland-Olson, *Texas Prisons: The Walls Came Tumbling Down*; Ben M. Crouch and James W. Marquart, *An Appeal to Justice: Litigated Reform of Texas Prisons*.

4. Arthur Raper, *The Tragedy of Lynching*, p. 10.

5. See, for example, George C. Wright, *Racial Violence in Kentucky, 1865–1940*, especially Chapters 7 and 8; and George C. Wright, "Executions of Afro-Americans in Kentucky, 1870–1940," *Georgia Journal of Southern Legal History* 1 (1991): 321–355.

6. See, for example, the Governor's Records for this time period housed in the Texas State Archives. The letters and speeches of James Webb Throckmorton are illustrative.

7. See, for example, Claude Elliott, "The Freedmen's Bureau in Texas," *Southwestern Historical Quarterly* 61 (1952): 1–24; Barry Crouch, "A Spirit of Lawlessness," *Journal of Social History* 18 (1984): 217–232; James Smallwood, "Perpetuation of Caste: Black Agriculture Workers in Texas," *Mid-America* 61 (1979): 5–23, Gregg Cantrell, "Racial Violence and Reconstruction Politics in Texas, 1867–1868," *Southwestern Historical Quarterly* 93 (1990): 331–355; and Eric Foner's comprehensive *Reconstruction, 1863–1877*.

8. See Crouch, "A Spirit of Lawlessness."

9. See D. W. Meinig, *Imperial Texas: An Interpretive Essay in Cultural Geography*; Terry Jordan, "A Century and a Half of Ethnic Change in Texas, 1836–1986," *Southwestern Historical Quarterly* 89 (1986): 385–422.

10. Cited in Crouch, "A Spirit of Lawlessness," p. 220, note 6.

11. Crouch, "A Spirit of Lawlessness."

12. These rates were constructed by dividing the total number of violent incidents compiled by Crouch ("A Spirit of Lawlessness," p. 220) by the respective population figures for 1870. The victimization rates for "killings" alone were 196.9 for white-offender/black-victim incidents and 2.7 for black-offender/white-victim incidents.

13. Cantrell, "Racial Violence."

14. Hon. Richard Coke, "The Killing of Joseph Hoffman, Washington County, Texas," speech of Senator Coke in the United States Senate, September 12, 1888 (Barker History Archives at the Center for American History, University of Texas at Austin).

15. See, C. L. Sonnichsen, *Ten Texas Feuds*; Richard Maxwell Brown, *Strain of Violence: Historical Studies of American Violence and Vigilantism*; W. Eugene Hollon, *Frontier Violence, Another Look*; Thomas J. Dimsdale, *The Vigilantes of Montana*; Henry Cabot Lodge, "Lynch Law and Unrestricted Immigration," *North American Review* 152 (1891): 602–612.

16. See Raper, *The Tragedy of Lynching*.

17. Ibid.

18. See Bruce A. Glasrud, "Enforcing White Supremacy in Texas, 1900–1910," *Red River Historical Review* 4 (1979): 65–74.

19. NAACP, *Thirty Years of Lynching in the United States: 1889–1918*, p. 98.

20. See, for example, *San Antonio Daily Express*, March 13, 1901; *Dallas Morning News*, May 22, 1902.

21. See Mark Jetton, "The NAACP's Campaign Against Lynching in Texas," Honors thesis in sociology, University of Texas at Austin, 1992, for more detailed discussion.

22. Quoted in Mary White Ovington, *The Walls Came Tumbling Down*, p. 100.

23. "'The Call'": A Lincoln Emancipation Conference," reprinted in Minnie Finch, *The NAACP: Its Fight for Justice*, p. 252.

24. See Glasrud, "Enforcing White Supremacy," p. 67.

25. Quoted in James M. SoRelle, "The 'Waco Horror': The Lynching of Jessie Washington," *Southwestern Historical Quarterly*, 86 (1983): 519.

26. Jessie Daniel Ames, *The Changing Character of Lynching*. For example, subscriptions to the *Crisis* had risen from about 1,000 in 1910 to approximately 100,000 by the end of the decade (see Finch, *The NAACP*, p. 49).

27. A number of detailed accounts of the Longview riot and the Red Summer of 1919 are available. See, for example, Arthur Waskow, *From Race Riot to Sit-in*, and Victoria K. Seligman, "The Worst of Times: Racial Violence in Longview, Texas, 1902–1919." In addition, the *Dallas Morning News* during that time period is a rich source of information.

28. See Papers of the NAACP, Part 7: The Anti-lynching Campaign, 1912–1955, Series A: Investigative Files, 1912–1953, Reel 18. For more detailed discussion of this and other correspondence, see Jetton, "The NAACP's Campaign," pp. 23–26.

29. Interview of Judge David J. Pickle by Walter Long, October 20, 1961. Transcript obtained from the Austin History Center.

30. Ovington, *The Walls Came Tumbling Down*.

31. Jacquelyn Dowd Hall, *Revolt against Chivalry: Jessie Daniel Ames and the Women's Campaign against Lynching*.

32. See Raper, *The Tragedy of Lynching*; Finch, *The NAACP*.

33. However, in Texas, the *Houston Post* weighed in on the side of federal antilynching legislation, noting that "No state which has a bloody record of mob law staining its escutcheon will have any right to protest." Cited in the *Crisis*, May 1919, p. 30.

34. The most useful source of information on these May 1922 events is the *Waco Times Herald*, Barker Archives at the Center for American History, University of Texas at Austin. Research on the episodic nature of such economic crises may be a useful supplement to the argument of E. M. Beck and S. E. Tolnay, "The Killing Fields of the Deep South," *American Sociological Review* 55 (1990): 526-539.

35. H. Crow, "A Political History of the Texas Penal System—1829-1951," Ph.D. dissertation, University of Texas at Austin, 1964, p. 4.

36. H. P. N. Gammel, *Laws of Texas*, vol. 1, *1822-1897*, pp. 1247-1254.

37. Watt M. Espy and John Ortiz Smykla, *Executions in the United States, 1608-1991: The Espy File*. Espy continues to uncover additional executions. For updates and other information, one can correspond with Watt Espy at P.O. Drawer 277, 100 East Main Street, Headland, AL 36345.

38. See Raper, *The Tragedy of Lynching*.

39. William J. Bowers, with G. L. Pierce and J. McDevitt, *Legal Homicide: Death as Punishment in America, 1864-1982*, pp. 45-58.

40. Hugo Adam Bedau, *The Death Penalty in America*; Richard Moran, "Executing a Businessman's Strategy," paper presented at American Society of Criminology Meetings, Reno, Nev., November 1989.

41. *In re Kemmler*, 136 U.S. 436 (1890).

42. Bowers, *Legal Homicide*.

43. See R. Neustadler, "The 'Deadly Current': The Death Penalty in the Industrial Age," *Journal of American Culture* 12 (1989): 79-87.

44. State of Texas, Senate, *Journal*, 38th Legislature, 2d Called Session, 1923, pp. 221-223.

45. "Hangman's Rope to Be Used to Tow Autos," *San Antonio Express*, February 9, 1924.

46. "Ex-Warden Sleeps as Five Negroes Die," *Dallas Morning News*, February 8, 1924.

47. "Johnson County Man New Prison Warden," *Austin American-Statesman*, February 6, 1924.

48. Ames, *The Changing Character of Lynching*.

49. There is some indication that this southern concentration may be diminishing, in that early 1992 saw four nonsouthern states—Delaware, Wyoming, Arizona, and California—join the list of states that have carried out executions.

50. See Orlando Patterson, *Slavery and Social Death: A Comparative Study*. The virtually universal link between social excommunication and slavery is developed in detail. For example, in the twenty-fifth chapter of Leviticus, God is found telling Moses not to enslave or sell his own brethren, "but of the *children of the strangers* that do sojourn among you, of them may ye buy, and of their families that are with you, which they have begotten in your land; and they may be your possession" (emphasis added).

51. See Joseph Campbell, *The Power of Myth*, p. 22. "Brotherhood in most of the myths I know of is confined to a bounded community. In bounded communities aggression is projected outward. For example, the Ten Commandments say, 'Thou shalt

not kill.' Then the next chapter says, 'Go into Canaan and kill everybody in it.' This is a bounded field. The myths of participation . . . pertain only to the in-group, and the out-group is totally other. This is the sense of the word 'gentile'—the person is not of the same order."

52. See William A. Gamson, Bruce Fireman, and Steven Rytina, *Encounters with Unjust Authority.*

53. Ibid., p. 14

54. Ibid., p. 5.

55. See, for example, Hall, *Revolt against Chivalry.*

56. See Roy Wilkins, "Nazi Plan for Negroes Copies Southern U.S.A.," *Crisis* 48 (1941): 71; Jeffrey Lee Olbrich, "American Civil Rights and Nazi Germany: An Analysis Using Resource Mobilization Theory," M.A. thesis, University of Texas at Austin, 1990.

2. The Initial "Harvest of Death": 1924–1972

1. Death warrant for Dwight Beard (#179), executed on June 4, 1937.

2. Melvin Johnson's attorney appealed to the Court of Criminal Appeals for reversal of his death sentence on the grounds that verdict was that Johnson should "hang by the neck" until dead. The court, however, let the death sentence stand because "the right to determine the method of execution is not within the scope of the jury's authority. The method of execution is fixed by law and any change in the mode is exclusively within the power of the legislature." See "Condemned Negro," *Austin American-Statesman,* February 8, 1924, p. 1.

3. "Midnight Appeal Causes Pause in Harvest of Death," *Austin American-Statesman,* February 7, 1924.

4. See Don Reid, *Eyewitness: I Saw 189 Men Die in the Electric Chair,* p. 109.

5. The authors gratefully acknowledge the cooperation of Gloria Duncan, deputy clerk of Titus County, who provided the trial records from Gray's murder case.

6. The six counties with the largest population in Texas between 1923 and 1972 were (and still are): Bexar (San Antonio), Dallas, El Paso, Harris (Houston), Tarrant (Fort Worth), and Travis (Austin). Offenders coming from these counties were categorized as urban. Offenders coming from all other counties regardless of size were considered non-urban.

7. See Richard Lempert, "Capital Punishment in the '80s: Reflections on the Symposium," *Journal of Criminal Law and Criminology* 74 (1983): 1101–1114.

8. See Crow, "A Political History of the Texas Penal System."

9. These files, still maintained in the Texas Department of Corrections Classification Office, were used throughout the analysis in this and subsequent chapters.

10. Reid, *Eyewitness,* pp. 22–25.

3. Rape, Race, and a "Peculiar Chivalry"

1. From the file of Bob White (#220), murdered by the victim's husband during trial in June, 1941.

2. See T. Sellin, *The Penalty of Death,* pp. 13–40; Bedau, *The Death Penalty in America,* pp. 58–61.

3. See, for example, Winthrop D. Jordan, *White over Black: American Attitudes toward the Negro, 1550–1812,* especially pp. 24–40.

4. Jordan (*White over Black,* p. 150) has reviewed much of the relevant literature, citing the following characterization from the West Indies:

Next comes a warmer race, from sable sprung,
To love each thought, to lust each nerve is strung;
The Samboe dark, and the Mullattoe brown,
The Mestize fair, the well-limb'd Quadroon,
And jetty Afric, from no spurious sire,
Warm as her soil, and as her sun—on fire.
These sooty dames, well vers'd in Venus' school,
Make love an art, and boast they kiss by rule.
(From "Jamaica, a poem, in three parts . . ." [London, 1777])

5. See, for example, Herbert Aptheker, *American Negro Slave Revolts.*

6. See Appendix A in Bowers, *Legal Homicide.* See also U.S. Bureau of Justice Statistics, Capital Punishment—1977, National Prisoner Statistics, p. 14.

7. See Bowers, *Legal Homicide,* Appendix A.

8. See undated typescript by Jessie Daniel Ames, cited in Hall, *Revolt against Chivalry.*

9. W. J. Cash, *The Mind of the South,* pp. 118–119.

10. See Bowers, *Legal Homicide,* p. 58.

11. See, for example, Beck and Tolnay, "The Killing Fields of the Deep South," pp. 526–539.

12. Elmer Johnson, "Selective Factors in Capital Punishment," *Social Forces* 36 (1956): 165–169.

13. Donald Partington, "The Incidence of the Death Penalty for Rape in Virginia," *Washington and Lee Law Review* 22 (1965): 43–75; Rupert Koeninger, "Capital Punishment in Texas, 1924–1968," *Crime and Delinquency* 15 (1969): 132–141; Marvin E. Wolfgang and Marc Riedel, "Rape, Race, and the Death Penalty in Georgia," *American Journal of Orthopsychiatry* 45 (1975): 658–668.

14. See John Hagan, "Extra-legal Attributes and Criminal Sentencing," *Law and Society Review* 8 (Spring 1974): 357–383; Gary Kleck, "Racial Discrimination in Criminal Sentencing: A Critical Evaluation of the Evidence with Additional Evidence on the Death Penalty," *American Sociological Review* 46 (December 1981): 783–805.

15. See also Robert J. Hunter, "The Death-Sentencing of Rapists in Texas, 1942–1971," master's thesis, Sam Houston State University, 1990.

16. For example, Myrdal's *An American Dilemma* was one of a series of studies referred to in *Brown v. Board of Education.* Marvin E. Wolfgang and his colleagues (see Wolfgang, A. Kelly, and H. Nolde, "Comparison of the Executed and the Commuted among Admissions to Death Row," *Journal of Criminal Law, Criminology, and Police Science* 53 (1962): 301–311; and Wolfgang and Riedel, "Rape, Race, and the Death Penalty in Georgia," pp. 658–668) compiled similarly influential information in the *Furman* case. For a discussion of some of the dilemmas the social scientist faced in this arena of advocacy, see Wolfgang, "The Social Scientist in Court," *The Journal of Criminal Law and Criminology* 65 (1974): 239–247.

17. *Richardson v. State,* 257 S.W. 2d 308 (1953).

18. "Negro Bob White Killed in Courtroom Here Tuesday," *Conroe Courier*, June 12, 1941. This same town, just north of Houston, would once again move center stage for its death-sentencing practices in the 1980s and 1990s. See Nick Davies, *White Lies: Rape, Murder, and Justice Texas Style*; Alan Sembera, "Brandley Urges Social Change," *Conroe Courier*, April 5, 1990.

19. "District Attorney McClain Receives Threatening Letter," *Conroe Courier*, June 19, 1941.

4. Capital Murder and Midnight Appeals

1. Taken from Henry Meyer's social summary, compiled on his admission to death row.
2. Details taken from Matura's social summary.
3. From the psychologist's report in Mouton's file.
4. Taken from Henderson's social summary.
5. From a letter seeking clemency for Leo Lera (#251).
6. See William Wilbanks, *The Myth of a Racist Criminal Justice System*.
7. Charles Mangum, *The Illegal Status of the Negro*.
8. Guy Johnson, "The Negro and Crime," *Annals of the American Academy of Political and Social Science* 217 (1941): 93–104.
9. Harold Garfinkel, "Research Note on Inter- and Intra-racial Homicide," *Social Forces* (1949): 369–381.
10. Elmer Johnson, "Selective Factors in Capital Punishment," pp. 165–169.
11. Marvin E. Wolfgang, *Patterns of Criminal Homicide*, p. 61.
12. Robert Bensing and Oliver Schroeder, *Homicide in the Urban Community*, p. 56.
13. Henry Bullock, "Significance of the Racial Factor in the Length of Prison Sentences," *Journal of Criminal Law, Criminology, and Police Science* 52 (1961): 411–416; Koeninger, "Capital Punishment in Texas," pp. 62–71.
14. Franklin Williams, "The Death Penalty and the Negro," *Crisis* 67 (1960): 503.
15. Charles Judson et al., "A Study of the California Jury in First-Degree Murder Cases," *Stanford Law Review* 21 (1967): 1297.
16. Kenneth Murchison and Arthur Schwab, "Capital Punishment in Virginia," *Virginia Law Review* 58 (1972): 97–142.
17. R. Farrell and V. Swigert, "Legal Disposition of Inter-group and Intra-group Homicides," *Sociological Quarterly* 12 (1978): 437–454.
18. Kleck, "Racial Discrimination in Criminal Sentencing," p. 788.
19. In the latter instance, we have restricted our analysis to 1942–1971 because detailed social summaries on the control group (murderers sentenced to prison) did not appear until 1942.
20. Bowers, *Legal Homicide*.
21. See Chapter 1 and T. R. Fehrenbach, *Lone Star: A History of Texas and the Texans*; Norman D. Brown, *Hood, Bonnet, and Little Brown Jug: Texas Politics, 1921–1928*.
22. For this purpose logit analysis (see D. Hosmer and S. Lemeshow, *Applied Logistic Regression*) was chosen.
23. These seven variables included whether an additional felony was involved; whether the offender had a prior prison record; whether codefendants were involved;

whether the case involved an offender who was a stranger to the victim; whether a white offender was involved, whether a white victim was involved, and whether a female victim was involved.

24. Bedau, *The Death Penalty in America*, pp. 18–21.

5. Spared the Chair and Sentenced to Life

1. *Texas Penal Code*, Title VII, Chapter V, Article 811, 1857.

2. Personal letter in the inmate file, seeking clemency, dated January 5, 1938. The letter writer's son, Albert Lee Hemphill (#188), was executed January 14, 1938.

3. Elkan Abramowitz and David Paget, "Executive Clemency in Capital Cases," *New York University Law Review* 39 (1964): 136–192; Deborah Leavy, "A Matter of Life and Death: Due Process Protection in Capital Clemency Proceedings," *Yale Law Review* 90 (1981): 889–911; Daniel T. Kobil, "The Quality of Mercy Strained: Wresting the Pardoning Power of the King," *Texas Law Review* 69 (1991): 569–641; Paul Cobb, "Reviving Mercy in the Structure of Capital Punishment," *Yale Law Journal* 99 (1989): 389–409; Solie Ringold, "The Dynamics of Executive Clemency," *American Bar Association Journal* 52 (1966): 240–243; Winthrop Rockefeller, "Executive Clemency and the Death Penalty," *Catholic University Law Review* 21 (1971): 94–102; Michael DiSalle, "Comments on Capital Punishment and Clemency," *Ohio State Law Journal* 25 (1964): 71–83. Clemency is a general term, used to cover at least four distinct acts of interest here: pardon, which provides sweeping forgiveness, generally to individual offenders; amnesty, often provided to categories of offenders, which may not forgive as much as a pardon, but which does forget in the sense that the punishment is foregone; commutation, which substitutes a lesser punishment for a more severe one; and reprieve, which provides only a temporary postponement of the punishment. Our major focus on this chapter is on commutations.

4. See Leon Radzinowicz and Roger Hood, *A History of English Criminal Law*; and Robert Hughes, *The Fatal Shore*.

5. See note 1 above.

6. *Texas Penal Code*, Title VII, Chapter V, Article 811, 1857.

7. *Texas Revised Criminal Statutes* (Vernon 1920, 1925).

8. With some variation on the themes, these events were echoed in other states at other times. For example, J. C. Walton, then Governor of Oklahoma, was impeached and removed from office in 1923. More recently, in the early 1980s, Governor Ray Blanton's administration in Tennessee found itself charged with widespread sale of pardons and commutations. Governor Edmund (Pat) Brown presents a more delicate political exchange in his book (with D. Adler) *Public Justice, Private Mercy*, where he recalls deciding against commuting a death sentence in exchange for support from a swing-vote legislator on an impending piece of legislation improving the lot of migrant workers (Kobil, "The Quality of Mercy Strained," p. 607).

9. *Texas Revised Criminal Statutes* (Vernon 1936).

10. Annual Report of the Texas Prison Board of the Texas Prison System, 1936. Filed in Texas State Archives.

11. We gratefully acknowledge the work of David Wagner for his extensive assistance in collecting much of the data used in this chapter. See David E. Wagner, "A

Commutation Study of Ex-Capital Offenders in Texas from 1924–1971," master's thesis, Sam Houston State University, 1988.

12. See Kobil, "The Quality of Mercy Strained," pp. 610–611.

13. *Furman v. Georgia*, 408 U.S. 238 (1972).

14. See Marvin E. Wolfgang, "Murder, the Pardon Board, and Recommendations by Judges and District Attorneys," *Journal of Criminal Law, Criminology, and Police Science* 50 (1959): 338–346. See also Hugo Adam Bedau, "Capital Punishment in Oregon: 1903–1964," *Oregon Law Review* 45 (1965):1–39; Bedau, "Post-Conviction Remedies in California Death Penalty Cases," *Stanford Law Review* 11 (1958): 94–135; Margaret Vandiver, "Race, Clemency, and Executions in Florida, 1924–1966," master's thesis, Florida State University, 1983; Lloyd Braithwaite, "Executive Clemency in California: A Case Study Interpretation of Criminal Responsibility," *Issues in Criminology* 1 (1965): 77–107.

15. Materials collected from Emma Oliver's file.

16. Hugo Adam Bedau and Michael L. Radelet, "Miscarriages of Justice in Potentially Capital Cases," *Stanford Law Review* 40, no. 1 (1987): 21–179.

17. Ibid., pp. 26, 38.

18. Davies, *White Lies*.

19. From *Charles v. State* (No. 12411), 16 S.W. 2d (1929), pp. 122–123.

20. Bedau and Radelet, "Miscarriages of Justice," p. 149.

21. See for example, Martin Shubik, ed., *Game Theory and Related Approaches to Social Behavior: Selections*; Robert Axelrod, *The Evolution of Cooperation*; William Poundstone, *Prisoner's Dilemma*.

22. From "The Mystery of Marie Rogêt," cited in Poundstone, *Prisoner's Dilemma*, p. 124.

23. See Fernando Rodriguez, "Patterns of Homicide in Texas: A Descriptive Analysis of Racial/Ethnic Involvement by Crime-Specific Categories", Ph.D. dissertation, University of Texas at Austin, May 1990.

24. See Donald Black, ed. *Toward a General Theory of Social Control*, vol. 1, *Fundamentals*; Allan V. Horwitz, *The Logic of Social Control*.

25. While this thesis is certainly a possibility, initial analysis of a sampling of public opinion polls (the General Social Surveys conducted by National Opinion Research Center in 1980, 1987, and 1990) indicates little difference among Protestants, Jews, and Catholics in this regard during these later years.

26. Hugo Adam Bedau, "Recidivism, Parole, and Deterrence," in *The Death Penalty in America*, ed. Bedau; see also T. Sellin, *The Penalty of Death*.

27. For a further description of inmate life in Texas prisons in the 1930s and 1940s, see Crouch and Marquart, *An Appeal to Justice*.

28. Interview with George J. Beto, October 20, 1989.

29. Ibid.; W. Kelly and Sheldon Ekland-Olson, "The Response of the Criminal Justice System to Prison Overcrowding," *Law and Society Review* 25 (1991): 601–620; Sheldon Ekland-Olson and W. Kelly, *Justice Under Pressure*.

30. Michael L. Radelet, ed., *Facing the Death Penalty: Essays on a Cruel and Unusual Punishment*; Michael Meltsner, *Cruel and Unusual Punishment: The Supreme Court and Capital Punishment*; Wolfgang and Riedel, "Rape, Race, and the Death Penalty in Georgia," p. 45.

31. 408 U.S. 238 (1972).

32. Ibid., p. 310 (J. Stewart, concurring).

33. See Sellin, *The Penalty of Death*, p. 103; also Gennaro Vito and Deborah Wilson, "Back from the Dead: Tracking the Progress of Kentucky's *Furman*-Commuted Death Row Population," *Justice Quarterly* 5 (1988): 101–111; James W. Marquart and Jonathan Sorensen, "Institutional and Post-release Behavior of *Furman*-Commuted Inmates in Texas," *Criminology* 26 (1988): 677–694.

34. See, for example, Vernon Fox, "Analysis of Prison Disciplinary Problems," *Journal of Criminal Law, Criminology, and Police Science* 49 (1958): 321–326.

35. See also Timothy Flanagan, "Time Served and Institutional Misconduct: Patterns of Involvement in Disciplinary Infractions among Long-term and Short-term Inmates," *Journal of Criminal Justice* 8 (1980): 357–367.

36. For comparable findings, see Terence Thornberry and Joseph E. Jacoby, *The Criminally Insane: A Community Follow-up of Mentally Ill Offenders*.

37. For another parallel estimate, see *Dallas Times Herald*, August 25, 1991, p. A1.

38. W. Kelly and Sheldon Ekland-Olson, "The Response of the Criminal Justice System to Prison Overcrowding," *Law and Society Review* 25 (1991): 601–620; Peter H. Rossi, R. A. Berk, and K. J. Lenihan, *Money, Work, and Crime: Experimental Evidence*. See also Henry Donnelly and Gerald Bala, *1977 Releasees: Five Year Post Release Follow-up*.

39. Roy Bragg, "Paroled Killer Arrested in Missouri," *Houston Chronicle*, May 5, 1992; Gary Cartwright, "Free to Kill," *Texas Monthly*, August 1992, pp. 90–95.

6. Adoption of Lethal Injection and Contemporary Death Rituals

1. C. L. Black, *Capital Punishment: The Inevitability of Caprice and Mistake*, 2d ed., pp. 114, 121.

2. *Jurek v. Texas*, 428 U.S. 153 (1976), pp. 275–276.

3. Dick Reavis, "Charlie Brooks' Last Words," *Texas Monthly*, February 1983, p. 176.

4. *Roberts v. Louisiana*, 428 U.S. 325 (1976); *Woodson v. North Carolina*, 428 U.S. 280 (1976); *Gregg v. Georgia*, 428 U.S. 153 (1976); *Proffitt v. Florida*, 428 U.S. 242 (1976); *Jurek v. Texas*, 428 U.S. 262 (1976).

5. *Roberts v. Louisiana* and *Woodson v. North Carolina*.

6. *Gregg v. Georgia*, *Proffitt v. Florida*, and *Jurek v. Texas*.

7. These figures are compiled by the NAACP Legal Defense and Educational Fund, continuing the tradition of those involved in the antilynching campaign decades earlier.

8. M. Kuhn, "House Bill 200: The Legislative Attempt to Reinstate Capital Punishment in Texas," *Houston Law Review* 11 (1974): 410.

9. *Texas Penal Code*, Section 19.03 (1974).

10. *Texas Penal Code*, Section 19.03 (1985).

11. *Texas Code of Criminal Procedure*, art. 37.071b (1985).

12. *Texas Code of Criminal Procedure*, art. 37.071 c–f (1985).

13. Justice Rehnquist, dissenting in *Adams v. Texas*, p. 2530.

14. Black, *Capital Punishment*, pp. 114, 121.

15. Ibid., p. 115.

16. *Jurek v. Texas*, 428 U.S. 262 (1976), pp. 272–273.

17. Quoted in *New York Times*, January 8, 1981, section A, p. 13, col. 1.

18. *Larry Leon Chaney et al., Appellants, v. Margaret M. Heckler, as Secretary of Health and Human Services*, 718 F. 2d 1174 (1983).

19. Ibid., pp. 1191–1192.

20. Ibid., p. 1198.

21. 105 S. Ct. 1649.

22. NAACP Legal Defense and Education Fund, Inc.

23. Differences in record-keeping practices make comparison of this differential sentencing pattern with figures compiled in earlier chapters somewhat suspect.

24. Three females were sentenced to death in the years we are considering. None were executed.

25. 448 U.S. 38 (1980).

26. 451 U.S. 454 (1981).

27. See B. Jackson and D. Christian, *Death Row*, for an excellent ethnography of Texas's death row, and P. Brasfield and J. Elliot, *Deathman Pass Me By: Two Years on Death Row*, for a first-hand account; see also R. Johnson, "Warehousing for Death: Observations on the Human Environment on Death Row," *Crime and Delinquency* 26 (1980): 545–562.

28. Jonathan Sorensen and James W. Marquart, "Working the Dead," in *Facing the Death Penalty*, ed. Michael L. Radelet, p. 169–177.

29. 503 F. Supp. 1265 (1980). See Crouch and Marquart, *An Appeal to Justice*; Martin and Ekland-Olson, *Texas Prisons*.

30. Interview, March 1988.

31. Interviews, March 1988.

32. Interview, March 1988.

33. Jackson and Christian, *Death Row*, p. 27, note 13.

34. Reavis, "Charlie Brooks' Last Words," p. 105.

35. See *Washington Post* editorial, "The Huntsville Mob," November 4, 1984.

36. Reavis, "Charlie Brooks' Last Words," p. 176.

37. Reporters and others with adequate reason are also allowed to witness executions.

38. *Atlanta Constitution*, April 23, 1992, section A, p. 6.

39. *The Houston Chronicle*, May 24, section A, p. 19.

7. Stages of Sentencing and Future Dangerousness of Convicts

1. Prosecuting attorney in *Granger v. Texas*, Tex. Cr. App., 605 S.W. 2d 602 (1979).

2. Prosecuting attorney in *Fortenberry v. State*, Tex. Cr. App., 579 S.W. 2d 482 (1977).

3. These questions have been discussed in greater statistical detail in Sheldon Ekland-Olson, "Structured Discretion, Racial Bias, and the Death Penalty," *Social Science Quarterly* 69 (1988): 853–873; and in James W. Marquart, Sheldon Ekland-Olson, and Jonathan Sorensen, "Gazing into the Crystal Ball: Can Jurors Accurately Predict Dangerousness in Capital Cases?" *Law and Society Review* 23 (1989): 449–468.

4. For example, Menachem Amir, in a 1971 study, *Patterns in Forcible Rape*, found that three-quarters of rapes with black offenders and white victims involved strangers, compared to 53 percent of the black-offender/black-victim cases and 41 percent of the white-offender/white-victim cases. This basic pattern has been more recently reconfirmed by Laurie Young (*Patterns of Victimization in Rape*) with data from the national crime surveys for the years 1979–1987.

5. D. Baldus, C. Pulaski, and G. Woodworth, "Comparative Review of Death Sentences: An Empirical Study of the Georgia Experience," *Journal of Criminal Law and Criminology* 74 (1983): 661–753. See also D. Baldus, C. Pulaski, and G. Woodworth, "Arbitrariness and Discrimination in the Administration of the Death Penalty: A Challenge to the State Supreme Courts," *Stetson Law Review* 15 (1986): 133–231; D. Baldus, C. Pulaski, and G. Woodworth, *Equal Justice and the Death Penalty: A Legal and Empirical Analysis*.

6. Lempert, "Capital Punishment in the '80s," p. 1114.

7. Ibid.

8. See U.S. General Accounting Office report to Senate and House Committees on the Judiciary, *Death Penalty Sentencing: Research Indicates Patterns of Racial Disparities*, for summary review of post-*Furman* research. For more specific treatment, see Kleck, "Racial Discrimination in Criminal Sentencing," p. 798; W. J. Bowers and G. L. Pierce, "Arbitrariness and Discrimination under Post-*Furman* Capital Statutes," *Crime and Delinquency* (1980): 611; Bowers, "The Pervasiveness of Arbitrariness and Discrimination under Post-*Furman* Capital Statutes," *Journal of Criminal Law and Criminology* 74 (1983): 1073; L. Foley, "Florida after the *Furman* Decision: The Effect of Extra-legal Factors on The Processing of Capital Offense Cases," *Behavioral Sciences and the Law* 5 (1987): 461; Michael L. Radelet, "Racial Characteristics and the Imposition of the Death Penalty," *American Sociological Review* 46 (1981): 922; Michael L. Radelet and G. Pierce, "Race and Prosecutorial Discretion in Homicide Cases," *Law and Society Review* 19 (1985): 598–609; Radelet and Pierce, "Choosing Those Who Will Die: Race and the Death Penalty in Florida," *Florida Law Review* 43 (1991): 1–34; L. Foley and R. Powell, "The Discretion of Prosecutors, Judges, and Juries in Capital Cases," *Criminal Justice Review* 7 (1982): 18; T. Keil and G. Vito, "Race, Homicide Severity, and Application of the Death Penalty: A Consideration of the Barnett Scale," *Criminology* 27 (1989): 520; J. Jacoby and R. Paternoster, "Sentencing Disparity and Jury Packing: Further Challenges to the Death Penalty," *Journal of Criminal Law and Criminology* 73 (1982): 383; R. Paternoster, "Race of the Victim and Location of Crime: The Decision to Seek the Death Penalty in South Carolina," *Journal of Criminal Law and Criminology* 74 (1983): 776; Paternoster, "Prosecutorial Discretion in Requesting the Death Penalty: A Case Study of Victim-based Racial Discrimination," *Law and Society Review* 18 (1984): 465; R. Paternoster and A. Kazyaka, "Racial Considerations in Capital Punishment: The Failure of Evenhanded Justice," in *Challenging Capital Punishment*, ed. K. Haas and J. Inciardi, p. 125.

9. See P. Lewis et al., "A Post-*Furman* Profile of Florida's Condemned—A Question of Discrimination in Terms of Race of the Victim and a Comment on *Spinkelink v. Wainwright*," *Stetson Law Review* 9 (1979): 31–35; Michael L. Radelet, "Rejecting the Jury: The Imposition of the Death Penalty in Florida," *University of California–Davis Law Review* 18 (1985): 1416; H. Zeisel, "Race Bias in the Administration of the Death

Penalty: The Florida Experience," *Harvard Law Review* 95 (1981): 460–461; D. Smith, "Patterns of Discrimination in Assessment of the Death Penalty: The Case of Louisiana," *Journal of Criminal Justice* 15 (1987): 282–283; M. Riedel, "Discrimination in the Imposition of the Death Penalty: A Comparison of Offenders Sentenced Pre-*Furman* and Post-*Furman*," *Temple Law Quarterly* 49 (1976): 275–283.

10. See Elizabeth Murphy, "Application of the Death Penalty in Cook County," *Illinois Bar Journal* 73 (1984): 91; S. Arkin, "Discrimination and Arbitrariness in Capital Punishment: An Analysis of Post-*Furman* Murder Cases in Dade County, Florida, 1973–1976," *Stanford Law Review* 33 (1980): 86–90; A. Heilbrun, A. Foster, and J. Golden, "The Death Sentence in Georgia, 1974–1987: Criminal Justice or Racial Injustice?" *Criminal Justice and Behavior* 16 (1989): 146–150.

11. See M. Radelet and M. Vandiver, "The Florida Supreme Court and Death Penalty Appeals," *Journal of Criminal Law and Criminology* 74 (1983): 919–924; Ekland-Olson, "Structured Discretion," pp. 853–873.

12. *McCleskey v. Kemp*, 107 S. Ct. 1756 (1987).

13. See Baldus, Pulaski and Woodworth, "Comparative Review," pp. 661–753.

14. See, generally, volume 47 of *Law and Contemporary Problems* (1984).

15. *New York Times*, January 6, 1989, section B, p. 9, col. 3.

16. 111 S. Ct. 1454 (1991).

17. See, for example, "Senate Blinks at Death and Race," *Legal Times*, May 28, 1990, p. 23; "House, Senate at Odds on Racial Justice Act," *National Law Journal*, September 3, 1990, p. 5; "Blacks Make up 40% of Death Row Inmates," *Chicago Tribune*, September 30, 1991, p. 6.

18. 448 U.S. 38 (1980), p. 2530.

19. *DeGarmo v. Texas*, 106 S. Ct. 337 (1985).

20. This population excluded two females and two offenders who killed Asians. Since the Houston Police Department did not report SHR data in 1982, ten offenders arrested for capital murder in Houston in 1982 who were later sentenced to death ($n = 8$) and life ($n = 2$) also were not included in the analysis.

21. See, for example, M. Maxfield, "Circumstances in Supplemental Homicide Reports: Variety and Validity," *Criminology* 27 (1989): 671–695.

22. Ibid., p. 675.

23. Ibid., p. 686.

24. Samuel R. Gross and Robert Mauro, "Note: Patterns of Death; An Analysis of Racial Disparities in Capital Sentencing and Homicide Victimization," *Stanford Law Review* 37 (1984): 27–153.

25. See notes 6–9 above.

26. Difference in total for victim-defined case categories and for offender-defined case categories are due to multiple-victim cases. Weighting of cases in this stage of the analysis is parallel to that described previously.

27. As before, variables included type of homicide, type of weapon used, presence of codefendants, number of victims (multiple or single), relationship between victim and offender, education and occupation of offender, age of offender and of victim, and ethnic mixture of victims and offenders.

28. *Jurek v. Texas*, 428 U.S. 262 (1976), pp. 275–276.

29. Ron Rosenbaum, "Travels with Dr. Death," *Vanity Fair*, May 1990, p. 143.
30. *Boulware v. Texas*, No. 52, 139 Tex. Crim. App. 1991–1992, 1974.
31. *Rodriguez v. Texas*, No. 62, 274 Tex. Crim. App. 2136, 1978.
32. Cited in Rosenbaum, "Travels with Dr. Death," p. 166, note 25.
33. *Estelle v. Smith*, 41 U.S. 454 (1981).
34. *Barefoot v. Estelle*, 463 U.S. 880 (1983).
35. G. Dix, "Administration of the Texas Death Penalty Statute: Constitutional Infirmities Related to the Prediction of Dangerousness," *Texas Law Review* 55 (1977): 1343; Bruce Ennis and Thomas Litwack, "Psychiatry and the Presumption of Expertise: Flipping Coins in the Courtroom," *California Law Review* 62 (1974): 693; J. Monahan, *Predicting Violent Behavior: An Assessment of Clinical Techniques*.
36. *Barefoot v. Estelle*, 463 U.S. 880 (1983), p. 3411.
37. See P. Applebaum, "Hypotheticals, Psychiatric Testimony, and the Death Sentence," *Bulletin of the American Academy of Psychiatry and Law* 12 (1984): 169–177; R. Bonnie, "Psychiatry and the Death Penalty: Emerging Problems in Virginia," *Virginia Law Review* 66 (1980): 167–189; G. Dix, "Expert Prediction Testimony in Capital Sentencing: Evidentiary and Constitutional Considerations," *American Criminal Law Review* 19 (1981): 1–48; C. Ewing, "'Dr. Death' and the Case for an Ethical Ban on Psychiatric and Psychological Predictions of Dangerousness in Capital Sentencing Proceedings," *American Journal of Law and Medicine* 8 (1983): 407–428; R. Gordon, "Crystal-balling Death?" *Baylor Law Review* 30 (1978): 35–64; C. Worrell, "Psychiatric Prediction of Dangerousness in Capital Sentencing: The Quest for Innocent Authority," *Behavioral Sciences and the Law* 5 (1987): 433–446.
38. The following is an extension of research reported in Marquart, Ekland-Olson, and Sorensen, "Gazing into the Crystal Ball."
39. H. Steadman and J. Cocozza, *Careers of the Criminally Insane: Excessive Social Control of Deviance*; Thornberry and Jacoby, *The Criminally Insane*.
40. See Cartwright, "Free to Kill," pp. 90–95.
41. *Houston Post*, magazine, June 28, 1987.
42. See Sheldon Ekland-Olson, "Crowding, Social Control, and Prison Violence: Evidence from the Post-*Ruiz* Years in Texas," *Law and Society Review* 20 (1986): 389–421.
43. To calculate the average yearly rates of serious rule violations for the former death row prisoners, we computed the rate per prisoner (4/90 = .044). We then divided this rate by the average number of years spent in prison by these offenders (.044/6.3 = .007). For the control cohort we followed the same procedure: 7/107 = .065; and then .065/7.2 (average time spent in prison) = .009. These figures were then multiplied by 100 to create the average yearly rate per 100 inmates.
44. Baldus, Pulaski, and Woodworth, *Equal Justice and the Death Penalty*, p. 403.

8. Some Closing Thoughts

1. From a letter seeking clemency for Leo Lera (#251).
2. *Austin American-Statesman*, January 8, 1972, p. A15.
3. Patterson, *Slavery and Social Death*, pp. 41–42.

4. Ibid., p. 5.

5. See, for example, Charles Phillips, "Exploring Relations among Forms of Social Control: The Lynching and Execution of Blacks in North Carolina, 1889–1918," *Law and Society Review* 21 (1987): 361–374; E. M. Beck, James Massey, and Stewart E. Tolnay, "The Gallows, the Mob, and the Vote: Lethal Sanctioning of Blacks in North Carolina and Georgia, 1882–1930," *Law and Society Review* 23 (1989): 317–331; James L. Massey and Martha A. Meyers, "Patterns of Repressive Social Control in Post-Reconstruction Georgia, 1882–1935," *Social Forces* 68 (1989): 458–488; E.M. Beck and Tolnay, "The Killing Fields," pp. 526–539.

6. Beck and Tolnay, "The Killing Fields."

7. Raper, *The Tragedy of Lynching*.

8. Carl Hovland and Robert R. Sears, "Minor Studies of Aggression: Correlations of Economic Indices with Lynchings," *Journal of Psychology* 9 (1940): 301–310.

9. For a discussion of this analytic technique, see Larry Isaac and Larry Griffin, "Ahistoricism in Time-Series Analyses of Historical Process: Critique, Redirection, and Illustrations from U.S. Labor History," *American Sociological Review* 54 (1989): 873–890.

10. See C. Vann Woodward, *The Strange Career of Jim Crow*. There were, of course, other changes taking place during this period. For example, social reform legislation dealing with child labor, compulsory school attendance, and old-age pensions clearly impacted the economic and social climate of the time.

11. *Plessey v. Ferguson*, 163 U.S. 537 (1896).

12. See the results reported in works cited in note 5 above.

13. Gamson, Fireman, and Rytina, *Encounters with Unjust Authority*.

14. David Snow et al., "Frame Alignment Processes, Micromobilization, and Movement Participation," *American Sociological Review* 51 (1986): 464–481.

15. Randall Collins, "On the Microfoundations of Macrosociology," *American Journal of Sociology* 86 (1981): 984–1014.

16. Gamson, Fireman, and Rytina, *Encounters with Unjust Authority*, p. 14.

17. Snow et al., "Frame Alignment Processes."

18. See, for example, Ovington, *The Walls Came Tumbling Down*; Hall, *Revolt Against Chivalry*; Finch, *The NAACP*.

19. See John D. McCarthy and Mayer Zald, "Resource Mobilization and Social Movements: A Partial Theory," *American Journal of Sociology* 82 (1977): 1212–1241.

20. Gamson, Fireman, and Rytina, *Encounters with Unjust Authority*, p. 5.

21. For example, the killing of Emmet Till in Mississippi in 1955 seemed to have a similar galvanizing effect. See Stephen J. Whitfield, *A Death in the Delta: The Story of Emmett Till*. Parallel potential, though fortunately less realized, is evident in the near execution of Clarence Brandley in Conroe, Texas; see Davies, *White Lies*.

22. Collins, "On the Microfoundations of Macrosociology."

23. Whitfield, *A Death in the Delta*.

24. Wilkins, "Nazi Plan for Negroes Copies Southern U.S.A.," p. 71; Olbrich, "American Civil Rights and Nazi Germany."

25. *Los Angeles Times*, April 16, 1992, p. A3, col. 5.

26. Gallup polls during this time period.

27. With the exception of 1979 and 1981.

28. In the 1991 General Social Survey, the western region of the country also reflects a less than majority approval among blacks of capital punishment. However, the number of respondents (14) makes this a statistically unstable estimate.

29. Cited in Welsh S. White, *The Death Penalty in the Nineties: An Examination of the Modern System of Capital Punishment*, p. 9.

30. Ibid., p. 10.

31. This trend has proceeded along two paths, revealed in a series of procedural default cases and decisions relating to the retroactive effect of "new" constitutional decisions. See ibid., pp. 16–21, as well as Michael Tigar, "Habeas Corpus and the Penalty of Death," *Columbia Law Review* 90 (1990): 255–275.

32. See, for example, J. P. Gibbs, *Crime, Punishment, and Deterrence*; R. Lempert, "Desert and Deterrence: An Assessment of the Moral Bases of the Case for Capital Punishment," *Michigan Law Review* 79 (1981): 1177–1231; R. Hood, *The Death Penalty: A World-wide Perspective.*

33. Gibbs, *Crime, Punishment, and Deterrence*, p. 1.

34. See I. Ehrlich, "The Deterrent Effect of Capital Punishment: A Question of Life and Death," *American Economic Review* 65 (1975): 397–417; Ehrlich, "Capital Punishment and Deterrence: Some Further Thoughts and Additional Evidence," *Journal of Political Economy* 85 (1977): 741–788; William J. Bowers and G. L. Pierce, "The Illusion of Deterrence in Isaac Ehrlich's Research on Capital Punishment," *Yale Law Journal* 85 (1975): 187–208; S. A. Layson, "Homicide and Deterrence: A Re-examination of the United States Time-Series Evidence," *Southern Economic Journal* 52 (1985): 68–69; Layson, "United States Time-Series Homicide Regressions with Adaptive Expectations," *Bulletin of the New York Academy of Medicine* 62 (1986): 589–600.

35. A. J. Blumstein, J. Cohen, and D. Nagin, eds., *Deterrence and Incapacitation: Estimating the Effects of Criminal Sanctions on Crime Rates*, pp. 336–360.

36. Public Law No. 98-473, 98 Stat. 1987 [codified as amended at 18 U.S.C. 3551–3742 and 28 U.S.C. 991–998 (1988)]. See Lewis J. Liman, "Note: The Constitutional Infirmities of the United States Sentencing Commission," *Yale Law Journal* 96 (1987): 1363–1388; Charles J. Ogletree, "The Death of Discretion? Reflections on the Federal Sentencing Guidelines," *Harvard Law Review* 101 (1988): 1938–1960; Julia L. Black, "Note: The Constitutionality of Federal Sentences Imposed under the Sentencing Reform Act of 1984 after *Mistretta v. United States*," *Iowa Law Review* 75 (1990): 767; Richard Husseini, "The Federal Sentencing Guidelines: Adopting Clear and Convincing Evidence as the Burden of Proof," *University of Chicago Law Review* 57 (1990): 1387–1411.

37. See Bedau and Radelet, "Miscarriages of Justice," pp. 21–179; Ronald J. Tabak and J. Mark Lane, "The Execution of Injustice: A Cost and Lack-of-Benefit Analysis of the Death Penalty," *Loyola University of Los Angeles Law Review* 23 (1989): 59–146.

38. The details of this case have been compiled in Davies, *White Lies.*

REFERENCES

■ ■ ■

Abramowitz, Elkan, and David Paget, "Executive Clemency in Capital Cases." *New York University Law Review* 39 (1964): 136–192.

Ames, Jessie Daniel. *The Changing Character of Lynching.* New York: AMS Press, 1942.

Amir, Menachem. *Patterns in Forcible Rape.* Chicago: University of Chicago Press, 1971.

Annual Report of the Texas Prison Board of the Texas Prison System, 1936.

Applebaum, P. "Hypotheticals, Psychiatric Testimony, and the Death Sentence." *Bulletin of the American Academy of Psychiatry and Law* 12 (1984): 169–177.

Aptheker, Herbert. *American Negro Slave Revolts.* New York: International Publishers, 1963.

Arkin, S. "Discrimination and Arbitrariness in Capital Punishment: An Analysis of Post-*Furman* Murder Cases in Dade County, Florida, 1973–1976." *Stanford Law Review* 33 (1980): 75–101.

Axelrod, Robert. *The Evolution of Cooperation.* New York: Basic Books, 1984.

Baldus, D., C. Pulaski, and G. Woodworth, "Arbitrariness and Discrimination in the Administration of the Death Penalty: A Challenge to the State Supreme Courts," *Stetson Law Review* 15 (1986): 133–231.

———. "Comparative Review of Death Sentences: An Empirical Study of the Georgia Experience." *Journal of Criminal Law and Criminology* 74 (1983): 661–753.

———. *Equal Justice and the Death Penalty: A Legal and Comparative Analysis.* Boston: Northeastern University Press, 1990.

Barnett, A. "Some Distribution Patterns for the Georgia Death Sentence," *University of California–Davis Law Review* 18 (1985): 1327–1374.

Beck, E. M., James Massey, and Stewart E. Tolnay. "The Gallows, the Mob, and the Vote: Lethal Sanctioning of Blacks in North Carolina and Georgia, 1882–1930." *Law and Society Review* 23 (1989): 317–331.

Beck, E. M. and S. E. Tolnay, "The Killing Fields of the Deep South: The Market for

Cotton and the Lynching of Blacks, 1882–1930." *American Sociological Review* 55 (1990): 526–539.

Bedau, Hugo Adam. "Capital Punishment in Oregon: 1903–1964." *Oregon Law Review* 45 (1965): 1–39.

———. *The Death Penalty in America*. New York: Oxford University Press, 1964.

———. "Post-Conviction Remedies in California Death Penalty Cases." *Stanford Law Review* 11 (1958): 94–135.

———. "Recidivism, Parole, and Deterrence." In *The Death Penalty in America*, ed. Bedau. New York: Oxford University Press, 1982.

Bedau, Hugo Adam, and Michael L. Radelet. "Miscarriages of Justice in Potentially Capital Cases." *Stanford Law Review* 40, no. 1 (1987): 21–179.

Bensing, Robert, and Oliver Schroeder. *Homicide in the Urban Community*. Springfield, Ill.: Charles C. Thomas, 1960.

Black, C. L. *Capital Punishment: The Inevitability of Caprice and Mistake*. 2d ed. New York: W. W. Norton, 1977.

Black, Donald. *Toward a General Theory of Social Control*, vol. 1, *Fundamentals*. New York: Academic Press, 1984.

Black, Julia L. "Note: The Constitutionality of Federal Sentences Imposed Under the Sentencing Reform Act of 1984 after *Mistretta v. United States*." *Iowa Law Review* 75 (1990): 767–789.

"Blacks Make Up 40% of Death Row Inmates." *Chicago Tribune*, September 30, 1991.

Blumstein, A. J., J. Cohen, and D. Nagin, eds. *Deterrence and Incapacitation: Estimating the Effects of Criminal Sanctions on Crime Rates*. Washington D.C.: National Academy of Sciences, 1978.

Bonnie, R. "Psychiatry and the Death Penalty: Emerging Problems in Virginia," *Virginia Law Review* 66 (1980): 167–189.

Bowers, William J. "The Pervasiveness of Arbitrariness and Discrimination under Post-*Furman* Capital Statutes." *Journal of Criminal Law and Criminology* 74 (1983): 1067–1100.

Bowers, William J., and G. L. Pierce. "Arbitrariness and Discrimination under Post-*Furman* Capital Statutes." *Crime and Delinquency* 26 (1980): 563–635.

———. "The Illusion of Deterrence in Isaac Ehrlich's Research on Capital Punishment." *Yale Law Journal* 85 (1975): 187–208.

Bowers, William J., with G. L. Pierce and J. McDevitt. *Legal Homicide: Death as Punishment in America, 1864–1982*. Boston: Northeastern University Press, 1984.

Bragg, Roy. "Paroled Killer Arrested in Missouri." *Houston Chronicle*, May 5, 1992.

Braithwaite, Lloyd. "Executive Clemency in California: A Case Study Interpretation of Criminal Responsibility." *Issues in Criminology* 1 (1965): 77–107.

Brasfield, P., and J. Elliot, *Deathman Pass Me By: Two Years on Death Row*. San Bernardino, Calif.: Borgo Books, 1983.

Brown, Norman D. *Hood, Bonnet, and Little Brown Jug: Texas Politics: 1921–1928*. College Station: Texas A & M University Press, 1984.

Brown, Richard Maxwell. *Strain of Violence: Historical Studies of American Violence and Vigilantism*. New York: Oxford University Press, 1975.

Bullock, Henry. "Significance of the Racial Factor in the Length of Prison Sentences." *Journal of Criminal Law, Criminology, and Police Science* 52 (1961): 411–416.

References

Campbell, Joseph. *The Power of Myth*. New York: Doubleday, 1988.

Cantrell, Gregg. "Racial Violence and Reconstruction Politics in Texas, 1867–1868," *Southwestern Historical Quarterly* 93 (1990): 331–355.

Cartwright, Gary. "Free to Kill." *Texas Monthly*, August 1992, pp. 90–95.

Cash, W. J. *The Mind of the South*. New York: Vintage Books, 1941.

Cobb, Paul. "Reviving Mercy in the Structure of Capital Punishment." *Yale Law Journal* 99 (1989): 389–409.

Collins, Randall. "On the Microfoundations of Macrosociology." *American Journal of Sociology* 86 (1981): 984–1014.

"Condemned Negro Fails to Save Life on a Technicality." *Austin American-Statesman*, February 8, 1924, p. 1.

Crime and Justice in Texas. Huntsville, Tex.: Sam Houston State University Press, 1988.

Crouch, Barry. "A Spirit of Lawlessness." *Journal of Social History* 18 (1984): 217–232.

Crouch, Ben M., and James W. Marquart. *An Appeal to Justice: Litigated Reform of Texas Prisons*. Austin: University of Texas Press, 1989.

Crow, H. "A Political History of the Texas Penal System—1829–1951." Ph.D. dissertation, University of Texas at Austin, 1964.

Crump, D. "Capital Murder: The Issues in Texas." *Houston Law Review* 14 (1977): 532–581.

Davies, Nick. *White Lies: Rape, Murder, and Justice Texas Style*. New York: Pantheon Books, 1991.

Davis, P. "Texas Capital Sentencing Procedures: The Role of the Jury and the Restraining Hand of the Expert," *Journal of Criminal Law and Criminology* 69 (1978): 300–310.

Dimsdale, Thomas J. *The Vigilantes of Montana*. Helena, Mont.: State Publishing Co., 1915.

DiSalle, Michael. "Comments on Capital Punishment and Clemency." *Ohio State Law Journal* 25 (1964): 71–83.

"District Attorney McClain Receives Threatening Letter." *Conroe Courier*, June 19, 1941.

Dix, G. "Administration of the Texas Death Penalty Statute: Constitutional Infirmities Related to the Prediction of Dangerousness." *Texas Law Review* 55 (1977): 1343–1414.

———. "Expert Prediction Testimony in Capital Sentencing: Evidentiary and Constitutional Considerations." *American Criminal Law Review* 19 (1981): 1–48.

Donnelly, Henry, and Gerald Bala. *1977 Releasees: Five Year Post Release Follow-up*. Albany, N.Y.: Department of Correctional Services, 1984.

Ehrhardt, Charles W., and L. Harold Levinson. "Florida's Legislative Response to *Furman*: An Exercise in Futility?" *Journal of Criminal Law and Criminology* 64 (1973): 10–21.

Ehrlich, I. "Capital Punishment and Deterrence: Some Further Thoughts and Additional Evidence." *Journal of Political Economy* 85 (1977): 741–788.

———. "The Deterrent Effect of Capital Punishment: A Question of Life and Death." *American Economic Review* 65 (1975): 397–417.

Ekland-Olson, Sheldon. "Crowding, Social Control, and Prison Violence: Evidence from the Post-*Ruiz* Years in Texas." *Law and Society Review* 20 (1986):389–421.

————. "Structured Discretion, Racial Bias, and the Death Penalty: The First Decade after *Furman* in Texas." *Social Science Quarterly* 69 (1988): 853–873.

Ekland-Olson, Sheldon, and W. Kelly. *Justice under Pressure.* New York: Springer-Verlag, 1993.

Elliott, Claude. "The Freedmen's Bureau in Texas. *Southwestern Historical Quarterly* 61 (1952): 1–24.

Ennis, Bruce, and Thomas Litwack. "Psychiatry and the Presumption of Expertise: Flipping Coins in the Courtroom." *California Law Review* 62 (1974): 693–752.

Espy, Watt M., and John Ortiz Smykla. *Executions in the United States, 1608–1991: The Espy File.* 2d ICPSR ed. Compiled by John Ortiz Smykla, University of Alabama. Ann Arbor, Mich.: Inter-university Consortium for Political and Social Research, 1992.

Ewing, C. "'Dr. Death' and the Case for an Ethical Ban on Psychiatric and Psychological Predictions of Dangerousness in Capital Sentencing Proceedings." *American Journal of Law and Medicine* 8 (1983): 407–428.

"Executive Clemency in Capital Cases." *New York University Law Review* 39 (1964): 136–192.

"Ex-Warden Sleeps as Five Negroes Die." *Dallas Morning News*, February 8, 1924.

Farrell, R., and V. Swigert. "Legal Disposition of Inter-group and Intra-group Homicides." *Sociological Quarterly* 12 (1978): 437–454.

Fehrenbach, T. R., *Lone Star: A History of Texas and the Texans.* Macmillan Press, 1985.

Fienberg, Stephen. *The Analysis of Cross-Classified Categorical Data.* Cambridge, Mass.: MIT Press, 1985.

Finch, Minnie. *The NAACP: Its Fight for Justice.* Metuchen, N.J.: Scarecrow Press, 1981.

Flanagan, Timothy. "Time Served and Institutional Misconduct: Patterns of Involvement in Disciplinary Infractions among Long-term and Short-term Inmates." *Journal of Criminal Justice* 8 (1980): 357–367.

Foley, L. "Florida after the *Furman* Decision: The Effect of Extra-Legal Factors on The Processing of Capital Offense Cases." *Behavioral Sciences and the Law* 5 (1987): 457–465.

Foley, L., and R. Powell. "The Discretion of Prosecutors, Judges, and Juries in Capital Cases." *Criminal Justice Review* 7 (1982): 16–22.

Foner, Eric. *Reconstruction, 1863–1877.* New York: Harper and Row, 1988.

Fox, Vernon. "Analysis of Prison Disciplinary Problems." *Journal of Criminal Law, Criminology, and Police Science* 49 (1958): 321–326.

Gammel, H. P. N. *Laws of Texas*, vol. 1, *1822–1897.* Austin: Gammel Book Co., 1898.

Gamson, William A., Bruce Fireman, and Steven Rytina. *Encounters with Unjust Authority.* Homewood, Ill.: Dorsey Press, 1982.

Garfinkel, Harold. "Research Note on Inter- and Intra-racial Homicide." *Social Forces* 27 (1949): 369–381.

Gibbs, J. P. *Crime, Punishment, and Deterrence.* New York: Elsevier Scientific Publishers, 1975.

Glasrud, Bruce A. "Enforcing White Supremacy in Texas, 1900–1910," *Red River Historical Review* 4 (1979): 65–74.

Gordon, R. "Crystal-balling Death?" *Baylor Law Review* 30 (1978): 35–64.

Gross, Samuel R., and Robert Mauro. "Note: Patterns of Death; An Analysis of Racial Disparities in Capital Sentencing and Homicide Victimization." *Stanford Law Review* 37 (1984): 27–153.

Hagan, John. "Extra-legal Attributes and Criminal Sentencing: An Assessment of a Sociological Viewpoint." *Law and Society Review* 8 (Spring 1974): 357–383.

Hall, Jacquelyn Dowd. *Revolt Against Chivalry: Jessie Daniel Ames and the Women's Campaign against Lynching.* New York: Columbia University Press, 1974.

"Hangman's Rope to Be Used to Tow Autos." *San Antonio Express,* February 9, 1924.

Heilbrun, A., A. Foster, and J. Golden. "The Death Sentence in Georgia, 1974–1987: Criminal Justice or Racial Injustice?" *Criminal Justice and Behavior* 16 (1989): 139–154.

Hollon, W. Eugene. *Frontier Violence, Another Look.* New York: Oxford University Press, 1974.

Hood, R. *The Death Penalty: A World-wide Perspective.* New York: Oxford University Press, 1989.

Horwitz, Allan V. *The Logic of Social Control.* New York: Plenum Press, 1990.

Hosmer, D., and S. Lemeshow. *Applied Logistic Regression.* New York: John Wiley and Sons, 1989.

"House, Senate at Odds on Racial Justice Act." *National Law Journal,* September 3, 1990, p. 5.

Hovland, Carl, and Robert R. Sears. "Minor Studies of Aggression: Correlations of Economic Indices with Lynchings." *Journal of Psychology* 9 (1940): 301–310.

Hughes, Robert. *The Fatal Shore.* New York: Knopf, 1986.

Hunter, Robert J. "The Death-Sentencing of Rapists in Texas, 1942–1971." Master's thesis, Sam Houston State University, 1990.

Husseini, Richard. "The Federal Sentencing Guidelines: Adopting Clear and Convincing Evidence as the Burden of Proof." *University of Chicago Law Review* 57 (1990): 1387–1411.

Isaac, Larry, and Larry Griffin. "Ahistoricism in Time-Series Analyses of Historical Process: Critique, Redirection, and Illustrations from U.S. Labor History." *American Sociological Review* 54 (1989): 873–890.

Jackson, B., and D. Christian. *Death Row.* Boston: Beacon Press, 1980.

Jacoby, J., and R. Paternoster. "Sentencing Disparity and Jury Packing: Further Challenges to the Death Penalty." *Journal of Criminal Law and Criminology* 73 (1982): 379–387.

Jetton, Mark. "The NAACP's Campaign against Lynching in Texas." Honors thesis in sociology, University of Texas at Austin, 1992.

Johnson, Elmer. "Selective Factors in Capital Punishment." *Social Forces* 36 (1956): 165–169.

Johnson, Guy. "The Negro and Crime." *The Annals of the American Academy of Political and Social Science* 217 (1941): 93–104.

Johnson, R. "Warehousing for Death: Observations on the Human Environment on Death Row." *Crime and Delinquency* 26 (1980): 545–562.

"Johnson County Man New Prison Warden." *Austin American-Statesman,* February 6, 1924.

Jordan, Terry. "A Century and a Half of Ethnic Change in Texas, 1836–1986." *Southwestern Historical Quarterly* 89 (1986): 385–422.

Jordan, Winthrop D. *White over Black: American Attitudes toward the Negro, 1550–1812.* Chapel Hill: University of North Carolina Press, 1968.

Judson, Charles, James Pandell, Jack Owens, James McIntosh, and Dale Matschullat. "A Study of the California Jury in First-Degree Murder Cases." *Stanford Law Review* 21 (1967): 1297.

Kalven, H., and H. Zeisel. *The American Jury.* Boston: Little Brown, 1966.

Keil, T., and G. Vito. "Race, Homicide Severity, and Application of the Death Penalty: A Consideration of the Barnett Scale." *Criminology* 27 (1989): 511–531.

Kelly, W., and Sheldon Ekland-Olson. "The Response of the Criminal Justice System to Prison Overcrowding: Recidivism Patterns among Four Successive Parolee Cohorts." *Law & Society Review* 25 (1991): 601–620.

Kleck, Gary. "Racial Discrimination in Criminal Sentencing: A Critical Evaluation of the Evidence with Additional Evidence on the Death Penalty." *American Sociological Review* 46 (1981): 783–805.

Kobil, Daniel T. "The Quality of Mercy Strained: Wresting the Pardoning Power of the King." *Texas Law Review* 69 (1991): 569–641.

Koeninger, Rupert. "Capital Punishment in Texas, 1924–1968." *Crime and Delinquency* 15 (1969): 132–141.

Kuhn, M. "House Bill 200: The Legislative Attempt to Reinstate Capital Punishment in Texas." *Houston Law Review* 11 (1974): 410–423.

Layson, S. A. "Homicide and Deterrence: A Re-examination of the United States Time-Series Evidence." *Southern Economic Journal* 1985: 68–69.

———. "United States Time-Series Homicide Regressions with Adaptive Expectations." *Bulletin of the New York Academy of Medicine* 62 (1986): 589–600.

Leavy, Deborah. "A Matter of Life and Death: Due Process Protection in Capital Clemency Proceedings." *Yale Law Review* 90 (1981): 889–911.

Lempert, Richard. "Capital Punishment in the '80s: Reflections on the Symposium." *Journal of Criminal Law and Criminology* 74 (1983): 1101–1114.

———. "Desert and Deterrence: An Assessment of the Moral Bases of the Case for Capital Punishment." *Michigan Law Review* 79 (1981): 1177–1231.

Lewis, P., H. Mannle, H. Allen, and H. Vetter. "A Post-*Furman* Profile of Florida's Condemned—A Question of Discrimination in Terms of Race of the Victim and a Comment on *Spinkelink v. Wainwright*." *Stetson Law Review* 9 (1979): 1–45.

Liman, Lewis J." Note: The Constitutional Infirmities of the United States Sentencing Commission." *Yale Law Journal* 96 (1987): 1363–1388.

Lodge, Henry Cabot. "Lynch Law and Unrestricted Immigration." *North American Review* 152 (1891): 602–612.

McCarthy, John D., and Mayer Zald. "Resources Mobilization and Social Movements: A Partial Theory." *American Journal of Sociology* 82 (1977): 1212–1241.

Mangum, Charles. *The Illegal Status of the Negro.* Chapel Hill: University of North Carolina Press, 1940.

Marquart, James W., and Jonathan Sorensen "Institutional and Post-release Behavior of *Furman*-Commuted Inmates in Texas." *Criminology* 26 (1988): 677–694.

Marquart, James W., Sheldon Ekland-Olson, and Jonathan Sorensen. "Gazing into the Crystal Ball: Can Jurors Accurately Predict Future Dangerousness in Capital Cases?" *Law and Society Review* 23 (1989): 449–468.

Martin, Steve J., and Sheldon Ekland-Olson. *Texas Prisons: The Walls Came Tumbling Down.* Austin: Texas Monthly Press, 1987.

Massey, James L., and Martha A. Meyers. "Patterns of Repressive Social Control in Post-Reconstruction Georgia, 1882–1935." *Social Forces* 68 (1989): 458–488.

Maxfield, M. "Circumstances in Supplemental Homicide Reports: Variety and Validity." *Criminology* 27 (1989): 671–695.

Meltsner, Michael. *Cruel and Unusual Punishment: The Supreme Court and Capital Punishment.* New York: Random House, 1973.

Meinig, D. W. *Imperial Texas: An Interpretive Essay in Cultural Geography.* Austin: University of Texas Press, 1969.

"Midnight Appeal Causes Pause in Harvest of Death." *Austin American-Statesman,* February 7, 1924.

Monahan, J. *Predicting Violent Behavior: An Assessment of Clinical Techniques.* Beverly Hills, Calif.: Sage, 1981.

Moran, Richard. "Executing a Businessman's Strategy." Paper presented at American Society of Criminology Meetings, Reno, Nev., November 1989.

Murchison, Kenneth, and Arthur Schwab. "Capital Punishment in Virginia." *Virginia Law Review* 58 (1972): 97–142.

Murphy, Elizabeth. "Application of the Death Penalty in Cook County." *Illinois Bar Journal* 73 (1984): 90–95.

NAACP. *Thirty Years of Lynching in the United States: 1889–1918.* New York, 1919.

Nakell, B., and K. Hardy. *The Arbitrariness of the Death Penalty.* Philadelphia: Temple University Press, 1987.

"Negro Bob White Killed in Courtroom Here Tuesday." *Conroe Courier,* June 12, 1941.

Neustadler, R. "The 'Deadly Current': The Death Penalty in the Industrial Age." *Journal of American Culture* 12 (1989): 79–87.

Newman, D., and P. Anderson. *Introduction to Criminal Justice.* New York, Random House, 1989.

Ogletree, Charles J. "The Death of Discretion? Reflections on the Federal Sentencing Guidelines." *Harvard Law Review* 101 (1988): 1938–1960.

Olbrich, Jeffrey Lee. "American Civil Rights and Nazi Germany: An Analysis Using Resource Mobilization Theory." M.A. thesis, University of Texas at Austin, 1990.

Ovington, Mary White. *The Walls Came Tumbling Down.* New York: Schocken Books, 1947.

Partington, Donald. "The Incidence of the Death Penalty For Rape in Virginia." *Washington and Lee Law Review* 22 (1965): 43–75.

Paternoster, R. "Prosecutorial Discretion in Requesting the Death Penalty: A Case Study of Victim-based Racial Discrimination." *Law and Society Review* 18 (1984): 437–478.

———. "Race of the Victim and Location of Crime: The Decision to Seek the Death Penalty in South Carolina." *Journal of Criminal Law and Criminology* 74 (1983): 754–785.

Paternoster, R., and A. Kazyaka. "Racial Considerations in Capital Punishment: The Failure of Evenhanded Justice." In *Challenging Capital Punishment*, edited by K. Haas and J. Inciardi. Beverly Hills, Calif.: Sage, 1988.

Patterson, Orlando. *Slavery and Social Death: A Comparative Study*. Cambridge: Harvard University Press, 1982.

Phillips, Charles. "Exploring Relations among Forms of Social Control: The Lynching and Execution of Blacks in North Carolina, 1889–1918." *Law and Society Review* 21 (1987): 361–374.

Poundstone, William. *Prisoner's Dilemma*. New York: Doubleday, 1992.

Radelet, Michael L. "Racial Characteristics and the Imposition of the Death Penalty." *American Sociological Review* 46 (1981): 918–927.

———. "Rejecting the Jury: The Imposition of the Death Penalty in Florida." *University of California at Davis Law Review* 18 (1985): 1409–1431.

———. *Facing the Death Penalty: Essays on a Cruel and Unusual Punishment*. Philadelphia: Temple University Press, 1989.

Radelet, Michael L., and G. L. Pierce. "Choosing Those Who Will Die: Race and the Death Penalty in Florida." *Florida Law Review* 43 (1991): 1–34.

———. "Race and Prosecutorial Discretion in Homicide Cases." *Law and Society Review* 19 (1985): 587–621.

Radelet, M., and M. Vandiver. "The Florida Supreme Court and Death Penalty Appeals." *Journal of Criminal Law and Criminology* 74 (1983): 913–926.

Radzinowicz, Leon, and Roger Hood. *A History of English Criminal Law*. London: Stevens, 1986.

Raper, Arthur. *The Tragedy of Lynching*. Chapel Hill: University of North Carolina Press, 1933.

Reavis, Dick. "Charlie Brooks' Last Words." *Texas Monthly*, February 1983.

Reid, Don. *Eyewitness: I Saw 189 Men Die in the Electric Chair*. Houston: Cordovan Press, 1973.

Richards, William. "Doctors Seek Crackdown on Colleagues Paid for Testimony in Malpractice Suits." *Wall Street Journal*, November 7, 1988.

Riedel, M. "Discrimination in the Imposition of the Death Penalty: A Comparison of Offenders Sentenced Pre-*Furman* and Post-*Furman*." *Temple Law Quarterly* 49 (1976): 261–287.

Ringold, Solie. "The Dynamics of Executive Clemency." *American Bar Association Journal* 52 (1966): 240–243.

Rockefeller, Winthrop. "Executive Clemency and the Death Penalty." *Catholic University Law Review* 21 (1971): 94–102.

Rodriguez, Fernando. "Patterns of Homicide in Texas: A Descriptive Analysis of Racial/Ethnic Involvement by Crime-Specific Categories." Ph.D. dissertation, University of Texas at Austin, May 1990.

Rosenbaum, Ron. "Travels with Dr. Death." *Vanity Fair*, (May 1990).

Rossi, Peter H., R. A. Berk, and K. J. Lenihan. *Money, Work, and Crime: Experimental Evidence*. New York: Academic Press, 1980.

Scofield, G. "Due Process in the United States Supreme Court and the Administration of the Texas Capital Murder Statute." *American Journal of Criminal Law* 8 (1980): 1–42.

Seligman, Victoria K. "The Worst of Times: Racial Violence in Longview, Texas, 1902–1919." Honors thesis, University of Texas at Austin, 1987.

Sellin, T. *The Penalty of Death*. Beverly Hills, Calif.: Sage, 1980.

Sembera, Alan. "Brandley Urges Social Change." *Conroe Courier*, April 5, 1990.

"Senate Blinks at Death and Race." *Legal Times*, May 28, 1990, p. 23.

Shubik, Martin, ed. *Game Theory and Related Approaches to Social Behavior: Selections*. New York: John Wiley & Sons, 1964

Smallwood, James. "Perpetuation of Caste: Black Agriculture Workers in Texas." *Mid-America* 61 (1979): 5–23.

Smith, D. "Patterns of Discrimination in Assessment of the Death Penalty: The Case of Louisiana." *Journal of Criminal Justice* 15 (1987): 279–286.

Snow, David, E. Burke Rochford, Steve Worden, and Robert Benford. "Frame Alignment Processes, Micromobilization, and Movement Participation." *American Sociological Review* 51 (1986): 464–481.

Sonnichsen, C. L. *Ten Texas Feuds*. Albuquerque: University of New Mexico Press, 1957.

SoRelle, James M. "The 'Waco Horror': The Lynching of Jessie Washington." *Southwestern Historical Quarterly* 86 (1983): 517–536.

Sorensen, Jonathan, and James W. Marquart. "Working the Dead." In *Facing the Death Penalty*, edited by Michael L. Radelet, pp. 169–177. Philadelphia: Temple University Press, 1989.

Southern Commission on the Study of Lynching. *Lynchings and What They Mean*. 1931.

Steadman, H., and J. Cocozza. *Careers of the Criminally Insane: Excessive Social Control of Deviance*. Lexington, Mass.: Lexington Books, 1974.

Stout, J. "Executive Clemency in Pennsylvania." *Shingle* 22 (May 1959): 111–115.

Tabak, Ronald J., and J. Mark Lane. "The Execution of Injustice: A Cost and Lack-of-Benefit Analysis of the Death Penalty." *Loyola University of Los Angeles Law Review* 23 (1989): 59–146.

Thornberry, Terence, and Joseph E. Jacoby. *The Criminally Insane: A Community Follow-up of Mentally Ill Offenders*. Chicago: University of Chicago Press, 1979.

Tigar, Michael. "Habeas Corpus and the Penalty of Death." *Columbia Law Review* 90 (1990): 255–275.

Trow, L. "Circus Happened outside the Prison." *Huntsville Item*, December 7, 1982.

U.S. Bureau of Justice Statistics. *Capital Punishment—1977, National Prisoner Statistics*. Washington, D.C.: Government Printing Office, 1978.

U.S. Department of Justice, Law Enforcement Assistance Administration. *Capital Punishment—1977, National Prisoner Statistics*, SD-NPS-CP-6. Washington, D.C.: Government Printing Office, November 1978.

U.S. General Accounting Office. *Death Penalty Sentencing: Research Indicates Patterns of Racial Disparities*. Washington, D.C.: Government Printing Office, February 1990.

Vandiver, Margaret. "Race, Clemency, and Executions in Florida, 1924–1966." Master's thesis, Florida State University, 1983.

Vito, Gennaro, and Deborah Wilson. "Back from the Dead: Tracking the Progress of Kentucky's *Furman*-Commuted Death Row Population." *Justice Quarterly* 5 (1988): 101–111.

Wagner, David E. "A Commutation Study of Ex-Capital Offenders in Texas From 1924–1971." Master's thesis, Sam Houston State University, 1988.

Walt, Robert S., Assistant Texas Attorney General. *Criminal Law Update.* October 19, 1988.

Waskow, Arthur. *From Race Riot to Sit-in.* Garden City, N.Y.: Doubleday, 1966.

White, Welsh S. *The Death Penalty in the Nineties: An Examination of the Modern System of Capital Punishment.* Ann Arbor: University of Michigan Press, 1991.

Whitfield, Stephen J. *A Death in the Delta: The Story of Emmett Till.* Baltimore: Johns Hopkins University Press, 1988.

Wilbanks, William. *The Myth of a Racist Criminal Justice System.* Belmont, Calif.: Brooks-Cole, 1987.

Wilkins, Roy. "Nazi Plan for Negroes Copies Southern U.S.A." *Crisis* 48 (1941): 71.

Williams, Franklin. "The Death Penalty and the Negro." *Crisis* 67 (1960): 501–512.

Wolfgang, Marvin E. "Murder, the Pardon Board, and Recommendations by Judges and District Attorneys." *Journal of Criminal Law, Criminology, and Police Science* 50 (1959): 338–346.

———. *Patterns of Criminal Homicide.* Philadelphia: University of Pennsylvania Press, 1958.

———. "The Social Scientist in Court." *The Journal of Criminal Law & Criminology* 65 (1974): 239–247.

Wolfgang, Marvin E., A. Kelly, and H. Nolde. "Comparison of the Executed and the Commuted among Admissions to Death Row." *Journal of Criminal Law, Crimonology, and Police Science* 53 (1962): 301–311.

Wolfgang, Marvin E., and Marc Riedel. "Rape, Race, and the Death Penalty in Georgia." *American Journal of Orthopsychiatry* 45 (1975): 658–668.

Woodward, C. Vann. *The Strange Career of Jim Crow.* Rev. ed. New York: Oxford University Press, 1966.

Worrell, C. "Psychiatric Prediction of Dangerousness in Capital Sentencing: The Quest for Innocent Authority." *Behavioral Sciences and the Law* 5 (1987): 433–446.

Wright George C. "Executions of Afro-Americans in Kentucky, 1870–1940." *Georgia Journal of Southern Legal History* 1 (1991): 321–355.

———. *Racial Violence in Kentucky, 1865–1940.* Baton Rouge: Louisiana State University Press, 1990.

Young, Laurie. *Patterns of Victimization in Rape.* Ph.D. dissertation, University of Texas at Austin, 1992.

Zeisel, H. "Race Bias in the Administration of the Death Penalty: The Florida Experience." *Harvard Law Review* 95 (1981): 456–468.

Court Cases

Adams v. Texas, 448 U.S. 38 (1980).

Barefoot v. Estelle, 463 U.S. 880 (1983).

Boulware v. Texas, No. 52, 139 Tex. Crim. App. 1991–1992 (1974).

Chaney et al. v. Heckler, 718 F. 2d 1174 (1983).

Charles v. State, No. 12411, 16 S.W. 2d (1929).

DeGarmo v. Texas, 106 S. Ct. 337 (1985).

Estelle v. Smith, 451 U.S. 454 (1981).
Fortenberry v. State, Tex. Cr. App., 579 S.W. 2d 482 (1977).
Franklin v. Lynaugh, 108 S. Ct. 2320 (1988).
Furman v. Georgia, 408 U.S. 238 (1972).
Granger v. State, Tex. Cr. App., 605 S.W. 2d 602 (1979).
Gregg v. Georgia, 428 U.S. 153 (1976).
In re Kemmler, 136 U.S. 436 (1890).
Jurek v. Texas, 428 U.S. 262 (1976).
McCleskey v. Kemp, 107 S. Ct. 1756 (1987).
Miranda v. Arizona, 384 U.S. 436 (1966).
Penry v. Lynaugh, 57 U.S.L.W. 4958 (1989).
Plessy v. Ferguson, 163 U.S. 537 (1896).
Proffitt v. Florida, 428 U.S. 242 (1976).
Pulley v. Harris, 465 U.S. 37 (1984).
Richardson v. State, 257 S.W. 2d 308 (1953).
Rodriguez v. Texas, No. 62, 274 Tex. Crim. App. 2136 (1978).
Roberts v. Louisiana, 428 U.S. 325 (1976).
Ruffin v. Commonwealth, 62 Va. 790 (1871).
Satterwhite v. Texas, 108 S. Ct. 1792 (1988).
Woodson v. North Carolina, 428 U.S. 280 (1976).

INDEX

■ ■ ■